Manifold Greatness

The Making of the King James Bible

VITA MIHI CHRISTVS ET MORS MIHI LVCR

AN DNI 1567   MAII 21 AETATIS SVÆ 6

Manifold Greatness

The *Making* of the King James Bible

Edited by Helen Moore and Julian Reid

Bodleian Library
UNIVERSITY OF OXFORD

First published in 2011 by the Bodleian Library
Broad Street
Oxford OX1 3BG

in association with the Folger Shakespeare Library

Folger SHAKESPEARE LIBRARY
Advancing knowledge & the arts

www.bodleianbookshop.co.uk

Reprinted 2012

ISBN: 978 185124 349 5

Contents

TO THE MOST
HIGH AND MIGHTIE

Prince, IAMES by the grace of God
King of Great Britaine, France and Ireland,
Defender of the Faith, &c.

THE TRANSLATORS OF *THE BIBLE*,
wish Grace, Mercie, and Peace, through IESVS
CHRIST our LORD.

Reat and manifold were the blessings (most dread
Soueraigne) which Almighty GOD, the Father
of all Mercies, bestowed vpon vs the people of
ENGLAND, when first he sent your Maiesties
Royall person to rule and raigne ouer vs. For
whereas it was the expectation of many, who
wished not well vnto our SION, that vpon the
setting of that bright *Occidentall Starre* Queene
ELIZABETH of most happy memory, some
thicke and palpable cloudes of darkenesse would so haue ouershadowed
ths land, that men should haue bene in doubt which way they were to
wake, and that it should hardly be knowen, who was to direct the vnsetled
Stae: the appearance of your MAIESTIE, as of the *Sunne* in his strength,
instantly dispelled those supposed and surmised mists, and gaue vnto all
that vere well affected, exceeding cause of comfort; especially when we beheld he gouernment established in your HIGHNESSE, and your hope-
full Sed, by an vndoubted Title, and this also accompanied with Peace
and tranquillitie, at home and abroad.

Bu amongst all our Ioyes, there was no one that more filled our hearts,
then tle blessed continuance of the Preaching of GODS sacred word a-
mongst vs, which is that inestimable treasure, which excelleth all the riches

Foreword

The Bible has never been far from the heart of the Bodleian Library through all of its four centuries of existence. Sir Thomas Bodley was himself a Protestant, who had been partly raised in exile among the Bible-reading reformers of Geneva. His first librarian, Thomas James, was a biblical scholar who tracked down manuscripts of the Bible in the libraries of Oxford and Cambridge, and who compiled scriptural reference works during his time in post. Among the most important early acquisitions of the Bodleian were biblical manuscripts, such as the Laudian Acts, gifted by Archbishop Laud, one of the Library's most important Benefactors. Throughout the rest of the Library's history, Bibles have featured among the list of great acquisitions among all parts of the Bodleian, and several library staff after Thomas James have been learned biblical scholars (as Benjamin Kennicott).

The King James Bible has featured prominently as part of this phenomenon. Sir Thomas Bodley's close collaborator in the foundation of the 'Publike librarie of the University of Oxford', Henry Savile, the Warden of Merton College, was deeply involved in the translation of the King James Bible. The King James version has also emerged in unexpected places, such as the Music collections, where Handel's conducting score of *Messiah* – with the libretto adapted richly from the King James Version – is one of the most celebrated musical manuscripts in the collection.

While geographically far removed from the birthplace of the King James Bible, the Folger Shakespeare Library has its own lessons to teach about the cultural importance of the Bible in early modern England and beyond. Henry and Emily Folger focused their collecting on William Shakespeare's life and times, and the collection they established includes extensive theological holdings documenting the Protestant Reformation's arrival in England and the ensuing religious controversies of the sixteenth and seventeenth centuries. The fact that the Folger collection came to rest in Washington DC conveys a great deal about English culture's westward migration and, more specifically, the enormous cultural legacy of two of the major literary achievements of the age: the King James Bible and, just twelve years later, Shakespeare's First Folio.

Among the Folger's rich holdings is a Bishop's Bible that belonged to Elizabeth I and a King James Bible bound for Queen Anne. Early editions of the Bible in the Folger collection reveal personal inscriptions, unique bindings and other evidence of the way early readers both used and treasured this most personal of texts.

Figure 1 The dedication to King James from the 1611 King James Bible. Oxford, Bodleian Library, Bib. Eng. 1611 b.1.

BEATI PACIFICI

HAEC HABEO QVAE SCRIPSI

HAEC HABEO QVAE DEDI

REGNANTE D. IACOBO REGVM DOCTISSIMO
MVNIFICENTISSIMO OPTIMO HÆ MVSIS
EXTRVCTÆ MOLES. CONGESTA BIBLIOTHECA
ET QVÆCVNQVE ADHVC DEERANT AD SPLE
DOREM ACADEMIÆ FELICITER TENTATA
COEPTA ABSOLVTA. SOLI DEO GLORIA.

It is therefore fitting that the Bodleian and the Folger Shakespeare Library should be the chosen venues for a major exhibition charting the genesis and development of this great religious, literary and cultural text. The exhibition, publication and website has been a rich collaboration between the Bodleian, the Folger Shakespeare Library and a group of academic staff at Corpus Christi College – an institution at the very heart of the King James Bible's history. We are hugely grateful to Helen Moore and Julian Reid for leading such a talented scholarly team in developing the project. Both institutions also owe a debt of gratitude to the National Endowment for the Humanities, and to David Parsons for generously providing the funds that have made this contribution to the 400th Anniversary celebrations of the King James Bible possible.

Sarah E. Thomas

Bodley's Librarian and Head of Bodleian Libraries

Stephen Enniss

Eric Weinmann Librarian, Folger Shakespeare Library

Figure 2 King James, as depicted on the Tower of the Five Orders, Bodleian Library, Oxford. The Tower was built as part of the expansion of the Bodleian Library in 1613–19. Photograph © Tim Rawle.

Preface and Acknowledgements

'Great and manifold were the blessings, most dread Sovereign, which Almighty God, the Father of all mercies, bestowed upon us the people of *England*, when first he sent Your Majesty's Royal Person to rule and reign over us'.

Thus begins the experience of reading the King James Bible in most of the editions published today, which still print the translators' dedication from the first edition of 1611, even though the rest of the original preliminary matter (preface, map, genealogies, almanac, table of psalms and lessons) has for the most part disappeared from sight for modern readers. The persistence of the dedication to King James is largely explained by the need to elaborate for modern readers the nature of the connection between that king and this translation of the Bible. James VI of Scotland faced many competing expectations on his accession to the English throne as James I of England in 1603. While on the one hand the King James Bible is very directly the product of those competing expectations, on the other hand it has over the years defied its origins in controversy and come to be seen as a unifying element in the English-speaking Christian church and a cultural touchstone across the world for believers and non-believers alike.

'Manifold' means 'abundant' and 'diverse'; it is therefore a fitting adjective to describe the ways in which the King James Bible (KJB) has influenced the English language and Anglophone culture across four hundred years. *Manifold Greatness* celebrates the abundance and diversity that characterise the KJB's beginnings and afterlives by taking a fresh look at the origins of the translation, its cultural, literary, religious and material contexts, and its role in establishment and non-conformist contexts in England up until 1769. This is the date of the first revision to the 1611 text. Known as the 'Oxford Standard Version' and prepared by Benjamin Blayney for Oxford University Press, the 1769 revision has served as the basis for the text of the KJB ever since.

Manifold Greatness is linked to two exhibitions mounted in the KJB quatercentenary year of 2011: 'Manifold Greatness: Oxford and the Making of the King James Bible' at the Bodleian Library, Oxford, UK and 'Manifold Greatness: The Creation and Afterlife of the King James Bible' at the Folger Shakespeare Library, Washington, DC. The Bodleian exhibition has a particular focus on the role played by Oxford in the first 150 years of the translation's life: it seeks to provide a glimpse into the world of books inhabited by the members of the two translating committees based in Oxford, and to celebrate the wealth of Bible-related material preserved by the Bodleian and the Oxford colleges. The Folger exhibition enlarges this interest in the early years of the KJB to include the profoundly significant role played by the KJB in American religious, cultural and political life. We are delighted that this book shares in the collective endeavour of the two exhibitions by incorporating chapters on the KJB in America, and on KJB-related holdings in the Folger Shakespeare Library.

We would like to extend our considerable thanks to those with whom we have worked on *Manifold Greatness* in all its aspects: the Oxford curatorial committee (Valentine Cunningham, Judith Maltby, Diarmaid MacCulloch, Peter McCullough, Elizabeth Solopova and Chris Rowland); the Bodleian Library (especially Madeline Slaven, Sarah Wheale, Samuel Fanous, Deborah Susman, Janet Phillips and Dot Little); and the Folger Shakespeare Library (Hannibal Hamlin, Steve Galbraith, Caryn Laruzzi and Garland Scott). In addition, we would like to record our gratitude to those persons and institutions who have supported *Manifold Greatness* through loans or other acts of generosity, whether institutional, practical or intellectual: the British Library; Lambeth Palace Library; the Right Reverend Colin Fletcher, Bishop of Dorchester; Mr David Parsons; Prof. Diarmaid MacCulloch; the President and Fellows of Corpus Christi College, Oxford; the Warden and Fellows of Merton College, Oxford; the Rector and Fellows of Lincoln College, Oxford; the Provost and Fellows of The Queen's College, Oxford; the Master and Fellows of University College, Oxford; and the staff of the Oxford Conservation Consortium.

Helen Moore
Julian Reid

Corpus Christi College, Oxford
November 2010

other women that were with them, which tolde theſe things vnto the Apoſtles.

11 And their words ſeemed to them as idle tales, and they beleeued them not.

*Iohn 20. 6.

12 *Then aroſe Peter, and ranne vnto the Sepulchre, and ſtowping downe, hee behelde the linnen clothes layd by themſelues, and departed, wondering in himſelfe at that which was come to paſſe.

*Marke 16. 12.

13 ¶*And behold, two of them went that ſame day to a village called Emaus, which was from Hieruſalem about threeſcore furlongs.

14 And they talked together of all theſe things which had happened.

15 And it came to paſſe, that while they communed together, and reaſoned, Ieſus himſelfe drew neere, and went with them.

16 But their eyes were holden, that they ſhould not know him.

17 And he ſaid vnto them, what maner of communications are theſe that yee haue one to another as yee walke, and are ſad?

18 And the one of them, whoſe name was Cleophas, anſwering, ſaide vnto him, Art thou onely a ſtranger in Hieruſalem, and haſt not knowen the things which are come to paſſe there in theſe dayes?

19 And hee ſaide vnto them, What things? And they ſaid vnto him, Concerning Ieſus of Nazareth, which was a Prophet, mighty in deede and word before God, and all the people.

20 And how the chiefe Prieſts and our rulers deliuered him to be condemned to death, and haue crucified him.

21 But wee truſted that it had bene hee, which ſhould haue redeemed Iſrael: and beſide all this, to day is the third day ſince theſe things were done.

22 Yea, and certaine women alſo of our company made vs aſtoniſhed, which were early at the Sepulchre:

23 And when they found not his bodie, they came, ſaying, that they had alſo ſeene a viſion of Angels, which ſaide that he was aliue.

24 And certaine of them which were with vs, went to the Sepulchre, and found it euen ſo as the women had ſaid, but him they ſaw not.

25 Then hee ſaide vnto them, O fooles, and ſlow of heart to beleeue

all that the Prophets haue ſpoken:

26 Ought not Chriſt to haue ſuffered theſe things, and to enter into his glorie?

27 And beginning at Moſes, and all the Prophets, hee expounded vnto them in all the Scriptures, the things concerning himſelfe.

28 And they drew nigh vnto the village, whither they went, and hee made as though hee would haue gone further.

29 But they conſtrained him, ſaying, Abide with vs, for it is towards euening, and the day is farre ſpent: And he went in, to tarrie with them.

30 And it came to paſſe, as hee ſate at meate with them, hee tooke bread, and bleſſed it, and brake, and gaue to them.

31 And their eyes were opened, and they knew him, and he ‖ vaniſhed out of their ſight.

‖ Or, ceaſed to be ſeene of them.

32 And they ſaid one vnto another, Did not our heart burne within vs, while hee talked with vs by the way, and while hee opened to vs the Scriptures?

33 And they roſe vp the ſame houre, and returned to Hieruſalem, and found the eleuen gathered together, and them that were with them,

34 Saying, The Lord is riſen indeed, and hath appeared to Simon.

35 And they told what things were done in the way, & how he was knowen of them in breaking of bread.

*Marke 16. 14.

36 ¶*And as they thus ſpake, Ieſus himſelfe ſtood in the midſt of them, and ſayeth vnto them, Peace bee vnto you.

37 But they were terrified, and affrighted, and ſuppoſed that they had ſeene a ſpirit.

38 And he ſaid vnto them, why are yee troubled, and why doe thoughts ariſe in your hearts?

39 Beholde my hands and my feete, that it is I my ſelfe: handle me, and ſee, for a ſpirit hath not fleſh and bones, as ye ſee me haue.

40 And when hee had thus ſpoken, hee ſhewed them his handes and his feete.

41 And while they yet beleeued not for ioy, and wondered, hee ſaide vnto them, Haue ye here any meat?

42 And they gaue him a piece of a broyled fiſh, and of an hony combe.

43 And he tooke it, and did eate before them.

44 And hee ſaid vnto them, Theſe are the words which I ſpake vnto you while I was yet with you, þ all things muſt be fulfilled, which were written the Law of Moſes, & in the Prophets, and in the Pſalmes concerning me.

45 Then opened he their vnderſtanding, that they might vnderſtand the Scriptures,

46 And ſaid vnto them, Thus written, & thus it behoued Chriſt to ſuffer, & to riſe from the dead the third day:

47 And that repentance and remiſſion of ſinnes ſhould be preached in his Name, among all nations, beginning

¶ The Goſpel

CHAP. I.

Gen. 1. 1.

IN the beginning was the Word, & the Word was with God, and the Word was God.

2 *The ſame was in the beginning with God.

Col. 1. 16.

3 *All things were made by him, and without him was not any thing made that was made.

4 In him was life, and the life was the light of men.

5 And the light ſhineth in darkneſſe, and the darkneſſe comprehended it not.

Mat. 3. 1.

6 ¶*There was a man ſent from God, whoſe name was Iohn.

7 The ſame came for a witneſſe, to beare witneſſe of the light, that all men through him might beleeue.

8 Hee was not that light, but ſent to beare witneſſe of that light.

9 That was the true light, which lighteth euery man that commeth into the world.

Heb. 11. 3.

10 Hee was in the world, and the world was made by him, and the world knew him not.

Hierusalem.
48 And yee are witnesses of these
ings.
49 ¶ *And behold, I send the prose of my Father vpon you: but tarie
in the citie of Hierusalem, vntill ye be
ued with power from on high.
50 ¶ And he led them out as farre
to Bethanie, and hee lift vp his
nds, and blessed them.
51 *And it came to passe, while hee
ssed them, hee was parted from
em, and caried vp into heauen.
52 And they worshipped him, and
urned to Hierusalem, with great ioy:
53 And were continually in the Tem=
-, praising and blessing God. Amen.

*Iohn 15.
26. actes
1.4.

*Mar. 16.
19. actes
1.9.

rding to S. Iohn.

1 Hee came vnto his owne, and his
one receiued him not.
12 But as many as receiued him, to
em gaue hee ‖ power to become the
nes of God, euen to them that beleeue
his Name:
13 Which were borne, not of blood,
 of the will of the flesh, nor of the will
man, but of God.
14 *And the word was made flesh,
d dwelt among vs (& we beheld his
ory, the glory as of the onely begotten
the Father) full of grace and trueth.
15 ¶ Iohn bare witnesse of him, and
ed, saying, This was he of whom I
ake, He that commeth after me, is pre=
rred before me, for he was before me.
16 And of his *fulnesse haue all wee
ceiued, and grace for grace.
17 For the Law was giuen by Mo-
s, but grace and trueth came by Ie-
s Christ.
18 *No man hath seene God at any
ne: the onely begotten Sonne, which
in the bosome of the Father, he hath
clared him.
19 ¶ And this is the record of Iohn,
hen the Iewes sent Priests and Le=
tes from Hierusalem, to aske him,
ho art thou?
20 And he confessed, and denied not:
t confessed, I am not the Christ.

‖ Or, the
right or pri-
uiledge.

*Mat. 1.16.

*Col. 1.19.

*1. Iohn 4.
12. 1. tim.
6.16.

I 3   21 And

I

Before the King James Bible

Diarmaid MacCulloch and Elizabeth Solopova

Figure 3 *pp 12–13* The opening
of the Gospel of St John in the
1611 King James Bible. Oxford,
Bodleian Library, Bib. Eng.
1611 b.1.

Figure 4 *right* A page from
the 'MacRegol Gospels',
showing St John's Gospel,
starting at 21:16 (*Dicit ei iterum:
Simon Joannis, diligis me?...*)
with a border of geometric
patterns, Old English gloss,
and the beginning of Owun's
note in the bottom margin.
Oxford, Bodleian Library, MS.
Auct. D. 2. 19,
fol. 168v.

T HE HISTORY OF THE BIBLE IN ENGLAND, at least as far as it
can be documented, begins with the Christianisation of the
Anglo-Saxons at the end of the sixth century. The earliest
biblical manuscripts were imported from Italy, some possibly with
or soon after Augustine's mission to Kent in 597. Such may be the
'Gospels of St Augustine', written in Italy in the sixth century, once at
St Augustine's, Canterbury, where they were used as an oath book for
incoming archbishops, and now in Corpus Christi College, Cambridge.[1]
Some time during the seventh century manuscripts started to be copied
in native scriptoria. A great achievement from Bede's Northumbria was
Codex Amiatinus, one of three huge, single-volume Bibles produced at
the monastery of Wearmouth-Jarrow around 700, and the earliest extant
complete Latin Bible. Complete Bibles, however, were rare in the early
Middle Ages; much more common was the circulation of Scriptures
as a selection of texts from the Old or New Testaments, such as the
Gospels, psalms, epistles and prophets. Such collections were portable
and cheaper to make. The gospel book and liturgical psalter, the two
most basic requirements for any monastic or secular church, survive in
particularly large numbers.

The Bible and Old English translation

Translations from the Bible may have been undertaken already at the
time of Bede, probably for use in teaching. A letter describing Bede's
death in 735, written by his pupil Cuthbert, later abbot of Wearmouth-
Jarrow, survives in manuscripts dating from the ninth century onwards.
This account, written for an acquaintance in another monastic house,
tells that during his final days Bede was working on a translation into
English of part of St John's Gospel. This translation does not survive,
but word-for-word interlinear glosses in Latin psalters and gospels are
known from the ninth century onwards. Such glosses probably had an
educational role and may have been used by younger or less learned
clergy and possibly, particularly in the case of psalters, by educated
wealthy lay people. Of forty psalters and psalter fragments surviving
from Anglo-Saxon England, fourteen, an impressively large number,
have an Old English gloss. Two Latin gospel books also have a gloss, the

16

17

18

19

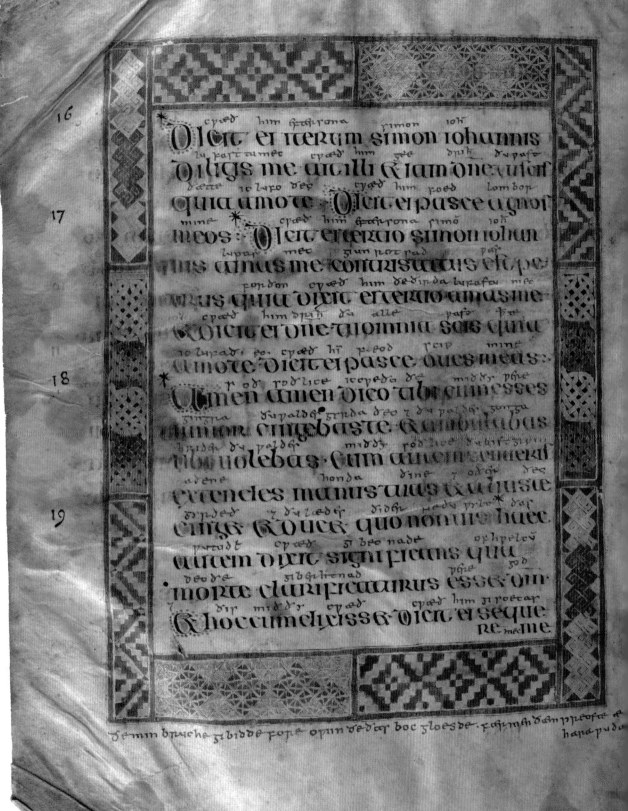

Lindisfarne Gospels in the British Library and the 'MacRegol Gospels' (or 'Rushworth Gospels') in the Bodleian Library. The 'MacRegol Gospels' (figure 4) were written around 800 in Irish half-uncial by a scribe whose name, MacRegol, appears on the last page in a request to the reader to pray for him. He is probably identifiable as the abbot of Birr, in modern County Offaly, Ireland, who died in 821 or 822. The book was imported into England where the Old English gloss was added throughout in the middle of the tenth century, around the same time as the Lindisfarne Gospels gloss, by a priest called Farman and a scribe called Owun, whose names also occur in the manuscript as part of prayers. Most glossed texts date from the second half of the tenth century onwards and are a product of the scholarly and educational activities of the Benedictine Revival.

Perhaps the most diverse and extensive evidence for biblical translation in Anglo-Saxon England are extracts from biblical books which survive in various prose works. Numerous short extracts from the Bible occur in Old English homilies, saints' lives, legal, pedagogical, historical and other texts. The earliest example of a continuous prose translation occurs as part of King Alfred's prologue to his law code, issued during the 880s or early 890s, and surviving at the end of the Parker manuscript of the Anglo-Saxon Chronicle (Cambridge, Corpus Christi College MS. 173). The prologue aims to put Alfred's laws into the context of Christian legislation, and contains portions of Exodus 20–23, describing Moses promulgating his laws, followed by a quotation from Acts 15:23–29, with an endorsement of Mosaic law by the Apostles. The translation is a mixture of close rendering and paraphrase.

Complete, or nearly complete, Old English translations of individual books and 'part-Bibles' – collections of books – also survive. Unlike glosses and quotations they are independent of Latin and other texts. An eleventh-century manuscript (Paris, Bibliothèque nationale de France, MS. lat. 8824), known as the 'Paris Psalter', preserves a full translation of the Book of Psalms, comprising a prose version of the first fifty psalms and a verse adaptation of the remaining hundred. It is unclear when or how the two translations were combined, but they were almost certainly originally independent. The author of the prose translation is probably King Alfred.[2] His work on the translation of the psalter, left unfinished at the time of his death, is mentioned by William of Malmesbury, and the prose version shares stylistic and linguistic features with his other compositions.

Alfred's translation of the psalms was part of a wider programme of educational reforms, literary activity and patronage aimed at re-establishing Christian scholarship and learning, which had been severely undermined by the Viking invasions. Very unusually, Alfred promoted literacy not only in Latin, but also in the vernacular, and not only among the clerical orders, but also among the laity. He saw the revival of learning not simply as a practical necessity for a functional political system but also as a foundation for moral and religious revival. His translation into Old English of texts which he considered 'most necessary for all men to know' made major works of Christian history and theology accessible for the first time to a lay and clerical reader educated in the vernacular.

By the end of the tenth century, a continuous translation of the four Gospels and substantial parts of the Pentateuch (the Books of the Law), Joshua and Judges also became available. Of the Old Testament books, Genesis was nearly complete, whereas large parts of the other books were omitted or summarised. Where the text was a direct translation, however, it was essentially faithful to the Latin Vulgate original. The translator of a substantial portion of the Old Testament was Ælfric (c. 950–c. 1010), abbot of Eynsham and one of the most prolific, learned and accomplished Old English writers. His surviving translations include Genesis up to 24:22, the second half of Numbers (from Chapter 13 onwards), and the whole but abbreviated version of Joshua, and Judges. The rest of the translation was the work of anonymous late tenth- to early eleventh-century authors. Their work was combined with Ælfric's, probably early in the eleventh century, to form a compilation which survives in nine versions, most of which are fragmentary. The two most important and complete copies are the lavishly illustrated British Library MS. Cotton Claudius B. IV, dating from the middle of the eleventh century, and Bodleian Library MS. Laud Misc. 509, written later in the eleventh century. Claudius contains the first six books of the Old Testament and is sometimes referred to as 'Old English Hexateuch', whereas Laud in addition to this has the seventh book, Judges, and is therefore known as 'Heptateuch'.

Ælfric discusses his attitudes to biblical translation in a Preface which precedes Genesis in both Claudius and Laud. He expresses concern about a possible misunderstanding of what he calls the 'naked narrative' by unlearned people, including clergy. His example is a priest who used to be his teacher and believed that polygamy was permissible based on the multiple marriages of patriarchs. Ælfric insists on the need for a historical understanding of texts, taking into account the differences between the 'old law' before and after Moses, and the 'new law' of Christ. He also explains the importance of a spiritual and Christological interpretation of the Old Testament. Ælfric discusses technical aspects of translation, such as the differences between Latin and English, and emphasises the need for accuracy, but admits that all languages differ in their word order and idiom. His translation is the most accomplished and learned part of the Heptateuch, but other translators also do not follow Latin slavishly. The Old English Heptateuch has didactic additions that provide commentary on the text. Occasionally translators attempt to explain, edit or shorten passages that are complex or can be misunderstood, such as the episodes that show biblical figures in a negative light and references to topics such as God's jealousy, sorcery, divination and circumcision. The work reflects a desire to control the interpretation of the text and to make it more accessible.[3]

The purpose and exact audience of the translations and compilation remain unclear. Ælfric tells that the translation of Genesis was made at the request of Ealdorman Æthelweard, a powerful nobleman and his patron. It may have been part of Ælfric's efforts to adapt materials for pious and learned laymen, evident in several of his works. As Marsden notes, however, Æthelweard himself was a Latinist who undertook translations *from* the vernacular, including a version of the Anglo-Saxon Chronicle.[4]

Old and New Testament stories and themes were also known to Anglo-Saxon audiences from poetic adaptations. The earliest surviving poem in English is a hymn about creation. A story of its divinely inspired composition in the late seventh century by an illiterate herdsman called Cædmon is told by Bede in his *Ecclesiastical History*. Bede reports that Cædmon composed many greatly admired poems, based on Genesis, Exodus and other Old and New Testament subjects. These poems do not survive, but the body of extant Old English verse uses similar narratives and themes. Bodleian Library MS. Junius 11 was written and illustrated, possibly as early as the late tenth century, at an unknown centre (Canterbury, Winchester, Glastonbury and Malmesbury have all been suggested). It has three poems based on Old Testament books, known by their modern titles as 'Genesis', 'Exodus' and 'Daniel', and a poem known as 'Christ and Satan', covering such subjects as the Harrowing of Hell, the Resurrection, the Ascension and the Day of Judgement. The longest poem, 'Genesis', consists of two originally independent compositions, the first recounting chronologically and in close detail the events of Genesis 1–22, from the Creation to Abraham's decision to sacrifice Isaac, and the second, telling about the Fall of the angels and of man, translated from Old Saxon. The poems were joined, probably already in the exemplar of the present manuscript, to create a single narrative comprising nearly 3,000 lines. The Junius manuscript also contains a series of ink illustrations completed only up to Abraham and Sarah's approach into Egypt, although planned, as can be seen from spaces left blank, for the whole of the Old Testament sequence (figure 5).

After the Norman Conquest, Old English homiletic and hagiographic texts, as well as parts of the translation of the Bible (Hexateuch,

Figure 5 Text and illustrations from Genesis (Adam and Eve in Paradise, with God beholding the beauty of his works). Oxford, Bodleian Library, MS. Junius 11 (late tenth century), p 11.

Gospels, psalter), continued to be copied in monastic centres, although manuscripts based on Old English exemplars are far fewer than Latin and Anglo-Norman works produced during the same period. One of the centres of Old English learning after the Conquest was Worcester, where the library had a collection of Old English manuscripts. A thirteenth-century scribe, known as the 'Tremulous Hand' of Worcester due to his recognisable handwriting, copied some texts and added Latin glosses to at least nineteen manuscripts in Old English. The 'Tremulous Hand' also copied some verse, known as the 'Worcester Fragments', which praises Old English monastic scholarship and the achievements of the Anglo-Saxon church. A short poem, known as the 'First Worcester Fragment', praises Bede and Ælfric for translating books, including the Pentateuch, and for teaching people in their own language. Old English bishops, such as John of Beverly, Cuthbert and Oswald of Worcester, are praised for preaching in English. The author of the 'Fragment' concludes that 'now this teaching is lost' and so the people are lost as well.

The Middle English period

Already towards the end of the twelfth century, however, important new texts were written in English, including adaptations of biblical books, such as the *Ormulum*, dating from around 1200 and containing a verse paraphrase of the Gospels and Acts. Verse and prose adaptations of biblical narratives were made throughout the Middle English period. Such are the *Cursor Mundi*, written around 1300, and *The Prick of Conscience*, dating from the middle of the fourteenth century, both very popular works containing an account of biblical history. Most of these texts were written for the laity, or for mixed clerical and lay audiences. Vernacular paraphrases and translations from the Bible had their opponents. Throughout the period there were doubts as to whether English was sufficiently flexible and developed to be the language of spiritual guidance, and whether people without a clerical education should have access to theology and the Scriptures. Throughout the period church authorities attempted to control the content and practice of preaching and translation, and to censor materials addressed to the laity. However, the growing emancipation and education of lay believers resulted in a greater number, variety and sophistication of texts made available to them.

A translation of the psalter by Richard Rolle (*c.* 1290–1349), a hermit and a mystical writer, who lived for some of his life and died in Hampole, Yorkshire, is one of three surviving Middle English translations, produced before the middle of the fourteenth century. According to a medieval tradition the translation was composed for Rolle's disciple and friend, anchoress Margaret Kirkeby. The work was widely circulated and survives in a large number of copies, but originally it may have been intended for use by a small circle of Rolle's educated and spiritually sophisticated followers. Rolle's translation is literal, intended to deviate as little as possible from the Latin, even in the word order. In manuscripts it accompanies the Latin text, laid out with the lines of the translation alternating with the lines of the original, and according to Rolle's Preface aims to assist the reading and understanding of Latin. The translation is accompanied by a verse-by-verse commentary, based on Peter Lombard's authoritative gloss on the psalter.

The Wycliffite Bible and medieval translation

The first full translation of the Bible in English, aiming to satisfy the need for wide lay access to the text of the Scriptures, was the Wycliffite Bible, produced by the followers of the Oxford theologian John Wyclif (c.1324–1384). The identity of the translators remains uncertain, but the magnitude and scholarly nature of the project must have required the involvement of several academic translators and access to libraries, making Oxford a likely place for their work. John Wyclif probably instigated the translation and it may have started in the 1370s at The Queen's College, Oxford, where he lived between 1374 and 1381. Early evidence also points to Nicholas Hereford and John Trevisa, both fellows of Queen's in the 1370s, as translators, though pre-Reformation attributions are rare and uncertain. The translation survives in two versions, the Earlier Version, a literal rendering of the Latin text, and the Later Version, a more idiomatic revision, preserved in a much larger number of copies. The textual tradition of the two versions is highly complex, partly because the revision was an ongoing process (figure 6).

The purpose and methods of the translation are discussed in the prologue, usually referred to as the General Prologue. Its author is unknown, but he represents himself as being in charge of the production of the Later Version, in which he was assisted by 'diverse fellows and helpers'. The translators were aware that one of the arguments against biblical translation was the use of a potentially corrupt text of the Latin Bible. To address this, as described in the final chapter of the Prologue, they started with establishing an authoritative Latin text through consulting many 'old bibles'. The work proceeded through studying the Latin text with the help of commentaries and glosses, consulting linguistic authorities to elucidate difficult words and phrases, and eventually producing a clear and accurate English translation. The General Prologue claims that the Later Version has less need to be corrected than the text of the common Latin Bibles.

The Lollards emphasised the need for direct knowledge of the text of the Scriptures, without mediation, and believed that the biblical text, as the word of God, had superior authority to the works of human authors, and should be kept separate from any additions, even those sanctioned by the church. According to the Prologue, the translators avoided adding words unnecessarily, though where the text was unclear they could include glosses within the text or in the margins. Unlike in the Old English Heptateuch and most earlier translations and adaptations, however, such commentary had to be kept strictly separate from the text. In existing manuscripts marginal glosses are clearly distinguished from the translation: those within the text are usually underlined in red, and prologues are explicitly identified. The work of the Wycliffite translators led to the development of scholarship focused on the text of the Bible, issues of authenticity and authority, textual criticism and presentation of the text. The Prologue discusses the textual condition of the Latin Bible, makes a distinction between canon and apocrypha, gives a definition of both and provides a list of canonical books. Surviving marginal glosses draw attention to the differences between the Latin text and the Hebrew original, and to issues of the authority and canonicity of individual passages.

The Wycliffite Bible was met with violent clerical opposition, resulting in the promulgation of legislation prohibiting the making of new translations and the use of any recent translations without episcopal approval of both the version and the owner. Concerns about access to scripture by the laity, the impossibility of translation adequately rendering a range of meanings present in the original, and the loss of control over the production and dissemination of the Bible, existed throughout the medieval period. It seems that the primary reason why the Wycliffite Bible became the first ever translation to be condemned by the English church was its association with John Wyclif, whose radical ideas about the church as an institution, its practices and its relationship with the state were perceived to be heretical. Archbishop Thomas Arundel's articles against heresy ('Constitutions') were issued at the Provincial Council at Oxford in 1407, and promulgated at the London Council at St Paul's in 1409. They were subsequently published as part of William Lyndwood's *Provinciale seu Constitutiones Anglie* (1433), a glossed collection of the most important ecclesiastical legislation of the province of Canterbury from 1222 up to the time of writing, and the principal authority for medieval English canon law.

The church was conscious of the demand for the Bible in English, and formally, at least, there was no outright prohibition, but rather a requirement that any translation be licensed. However, very little evidence survives for the existence of a system of licences and its operation.

Figure 6 The beginning of the Song of Songs in one of the earliest and most important manuscripts of the Wycliffite Bible, dating from *c*.1380–1390, possibly copied directly from the translators' original and containing corrections witnessing continuous work on the text. MS. Bodl. 959, fol. 269v.

Here begynneth ye book yt is clepid songis of songis of ye bridale of crist & of ye chirche. ye chirche of ye comyns of crist spekey seiynge. kisse he me wt ye cosse of his mouy. for bettre be y tetis yan wyn. smellynge wt best oynementis. oile held out y name. þore ye ȝunge maydyns wy me loueden. reeful myche ye vois of ye chirche to crist. drawe me aftir þee. wee shul renen i ye smel of þyn oynementis. ye chirche seiy of crist. broȝte me in to his celeris. wee shul ful out ioȝe & glade i þee. myndeful of ye tetys vp on wyn. riȝt me loue þee. ye chirche of his tribulaciouns. o ȝee doȝtris of irl sublie I am blac but shaply. as ye tabernaclis of cedar as ye skynnes of salamon. wileȝ not beholden yt I be broun. for distoisou haȝ me chaunged ye sunne. ye sones of my modir foȝte aȝein me. þei setteden me kepere i vynes. my vyneȝerd I kepte not ye vois of ye chirche to crist. shew y to me whom loueey my soule. wher y ȝifuest. leswe. wher y liggest i mydday. lest I bigynne to go aftir ye flockis of þi felawes. ye vois of crist to ye chirche. if y knowest not þee o þ most fair a mong wymmen. go out & go aftir ye steppis of þi flockis. & fede þi got beside ye tabernacle of shepperdes. to my ridise i charis of pha rao I lickenede þee o my leef. faire be þy chekis as of a turtil. þi necke as brochis. siluerne rnbaied. wee shul make to þee mayd fir reed wt selur. ye vois of ye chirche of crist whan ye kis was i his lugyng place. my mad eucense ȝaf his smel. A bundel of myrre my leman is to me betwen my tetis he shal dwelle. ye cluster of cipresse my leman to me i þe vynes of engaddy. ye vois of crist to ye chirche lo y art faire my leef. lo y a faire wyn eȝen of culueris. ye vois of ye chirche to crist lo y art faire my leman & semely. oure bed shynys. ye trees of oure houses cedre. oure coupsis cipresse. ye vois of crist. I of ye flour of ye feeld & ye lilie chirchia of askyes. as a lelye amons þornes. so my leef amons doȝtris. ye vois of ye chirche of crist. as an appil tree amons þe trees of woodis. so my leman amons sones. vnder ye shadewe of hym whom I hadde de sired I sit. & his frute swete to my þrote. ye kis ladde me i to his wyn celer. he ordeynede i me charite. vnderleȝ ȝee me

wt floures. setteȝ me aboute wt apples. for I langu ysshe for loue. ye vois of ye chirche of crist. þe lift hond of hym vnder myn heued. þis riȝt hond shal clippe me. ye vois of crist of ye chirche. I adiure ȝou ȝee doȝtris of irl bi ye capronis & ye hertis of feeldis. ne reise ȝee ne make ȝe leef to wake. to ye tyme yt she wile. ye vois of ye chirche of crist. ye vois of my leman to vis coney lepinge i mounteynes & ou lepinge hillis. lic is my leman to a capret & to an hert calf of hertis. lo he stant bihynden oure wal biholdinge bi ye wyndowis. afer lookinge þuriȝ ye la tisis. lo my leman spekey to me. ris vp y my leef my culu my shaply & cu. now forsoþe wynt passede weder ȝede fro & is gon awei. floures apeiede i oure loud dryue of kuttis is comen. ye vois of ye turtle is herd i oure loud. ye fiȝt tree broȝte forþ his firste fiȝis. ye vynes flourise ȝyuen y smel. ye vois of crist to ye chirche. ris vp my leef my shaply & cu y my culu. i ye holis of ye stoon i ye clyue of a stoon wal. shewe y to me y face. sowne y vois i myn eris. y vois forsoye is sweete & y face semely. ye vois of crist to ye chirche aȝen heretikes. take ȝee to vs litle foxes yt destroȝe vy nes. for oure vyne flowryde ye vois of ye chirche of crist. my leoued to me & I to hym yt is fed amons lilies. to ye tyme yt ye day springe & shadewes bo bowed in. turne aȝein lice be y o my leman to a ca pret & to ye hert calf of hertis. vp on ye mounteynes of bettel. ye vois of ye chir chia. I my litil bed bi þe nyȝte gedered to gidere of nyȝtis I soȝte whom loueede my ȝeutu tis soule. I soȝte by & I fond not. I shal ris & gon aboute ye cite bi toburwis & stiȝts. I shal seche whom loueey my soule. I soȝte by & fond not. y foude me ye waccheris yt kepe ye cite. ye chirche seiy of crist to ye apostolis. wheyr whom loueey my soule ȝee seeȝen. a litil whan I hadde passed ye I foud whom loueey my soule. I heeld hy & I shal not leten to ye tyme yt I brynge hy i to ye hous of my modir & to ye bed of hir yt gat me. & ye vois of crist of ye chirche. I adiure ȝou ȝee doȝtris of irl bui capris & hertis of feeldis. ne reise ȝee ne make ȝee my leef to wake. to ye tyme yt she ruse. ye spuasodr of ye chirche. whan is she yt stieȝy up bi deseit as a litil ȝerde of smoke. of ye swote spices. off

ye vois of ye fadir
ye vois of ye chirche
v
of a turtle
iii c·2
i
iiii vois
go
iii c 3

The best-known example of an officially sanctioned text is *The Mirror of the Blessed Life of Jesus Christ*, written early in the fifteenth century by Nicholas Love (d. 1424), prior of Mount Grace Charterhouse in Yorkshire. It was a free translation of an immensely popular Franciscan devotional work, *Meditationes vitae Christi*, ascribed in the Middle Ages to St Bonaventura. Like the Wycliffite Bible it was among the most successful works in Middle English, surviving in forty-nine complete or nearly complete manuscripts and found as extracts and fragments in twelve more. Love was writing for a secular audience, and seems to have conceived his work as an authorised scripture for laity, and an 'official alternative' to the Wycliffite Bible.[5] The work was licensed by Archbishop Arundel in 1410 and a certificate of approval is found attached to nineteen copies of the text. Intended to be used for meditation, it recounts events in the life and passion of Christ accompanied by orthodox interpretative and devotional material. The *Meditationes* contains polemical additions addressing Lollard views on confession, the Eucharist, the giving of tithes and the authority of priests. In many manuscripts such passages have the marginal note '*contra lollardos*'. The work's sharp opposition to Wycliffite ideology is, however, most obvious in the decision to provide a highly limited and thoroughly mediated access to the biblical text, entirely dependent on the interpretative authority of the church.

Arundel's Constitutions remained in force until 1529, and the persecutions that they initiated continued and increased in severity throughout the fifteenth century. Possession of the Bible or indeed any other religious text in English could result in a trial for heresy, ending in imprisonment or death. Considering this, it is particularly striking how successful was the Wycliffite translation. It started as a highly learned and specialised scholarly enterprise, but left the confines of academia to reach the widest possible audience. Much is unclear about the medieval ownership of the Wycliffite Bibles, but their known owners range from a king to clerics, members of religious orders, women and tradesmen. In spite of the extensive destruction of Wycliffite texts throughout the fifteenth century, the Bible survives in about 250 copies, significantly more than any other Middle English text. A great majority of manuscripts are professionally executed to a high standard, and in many the presentation of the text and accompanying materials suggest a possible liturgical use. About one-third of the manuscripts have lectionaries, and some have liturgical calendars, rubrics explaining how the texts were read or sung in church, and *mise-en-page* supporting the use of the texts in liturgy. However, it remains entirely obscure where or by whom the manuscripts were made, or how they were disseminated. In the situation of censorship the scribes and artists who wrote and illuminated the Bibles and the early owners of the books were unwilling to leave their names on their copies, and any other contemporary records were unlikely to survive.

The medieval history of English biblical translation anticipates subsequent history by offering examples of royal patronage, collaborative work, the crucial role of monastic and, later, university scholarship, and by exposing polarised attitudes towards vernacular scripture. Much is unclear about the use of medieval translations by later scholars, but it has been noticed that some phrases from the Wycliffite Bible are familiar to a modern reader because they appear in the King James Bible.[6] The famous example is Matthew 25:21, where at the end of the Parable of the Talents the KJB has 'enter thou into the joy of thy lord'. These admired words appear in the Wycliffite Bible and Coverdale's 1535 revision of Tyndale's New Testament. A curious example of continuity in English translations of the Bible is a much ridiculed reading 'breeches' in the story of the Fall of man in the Geneva Bible: 'Then the eyes of them both were opened, and they knew that they were naked, and they sewed fig tree leaves together, and made themselves breeches.' (Genesis 3:7), which actually has a very respectable ancestry:

> καὶ ἐποίησαν ἑαυτοῖς περιζώματα (Septuagint)
> et fecerunt sibi perizomata (Vulgate)
> and worhton him wǣdbrēc (Ælfric)
> and maden hem brechis (Wycliffite Bible Earlier Version)
> and maden brechis to hem silf (Wycliffite Bible Later Version)
> and made them apurns (Tyndale)
> and made them apurns (Coverdale Bible)
> and made them selues aperns (Great Bible)
> and made them apurns (Matthew Bible)
> & made them selues apernes (Bishops' Bible)
> and made themselues aprons (Rheims Douai)
> and made them selues breeches (Geneva Bible)
> and made themselves aprons (KJB)

It would appear that all translators struggled with this text and most copied earlier work, starting with the Vulgate, which simply borrows a word from the Greek. The readings are unlikely to be independent and point to a need for further research into the late medieval and early modern awareness and use of earlier translations.

The English Bible in the Tudor Age

Once the official English church had confined access to the Lollard Bible translation to those who could be trusted to read it without ill consequence, England's lack of provision for vernacular Bibles stood

bus expofito digno fide fomnio: per
qd vniuerfos letificauit. Erat aūt bu
iufcemodi vifus oniāqui fuerat fum
mus facerdos virū bonū z benignum
verecundū vifu: modeftā mozib? z elo
quio decoꝝ: z qui a puero in virtutib?
exercitatus ſit manus ptendentē: oꝛa
re pꝛo omni pplo iudeoꝝ. Poft ħ ap
paruiffe z aliūvirū etatez gła mirabi
lem: z magni decoꝛis babitudinē cir
ca illū. Rñdentē vero oniam dixiffe.
Hic eft fratrū amatoꝛ z ppłi ifł. Hic
eft q multū oꝛat pꝛo pplo z vniuerfa
fcta ciuitate bieremias ppħa dei. Et
tēdiffe añt bieremiā dexterā z dediffe
iude gladiū aureū dicente. Accipe fan
ctū gladiū munus a deo: in q deijcies
aduerfarios pplī mei ifrael. Exhorta
ti itaꝗ iude fmonib? bonis valde de
qbus extolli poffet imper? z animi iu
nenū pfoꝛtari: ftatueſt dimicare z cō
fligere foꝛtiter vt ꝗtus d negochs in
dicaret: eo ꝗ ciuitas fancta z tēplum
periclitarent. Erat eñ pꝛo vxoribus
z filijs: iteꝗ pꝛo fratribuz cognatis
minoꝛ follicitudo: maximus ꝙ oꝛpm?
pꝛo fanctitate timoꝛ erat tēpli. Sed
z eos q in ciuitate erant non minima
follicitudo bēbat pꝛo bis ꝗ cōgreffu
ri erāt. Et cū iam oēs fperarēt iudici
um futurū boftefꝗ adeffent atꝗ exer
citus erat oꝛdiatus: beftie eꝗteſꝗ op
poꝛtuno in loco cōpofiti ꝓfiderās ma
cbabeus aduentū multitudinis z ap
paratū variū armoꝛ ac ferocitatē be
ftiaꝝ extendēs manus in celū: pdigia
facientē dñm inuocauit: q non ſm ar
moꝛ potentiā fed ꝓut ipſi placet dat
dignis victoꝛiaz. Dixit autē inuocans
boc modo. Tu dñe qui mififti angelū
tuū fub ezechia rege iuda: z interfeci
fti de caftris fennacberib centū octo
gintaquinꝗ milia: z nūc dñatoꝛ celoꝛ
ruz mitte angelū tuuz bonum añ nos
i timoꝛe z treinoꝛe magnitudinis bꝛa
chij tui: vt metuant q cuz blafpbemia
veniunt aduerfus fanctū pplm tuum
Et bic qdem ita poꝛauit. Nicanoꝛ āt
z q cum ipo erant cū tubis z canticis
admouebāt. Iudas ꝓo z q cū eo erāt
inuocato deo: per oꝛoꝛes ꝓgreffi funt
manu qdě pugnātes: fed z dñm coꝛdi
bus oꝛates pftrauerunt nō minus tri
gintaꝗnꝗ milia pñtia dei magnifice
delectati. Cunꝗ ceffaffent z cū gau
dio redirent: cognouerunt nicanoꝛem
ruiffe cuz armis fuis. Facto itaꝗ cla
moꝛe z ꝑturbatioe excitata pfia voce

oſpotentē ofiꝗ. bñdicebant. z pcepte
autez iudas qui per oīa coꝛpoꝛez aīo
moꝛi pꝛo ciubus paratus erat caput
nicanoꝛis z manū cum bumero abfcif
fam bierofolymā pferri. Quo cuz pue
niffet ꝓuocatis ꝓtribulibus z facerdo
tib? ad altare acceffit ad eos q in ar
cerant. Et oftēfo capite nicanoꝛis z
manu nefaria quā extenderat ꝺ domū
fanctā omnipotētis dei magnifice glo
riatus eft. Linguaz etiā impij nicano
ris ꝓciffam iuffit pticulatim auibus
dari: manum aūt dementis ꝺ templū
fufpendi. Oēs igitur celi bñdixerunt
dñm dicentes: bñdictus qui locū fuuz
incontaminatum fuauit. Sufpendit
aūt nicanoꝛis caput in fumma arcevt
euidēs eēt māifeftū fignū auxilij dei
Itaꝗ oēs cōmuni ꝓfilio decreuerunt
nullo modo diē iftum abfꝗ celebrita
te pterire: babere autem celebritatem
tertiadecima die menfis adar: que dſ
voce fyriaca ꝓdie mardochei die Igit
bis erga nicanoꝛē geftis: z ex illis tpi
bus ab bebꝛeis ciuitate poffeffa: ego
ꝗ in bis faciam finē fermonis. Et ſi
quidē bene z vt biftoꝛie cōpetit boc: z
ipfe velim: ſi aūt minus digne conce
dendus eft mibi. Sicut eñ vinuz fem
per bibere: aut femp aquam cōtrariū
eft alternis añt vti delectabile: ita le
gentib? ſi femp exactus ſit fmo: non
erit gratus: ꝺ ergo erit cōfummatus.

¶ Scōs liber Machabeoꝝ explicit.
¶ Epiftola beati bieronimi ad dama
fum papa in ꝗttuoꝛ euāgeliftas icipit

Beatiffimo pape damafo. Hiero
nimus. Si nouū op? me facere co
gis ex veteri: vt poft exemplaria fcri
pturarū toto oꝛbe difperfa quaſi qui
dam arbiter fedeam: z qꝛ inter fe vari
ant que ſint illa que cum greca cōfen
tiant veritate decernam. Pius laboꝛ
fed periculofa pfumptio iudicare de
ceteris ipm ab oībus iudicandum: fe
nis mutare linguā z canefcentem iam
mundū ad initia retrabere paruuloꝝ
Quis eñ doctus pariter vel indoct?:
cum in manus volumen affumpferit
z a faliua quam femel imbibit viderit
difcrepare qd lectitat: non ftatim erū
pat in vocez: me falfarium me clamās
effe facrilegum: qui audea in aliqd in
veteribus libꝛis addere: mutare coꝛ
rigere. Aduerfus quam inuidiam du
plex caufa me cōfolatur: quod et tu q

ꝺ
1. mac. 7ꝺ

E
ſ. 8. ꝺ
4. reg. 19. ꝺ
Eccl. 48. ꝺ

fummus facer
rum nō effe qd
rum teftimoni
nis exēplarib?
rñdeant qbus
quot codices.
renda de plurib
ginem reuerter
ſis interpretib?
fumptoꝛib? im
uerfiusvel a li
aut addita ſu
mus. Neꝗ ver
to teftō: qd a ſ
in grecam ling
du ad nos vſꝗ
quid aquila: q
quare tbedodo
res medius in
terpꝛetatio in
De nouo nunc
cum effe non ꝛ
ftolo mattheo
geliuz chꝛifti ꝛ
boc certe cū m
datꝛ in diuerfo
cit: vno de font
mitto eos cod
esꝛto nuncupa
rit puerfa com
in toto veteri i
interpretes en
nouo ꝓfuit ꝛ
gentiū linguis
ta doceat falſ
Igitur bec pꝛe
licetur: ꝗttuoꝛ
do eft ifte. Aꝺ
iobannes cod
ta collatione:
tuꝛ a lectioni
creparent: ita
bis tm que ſe
coꝛrectis: reli
vt fuerant. La
cefarienfis cp
ammonium in
nauit: ſicut in
fimus. Qd ſi
rit noffe que a
vel vicina ful
ne cognofcer.
in noftris cod
qd in eadē re
ſit: in alio qꝛ
rūt. Uel dū ꝑ
preffit: ille qu
rat ad eius e

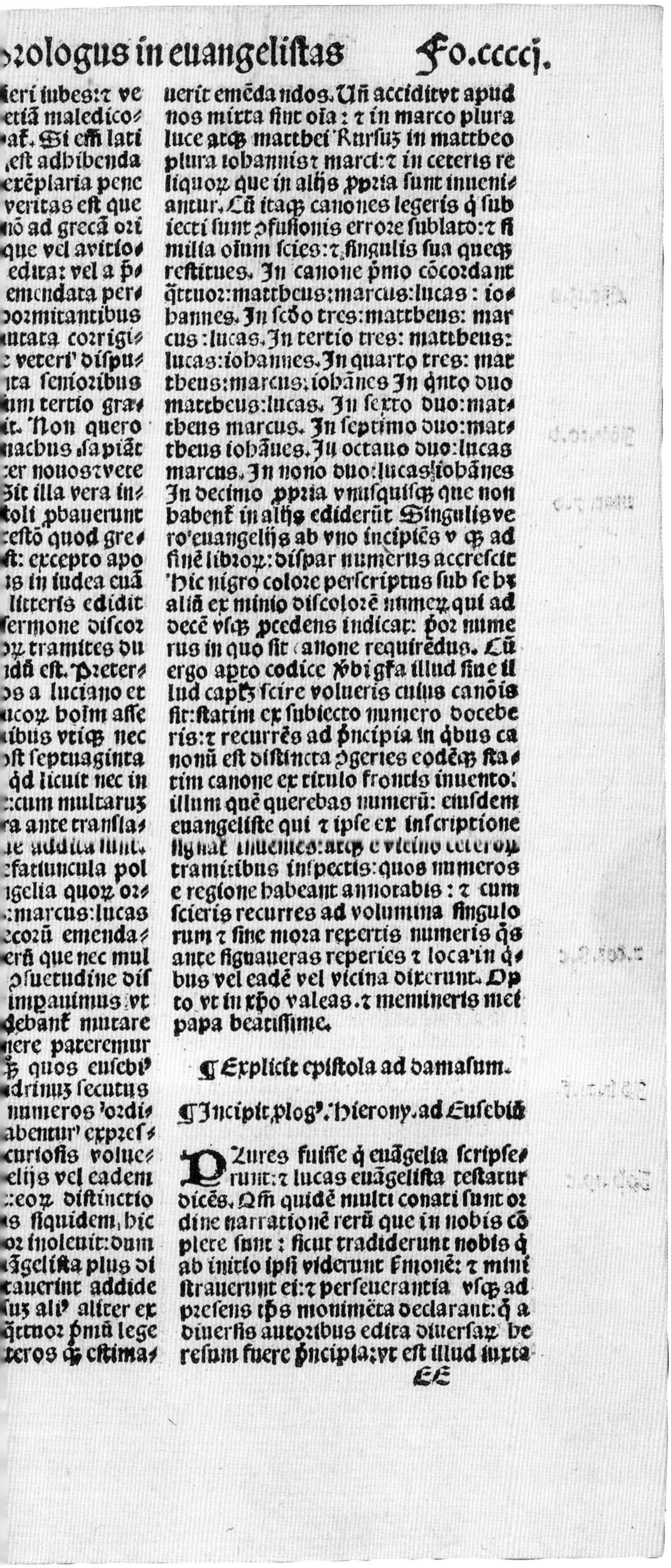

prologus in euangelistas Fo.cccci.

eri iubes: ⁊ ve
etiā maledico-
rum. Si enim lati
est adhibenda
exēplaria pene
veritas est que
nō ad grecā ori
que vel a vitio-
edita: vel a p-
emendata per-
dormitantibus
mutata corrigi-
: veteri dispu-
ita senioribus
um tertio gra-
it. Non quero
nachus, sapiāt
ter nouos ⁊ vere
sit illa vera in-
toli pbauerunt
estō quod gre-
st: excepto apo
is in iudea euā
litteris edidit
sermone discor
oꝝ tramites du
ndū est. Preter-
os a luciano et
ucoꝝ hoim asse
ibus vtriq₃ nec
ost septuaginta
q̄d licuit nec in
cum multaruꝝ
ra ante transla-
e addita sunt.
fatiuncula pol
gelia quoꝝ or-
marcus: lucas
corū emenda-
erā que nec mul
ꝯsuetudine dis
impauimus: vt
debant mutare
nere pateremur
p quos eusebi⁹
drinus secutus
numeros ordi-
abentur expres-
curiosis volue-
eliis vel eadem
eoꝝ distinctio
s siquidem, hic
or inoleuit: dum
āgelista plus di
cauerint addide
sus ali⁹ aliter ex
qttuor pmū lege
teros q̄ estima-

uerit emēdandos. Vñ accidit vt apud
nos mixta sint oīa: ⁊ in marco plura
luce atq₃ matthei. Rursus in mattheo
plura iohannis ⁊ marci: ⁊ in ceteris re
liquoꝝ que in aliis ꝓpria sunt inueni-
antur. Cū itaq₃ canones legeris q̄ sub
iecti sunt ꝯfusionis errore sublato: ⁊ si
milia oīum scies: ⁊ singulis sua queq₃
restitues. In canone pmo cōcordant
q̄ttuor: mattheus: marcus: lucas: iohannes. In scdo tres: mattheus: mar
cus: lucas. In tertio tres: mattheus:
lucas: iohannes. In quarto tres: mat
theus: marcus: iohānes In q̄nto duo
mattheus: lucas. In sexto duo: mattheus marcus. In septimo duo: mattheus iohānes. In octauo duo: lucas
marcus. In nono duo: lucas: iohānes
In decimo ꝓpria vnusquisq₃ que non
habent in aliis ediderūt. Singulis ve
ro euangeliis ab vno incipiēs vsq₃ ad
finē libroꝝ: dispar numerus accrescit
Hic nigro colore perscriptus sub se ha
liū ex minio discolorē numeꝝ qui ad
decē vsq₃ ꝓcedens indicat: hoc nume
rus in quo sit canone requirēdus. Cū
ergo aperto codice verbi gratia illud siue il
lud capitulū scire volueris cuius canōis
sit: statim ex subiecto numero docebe
ris: ⁊ recurrēs ad pncipia in q̄bus ca
nonū est distincta ꝯgeries eodēq₃ statim canone ex titulo frontis inuento:
illum quē querebas numerū: eiusdem
euangeliste qui ⁊ ipse ex inscriptione
signat inuenies: atq₃ e vicino ceteroꝝ
tramitibus inspectis: quos numeros
e regione habeant annotabis: ⁊ cum
scieris recurres ad volumina singulo
rum ⁊ sine mora repertis numeris q̄s
ante signaueras reperies ⁊ loca in q̄-
bus vel eadē vel vicina dixerunt. Op
to vt in xp̄o valeas. ⁊ memineris mei
papa beatissime.

¶ Explicit epistola ad damasum.

¶ Incipit plog⁹. hierony. ad Eusebiū

PLures fuisse q̄ euāgelia scripse-
runt: ⁊ lucas euāgelista testatur
dicēs. Qm̄ quidē multi conati sunt or
dine narrationē rerū que in nobis cō
plete sunt: sicut tradiderunt nobis q̄
ab initio ipsi viderunt smonē: ⁊ mini
strauerunt ei: ⁊ perseuerantia vsq₃ ad
presens tp̄s monimēta declarant: q̄ a
diuersis autoribus edita diuersaꝝ he
resum fuere pncipia: vt est illud iuxta
EE

Figure 7 Double-page spread from a 1511 Lyon Vulgate (fols. 400v–401r), showing the end of Maccabees and the prefatory material to the Gospels. In this copy the word 'papa' is carefully erased in ink from Jerome's letter to Pope Damasus, as Henry VIII ordered in 1535. Courtesy Diarmaid MacCulloch.

in stark contrast to their presence in the rest of western Europe. That was quickly expanding, despite the disapproval of individual prelates, notably Pope Leo X. Between 1466 and 1522 there were twenty-two editions of the Bible in High or Low German; the Bible reached Italian in 1471, Dutch in 1477, Spanish in 1478, Czech around the same time and Catalan in 1492. In England, there simply remained the Vulgate, though thanks to printing that was readily available. 156 complete Latin editions of the Bible were published across Europe up to 1520, and in a well-regulated part of the Western Church like England, it was likely that every priest with any pretence to education would have possessed one (figure 7).[7] The traditional Latin of the Vulgate was to see off any competitor in Latin even among Protestants: in the latter part of the century, such a militant champion of the new faith as John Knox's friend Anne Vaughan, whose second husband was the brilliant Puritan preacher Edward Dering, made use of it in her pioneering sonnet versions of the psalms.[8]

William Tyndale

The biblical scholarship of Desiderius Erasmus represented a dramatic break with any previous biblical tradition in England, for when he translated the New Testament afresh into Latin and published it in 1516 he went back to the original Greek. When he commented on scripture, his emphasis was on the early commentators in the first five Christian centuries (with pride of place going to that most audacious among them, Origen); his work is notable for the absence of much reference to the great medieval commentators. This attitude was fully shared by William Tyndale, the creator of the first and greatest Tudor translation of the Bible, although Tyndale's judicial murder at the hands of the Holy Roman Emperor and indirectly Henry VIII prevented his work reaching beyond the New Testament and the Pentateuch (figure 8). Tyndale came from the remote west-country Forest of Dean on the borders of Wales, and it is not fanciful to see his fascination with translation as springing out of market days in his childhood, listening to the mixed babble of Welsh and English around him.[9] His is the ancestor of all Bibles in the English language, especially the King James version; Tyndale's biographer David Daniell has bluntly pointed out that 'Nine-tenths of the Authorised Version's New Testament is Tyndale's.'[10]

There was no reason why this pioneer should have had the talent of an exceptional writer as well as being an exceptional scholar, but Tyndale was a gourmet of language: it pleased him to discover as he moved into translating the Old Testament that Hebrew and English

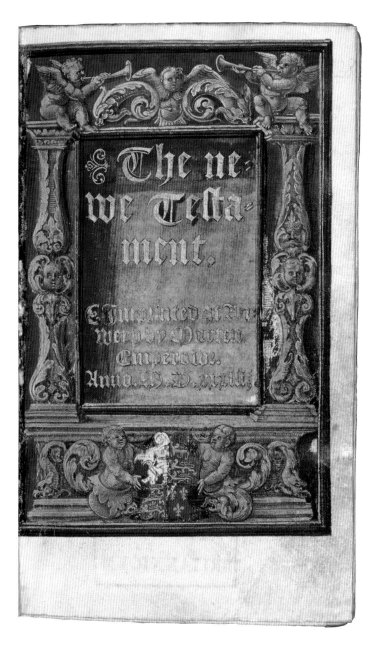

Figure 8 The second title page of Anne Boleyn's 1534 copy of Tyndale's New Testament. © British Library Board C.23.A.8.

were so much more compatible than Hebrew and Greek. He was an admirer of what Luther was achieving in Wittenberg in the 1520s, and visited the town during his years of exile at the end of that decade, but he was also his own man. When creating his New Testament translations, he drew generously on Luther's own introductions to individual books, but as he came to translate the books of the Pentateuch his own estimate of their spiritual worth began to diverge from Luther's strong contrast between the roles of Law and Gospel, and the plagiarism of Luther's German ceased, to be replaced by his own thoughts.

ראשית
אלהים

Ἐν ἀρχῇ ἦν πρὸς τὸν
ἦν ὁ Λόγος Θεὸν καὶ Θεὸς
καὶ ὁ Λόγος ἦν ὁ Λόγος

MEN·SPAKE·FROM·GOD·
BEING·MOVED·BY·THE·HOLY·GHOST

JEROME

CAREY

CYRIL
METHODIUS

MORRISON

LUTHER

MARTYN

WILLIAM   TINDALE

ELIOT

MOFFAT

·EVERY·MAN·IN·HIS·OWN·LANGUAGE·

·WORD·OF·GOD·GREW·AND·MULTIPLIED·

TO THE GLORY OF GOD   AND IN GRATEFUL ACKNOWLEDGMENT OF HIS BLESSING   UPON THE CENTENARY
OF THE BRITISH AND   FOREIGN BIBLE SOCIETY 1804–1904 THE GIFT OF WILLIAM   SON LAMPLOUGH 1911

Surreptitiously read and discussed during the 1520s and 1530s, Tyndale's still incomplete Bible translation worked on the imaginations of those who so far had virtually no access to public evangelical preaching in England. It may be significant that even before King Henry's quarrel with the Pope, during the 1520s there was a perceptible nationwide decline in ordinations in England: perhaps the traditional church was losing its grip on those thinking of a clerical career. By the time of Tyndale's martyrdom in 1536, perhaps 16,000 copies of his translation had passed into England, a country of no more than two and a half million people, with at that stage a very poorly developed market for books.[11] And this new presence of the vernacular Bible in Henry VIII's England entwined itself in a complex fashion around the King's own eccentric agenda for religious change in his realm, as the monarch, his leading churchmen and secular politicians all puzzled about the meaning of the King's quarrel and break with the Pope, which had begun in matters remote from the passionate theological claims of religious Reformers.

'The New Learning' was the hostile term applied by religious traditionalists to what we call Protestantism, yet many of the leading figures among those defending traditional religion also wanted to reform the church in their own way, and they were aware of how anomalous it was that England did not have a good Catholic vernacular version of the Bible. Bishop John Fisher, the prime scholar among the English bishops of the 1520s, made a point in late 1527 of arguing for such a project, and Sir Thomas More, a fierce controversialist with Tyndale, was also very ready to support biblical translation in principle. He claimed that his friends among the bishops were prepared to give their approval to such a translation project, should the church approve.[12] Yet simultaneously Bishop Tunstall of London, as cultivated a humanist as Fisher, was buying up Tyndale's New Testaments in order to burn them, an action which has rather outshone in the historical record the initially very tepid efforts with royal encouragement to begin work on a replacement that would not be tainted by the 'New Learning'. A royal proclamation inspired by Chancellor More on 22 June 1530 announced that not only should all existing translations be surrendered to the bishops, but that, 'having respect to the malignity of this present time', it was better to have scripture expounded in reliable sermons; it was not necessary for the Bible to be in the hands of common people. If Tyndale's Bibles 'and all other books of heresy' were given up, then that would be the time for the King to implement his intention of a translation by 'great, learned and Catholic persons'. This highly conditional offer represented a turning back from More's earlier agreement that an English vernacular translation was overdue; he had even made proposals for preparing such a project.[13]

Figure 9 A stained glass depiction of William Tyndale at Hertford College, Oxford. This nineteenth-century window was moved from the Bible Society in London and installed in the chapel of Hertford College in 1994.

This talk of an official Bible translated under the supervision of the existing episcopal hierarchy persisted through the next decade. On 19 December 1534, after the discreet evangelical Thomas Cranmer had become Archbishop of Canterbury, the Convocation of Canterbury (the church's counterpart to Parliament) put a positive spin on the 1530 proclamation by petitioning the King not only for the suppression of heretical books but also for a new effort of translation.[14] It was the memory of Elizabeth I's Archbishop Matthew Parker later that the arch-traditionalist Stephen Gardiner, Bishop of Winchester, did everything he could to oppose this move, though six months after Convocation's petition Gardiner claimed to be worn out by his efforts in translating the Gospels of Luke and John which Convocation had assigned to him.[15] Indeed that summer of 1535, with Henry VIII in one of the sunniest phases of his marriage to Queen Anne Boleyn and with evangelicals in high favour, it was a good time to be seen to favour the English scriptures: 'that same yere beganne the new testament in English' commented one conservative London chronicler who was not greatly enamoured of the new situation.[16] King Henry himself, never predictable in matters religious, achieved a first at the same time by commissioning the first Bible printed in the British Isles – yet not an English but a Latin text, selected edited highlights from the Vulgate Old Testament and the whole of the New Testament. Henry took a keen interest in this project, furnishing it with a very personal preface, which among other things commended the typeface, which he had himself chosen for ease of reading; he was beginning to have trouble with his eyesight and was using spectacles for reading, though he did not confide in his subjects on this matter.[17]

The Coverdale Bible

That idiosyncratic royal enterprise proved a dead end in comparison with a march of the vernacular through Henry's kingdom, which nevertheless owed little to most of his bishops. The apparent disappearance of all the sections of the Bible allotted to various divines in the 1534 Convocation remains one of the literary mysteries of the English Reformation, and one suspects that these labours were not as complete as their undertakers claimed. Certainly by 1537, Archbishop Cranmer was sarcastically commenting that it would 'not be till a day after doomsday' before the episcopate completed a translation, and he was now enthusiastically commending for public use a rival completed Bible: England's first since the time of the Lollards.[18] Its first version, optimistically dedicated to Henry VIII, had appeared from an Antwerp press in summer 1535, a completion of Tyndale's truncated work by the fugitive Augustinian friar Miles Coverdale (known now as the Coverdale Bible).[19] Only a year passed before Thomas Cromwell was using his newly acquired powers as vicegerent to issue injunctions that ordered the provision of a Bible in English and Latin in all churches: so while King Henry's shortened Vulgate would have fitted the bill on the Latin side, Coverdale's was the only English option available. The man who had translated most of it, Tyndale, was that same year trapped and executed as a heretic by the imperial authorities in Brussels, after a plot involving not merely the Bishop of London but the King in whose name Cromwell now acted: one of the many ironies that characterised Henry's convoluted religious policies.

The incongruity deepened when (after what was evidently a good deal of passive resistance to the vicegerential injunctions from traditionalist higher clergy) the order was intensified and repeated during 1537 and 1538. Probably the King never realised that his power was being used to spread the inspired translation of the man whom he had grown to hate and whose destruction he had helped to engineer.[20] Thanks to Cranmer and Cromwell, King Henry was now actually giving his royal licence to a further presentation of the complete Coverdale translation with further prefaces and commentary. The editing had been done by a former associate of Tyndale's called John Rogers, although his work went under the pseudonym of Thomas Matthew – apparently derived from some rather approximate anagram work around the name of the editor of topical apparatus which Rogers had lifted and translated from the first French Protestant Bible of 1535.[21]

The Great Bible

Hot on the heels of the Matthew Bible, Coverdale produced yet another refinement of his completed text, which despite traditionalist attempts to get it revised in Henry's last years was to remain definitive for more than two decades. It has acquired the nickname of the 'Great Bible'; thanks to a preface provided in 1541 by the Archbishop, it has with little justification often been called 'Cranmer's Bible'. More than any other version of the Henrician period, it gained the aura of an official translation, helped by the coincidence of optimistic preparations for Henry's disastrous marriage to Anne of Cleves in 1540. The ceiling of the Chapel Royal in St James's Palace, installed exactly at this time, displays five times the phrase VERBUM DEI, the only motif prominent in it apart from royal and dynastic symbols, and the same phrase is much repeated on the famous title page of the Great Bible probably not designed by Hans Holbein, as often asserted, but by a French master-engraver (figure 10).[22] Here the King is depicted as the benevolent provider of Bibles to clergy and laity alike, each layer of society in turn delivering it to the order below, all duly signifying their social superiority or inferiority by their covered or bare heads. The picture is a fine diagram of the hierarchy of the kingdom, as is the prison menacingly placed at the bottom right, showing what happens to those who violate the hierarchical rules and reject the good news of divine mercy as interpreted by the royal donor of the text. One of the most remarkable features of its text is that at 2 Chronicles 36:8 it actually amplifies the biblical original by adding a sin to the many committed by King Jehoiakim of Judah: he allowed carved images. Roman Catholics were gleeful when they discovered this gratuitous piece of evangelical spin.[23]

Even after Cromwell's fall and execution in 1540 (his heraldry on the title page of the Great Bible then became an unexplained blank in the busy design), Henry himself gave the parishes an effective extra spur to provide Bibles in a proclamation of 1541 which threatened fines if they did not.[24] Alas for his enthusiasm, not all took the hint that the picture of the prison provided. Popular excitement at the Bible was sufficiently noticeable for the King to take fright. Ever since 1539 he had been complaining about unruly public reading of the Bible now to be found in the kingdom's churches, and he was deeply troubled at the possibility that the lower orders might have radical thoughts as a result of irresponsible thumbing through its pages. In 1543 Henry pushed Parliament into ordering that only upper-status groups in society, presumably deemed less excitable, should be allowed to read it at all. Interestingly, in the same year the Scots Parliament, dominated after King James V's death by a regency regime toying with church reform, passed an Act which for the first time allowed lieges, that is landowners, to possess the Bible; the Scots were thus newly allowed access to the Bible approximately equivalent to its newly restricted access in England. It was a brief moment of concession: for the most part, successive Scots governments in the 1530s and 1540s remained hostile to the Reformation, and did their best to curb its growth, with only short-term success.

The Geneva Bible and the Bishops' Bible

The greater evangelical freedom of Edward VI's reign produced new editions of the biblical versions made before the Great Bible. These were kitted out with fresh notes taking notice of new theological departures in the Protestant churches of Switzerland and Geneva, particularly the agreement on the Eucharist achieved by Bullinger and Calvin in 1549, later termed the *Consensus Tigurinus*. For now Geneva and its large community of French exiles had emerged as a major force in European Reformation. It was in Geneva that the French Bible publisher Robert Estienne (Stephanus)

¶ The Byble in Englyshe, that is to saye the content of all the holy scrypture, bothe of ý olde and newe testament, truly translated after the veryte of the Hebrue and Greke textes, by ý dylygent studye of dyuerse excellent learned men, expert in the forsayde tonges.

¶ Prynted by Rychard Grafton & Edward Whitchurch.

Cum priuilegio ad imprimendum solum.

1539.

produced a French New Testament with a system of verse divisions which has survived to the present day, even in Catholic Bibles. It was soon taken up in a new translation produced in the late 1550s by a number of English exiles from Queen Mary Tudor's Catholic England.

Finally published as a whole in 1560 after the death of Mary, this 'Geneva Bible' showed all the enterprise of Geneva's publishing industry, then the city's greatest money-spinner. It was designed deliberately to be a popular edition for the whole anglophone market, not a lectern Bible in folio, with maximum aids to individual study: not just the verse numbering but also attractive features such as maps of the Holy Land and the Garden of Eden, plus a generous marginal commentary (figure 11). It drew on the considerable biblical scholarship available in a city which boasted such distinguished scholars as Calvin himself and his colleague Theodore Beza; hence its interesting improvements on previous English versions, which were not confined to the famous 'breeches' translation discussed above. Frequently editions were bound up with a metrical psalter, much less frequently with a bowdlerized version of the Book of Common Prayer, so that altogether it might be a complete kit for worship and education in the home.

The Geneva Bible got off to a slow start in circulation in the home country, but Queen Elizabeth's ministers never forbade its importation, despite her considerable personal hostility to the Genevan form of Reformed Protestantism, and from its first English printing in 1576 it became a firm favourite with the reading public. The Church of England's establishment had brought out a revision of the Great Bible in 1568, known appropriately as the Bishops' Bible, which became the dignified folio version for use in worship, but one should not see these two versions necessarily as rivals: people would expect to hear one in church and use the other at home. Shakespeare evidently drew on both in his quotation of scripture in his plays. One highly significant feature of the Geneva Bible was its use in the Church of Scotland, which after its turbulent Reformation in 1560 tended to out-Calvin Calvin in its enthusiasm for Reformed Protestant change. Along with the Genevan-inspired Book of Common Order, Scotland's adoption of the Geneva Bible meant that the official English used in the worship of England's neighbour-kingdom was that of London and not the Lowland Scots of Edinburgh. It was the beginning of the binding-in to a common Protestant purpose of the two polities, which had been enemies for centuries.

Figure 11 A 1606 copy of the Geneva Bible, sig.A2r, showing the Geneva Bible reading 'breeches' (Genesis 3:7) and a map of the geographical location of the Garden of Eden (near Baghdad). Courtesy Diarmaid MacCulloch.

THE SITVATION OF THE
GARDEN OF EDEN.

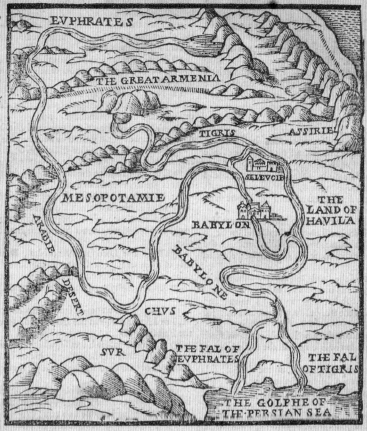

Within the map:
EVPHRATES
THE GREAT ARMENIA
TIGRIS   ASSIRIE
SELEVCIE
MESOPOTAMIE   THE LAND OF HAVILA
BABYLON
BABYLONE
ARABIE
DESERT
CHVS
SVR   THE FAL OF EVPHRATES   THE FAL OF TIGRIS
THE GOLPHE OF THE PERSIAN SEA

Right margin labels:
Armenia the great.

The land of Hani-lah.

The fall of Euphra-tes.
The fall of Tygris.

The goulfe of the Persian sea.

Left margin note:
Because mention is made in the tenth verse of this Chapter, of the riuer that watered the garden, wee must note that Euphrates and Tygris, called in Hebrew, Perash & Hiddekel, were called but one riuer where they ioyned together, els they had foure heads: that is, two at their springs, and two where they fell into the Persian sea. In this countrey and most plentifull land Adam dwelt, and this was called Paradise, that is, a garden of pleasure, because of the fruitfulnesse and abondance thereof. And whereas it is said that Pishon compasseth the land of Hauilah, it is meant of Tygris, which in some countreys, as it passed by diuers places, was called by sundry names, as sometime Diglitto, in other places Pasitygris, and of some Phasin or Pishon. Likewise Euphrates toward the countrey of Cush or Ethiopia, or Arabia, was called Gihon. So that Tygris and Euphrates (which were but two riuers, and sometime when they ioyned together, were called after one name) were according to diuers places called by these foure names, so that they might seeme to haue bene foure diuers riuers.

CHAP. III.

1 The woman seduced by the serpent, 6 enticeth her husband to sinne. 8 They both flee from God. 14 They three are punished. 15 Christ promised. 19 Man is dust. 22 Man is cast out of Paradise.

NOW* the serpent was more ¹ subtil then any beast of the fielde, which the Lord God had made: and he ᵇ said to the woman, Yea, hath God indeede said, Ye shall not eat of euery tree of the garden?

2 And the woman sayd vnto the serpent, We eat of the fruit of the trees of the garden.

3 But the fruite of the tree which is in the mids of the garden, God hath said, Ye shal not eat of it, neither shall ye touch it, ᶜ lest ye die.

4 Then * the serpent said to the woman, Yee shall not ᵈ † die at all,

5 But God doth know that when ye shall eat thereof, your eyes shalbe opened, and ye shal be as gods, ᵉ knowing good and euill.

6 So the woman (seeing that the tree was good for meat, & that it was pleasant to the eyes, and a tree to be desired, to get knowledge) tooke of the fruit thereof, and did * eat, and gaue also to her husband with her, and he ᶠ did eat.

7 Then the eyes of them both were opened, and they ᵍ knew that they were naked, and they

sewed figge tree leaues together, and made themselues † breeches.

8 ¶ Afterward they heard the voice of the Lord God walking in the garden in the ‖coole of the day, and the man and his wife ʰ hid themselues from the presence of the Lord God among the trees of the garden.

9 But the Lord God called to the man, and sayd vnto him, Where art thou?

10 Who said, I heard thy voice in the garden, and was afraid: because I was ⁱ naked, therefore I hid my selfe.

11 And he said, Who told thee that thou wast naked? Hast thou eaten of the tree whereof I commanded thee that thou shouldest not eate?

12 Then the man said, The woman which thou ᵏ gauest to be with mee, shee gaue mee of the tree, and I did eate.

13 And the Lord God saide to the woman, Why hast thou done this? And the woman said, ˡ The serpent beguiled me, and I did eate.

14 ¶ Then the Lord God sayd to the serpent, ᵐ Because thou hast done this, thou art cursed aboue all cattel, and aboue euery beast of the field: vpon thy belly shalt thou goe, and ⁿ dust shalt thou eate all the dayes of thy life.

Left margin notes:
* Wisd. 2. 24.
a As Satan can change himselfe into an Angel of light, so did hee, abuse the wisdome of the serpent to deceiue man.
b God suffered Satan to make the serpent his instrument to speake in him.
c In doubting of Gods threatning shee yeelded to Satan.
2. Cor. 11. 2.
d This is Satans chiefest subtiltie, to cause vs not to feare Gods threatnings.
† Ebr. die the death.
e As though he should say, God doeth not forbid you to eat of the fruit, saue that he knoweth that if ye should eate thereof, yee should be like to him. * Ecclus 25. 26. 1. Tim. 2. 14. f Not so much to please his wife as moued by ambition at her perswasion. g They began to feele the misery, but they sought not to God for remedie.

Right margin notes:
† Ebr. things to gird about them to hide their priuities.
‖ Or, winde.
h The sinfull conscience flieth Gods presence.

i His hypocrisie appeareth in that he hid the cause of his nakednesse, which was the transgression of Gods commandement.
k His wickednes and lacke of true repentance appeareth in this, that he burdeneth God with his fault, because he had giuen him a wife.
l Instead of confessing her sinne, shee increaseth it by accusing the serpent.

m Hee asked the reason of Adam and his wife, because hee would bring them to repentance, but he asketh not the serpent, because hee would shew him no mercie.
n As a vile and contemptible beast, Isa, 65. 25.

A 2   15 1

The Douai–Reims Bible

Roman Catholics remained highly suspicious of lay use of the vernacular Bible. Even if they could not ban it outright in northern Europe, as became the case in southern Europe generally (even Queen Mary Tudor confined herself to ordering the Great Bible out of her churches rather than banning vernacular Bible-reading altogether), Catholics saw reading the Bible primarily as a professional necessity in arguing with Protestantism. The result was that when English Roman Catholics created their first English biblical translation in exile at Douai and Reims, it was not for ordinary folk to read, but for priests to use as a polemical weapon – the explicit purpose that the 1582 title page and preface of the Reims New Testament proclaimed. Part of the polemic in the Catholic literature that accompanied the publication was in pointing out tendentious readings in the Protestant English Bibles, and in this the Catholic scholars scored some palpable hits. This was one good reason for King James commissioning a new translation, and when it was completed it was possible to see some of the readings of the Douai–Reims version amid all the work of Tyndale, Coverdale and the Geneva translators.

Notes

1. Cambridge, Corpus Christi College MS. 286.
2. The attribution of any texts to King Alfred is uncertain; see a recent discussion in Malcolm Godden, 'Did King Alfred Write Anything?', *Medium Ævum* 76 (2007), 1–23; and Janet Bately, 'Did King Alfred Actually Translate Anything? The Integrity of the Alfredian Canon Revisited', *Medium Ævum* 78 (2009), 189–215.
3. See Rebecca Barnhouse, 'Shaping the Hexateuch Text for an Anglo-Saxon Audience', in Rebecca Barnhouse and Benjamin C. Withers (eds), *The Old English Hexateuch: Aspects and Approaches* (Kalamazoo, Mich., 2000), pp. 9–108.
4. Richard Marsden, *The Text of the Old Testament in Anglo-Saxon England* (Cambridge, 1995), p. 405.
5. Kantik Ghosh, *The Wycliffite Heresy: Authority and the Interpretation of Texts* (Cambridge, 2002), p. 147.
6. See a discussion of similar readings in the Wycliffite Bible and KJB, and a possible influence of the Wycliffite Bible on Tyndale, in David Daniell, *The Bible in English* (New Haven, Conn. and London, 2003), pp. 85–90; and Mary Dove, *The First English Bible* (Cambridge, 2007), pp. 190–93.
7. Jerzy Kloczowski, *A History of Polish Christianity* (Cambridge, 2000), p. 84.
8. David Daniell, 'William Tyndale, the English Bible, and the English Language', in Orlaith O'Sullivan (ed.), *The Bible as Book: The Reformation* (London, 2000), pp. 39–50; at pp. 3 and 65f.

9. Andrew J. Brown, *William Tyndale on Priests and Preachers with New Light on His Early Career* (London, 1996). Chapters 1 and 2 provide a persuasive relocation of Tyndale's boyhood.

10. David Daniell, *William Tyndale: A Biography* (New Haven, Conn. and London, 1994), p. 1.

11. Daniell, 'William Tyndale', p. 47.

12. Richard Rex, *The Theology of John Fisher* (Cambridge, 1991), pp. 149 and 158–60.

13. Paul L. Hughes and James F. Larkin (eds), *Tudor Royal Proclamations*, 2 vols (New Haven, Conn. and London, 1964, 1969), Vol. I, pp. 193–7, no. 129; cf. G.R. Elton, *Policy and Police: The Enforcement of the Reformation in the Age of Thomas Cromwell* (Cambridge, 1972), pp. 218–20; and Alastair Fox, *Thomas More: History and Providence* (Oxford, 1982), pp. 169–70.

14. J.S. Brewer et al. (eds), *Letters and Papers, Foreign and Domestic, of the Reign of Henry VIII, 1509–47*, 21 vols and 2 vols addenda (London, 1862–1932), Vol. VII, no. 1555.

15. Parker's reminiscence is in Matthew Parker, *De Antiquitate Britannicae Ecclesiae …* (London, 1572), p. 385. Gardiner's letter is printed in *State Papers Published Under the Authority of His Majesty's Commission: King Henry VIII*, 11 vols (London, 1830–52), Vol. I, pp. 430–31 (*Letters and Papers* VIII, no. 850). James Gairdner, the historian of Lollardy, charitably suggested that Gardiner's translations were destroyed in the sack of his library in 1554 by Sir Thomas Wyatt's rebels: see James Arthur Muller, *Stephen Gardiner and the Tudor Reaction* (London, 1926), p. 350 n. 23.

16. John Gough Nichols (ed.), *Chronicle of the Grey Friars of London*, Camden Society 1st Ser. 53, (London, 1852), p. 38.

17. A. Freeman, 'To Guard His Words', *Times Literary Supplement*, 14 December 2007, pp. 13–14.

18. John Edmund Cox (ed.), *Works of Archbishop Cranmer*, 2 vols (Parker Society, 1844, 1846), Vol. II, p. 344 (*Letters and Papers* XII/2, no. 434; TNA, SP1/123, ffo. 198–9).

19. On its printing in Antwerp, see Guido Latré, 'The 1535 Coverdale Bible and Its Antwerp Origins', in O'Sullivan (ed.), *The Bible as Book*, pp. 89–102, at pp. 92–8.

20. On the first launch of Cromwell's injunction about Bible provision and its slow take-up, see Diarmaid MacCulloch, *Thomas Cranmer: A Life* (New Haven, Conn. and London, 1996), p. 166n.

21. Nicholas Tyacke, 'Introduction', in Nicholas Tyacke (ed.), *England's Long Reformation* (London, 1998), pp. 1–32; at pp. 7–8, 28.

22. M. Dickman Orth, 'The English Great Bible of 1539 and the French Connection', in S. L'Engle and Gerald B. Guest (eds), *Tributes to Jonathan J.G. Alexander: the Making and Meaning of Illuminated Medieval & Renaissance Manuscripts, Art and Architecture* (London and Turnhout, 2006), pp. 171–184.

23. I (Diarmaid MacCulloch) owe this point to my former student Dr Ellie Bagley.

24. Hughes and Larkin (eds), *Tudor Royal Proclamations*, Vol. I, pp. 296–8, no. 200.

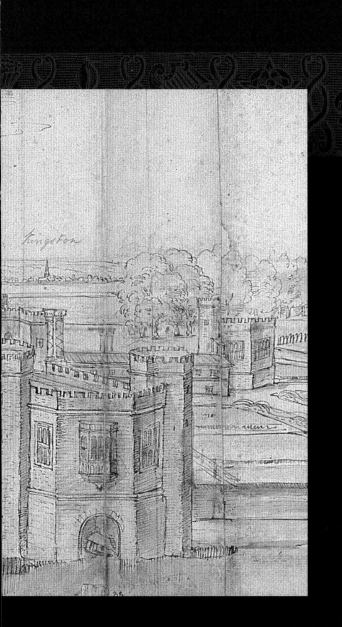

2

Origins of the Project

*Judith Maltby and
Helen Moore*

THE IDEA OF A NEW ENGLISH TRANSLATION of the Bible was proposed at a conference called by King James at Hampton Court in 1604 (figure 12). The purpose of the conference was to bring together at the beginning of the new King's reign those holding differing views about the theological and ecclesiastical direction and character of the Church of England. There is no question that the Church of England at the beginning of the seventeenth century was a complex institution, containing a variety of religious practices and theological outlooks. The Elizabethan Settlement of 1559, through the Act of Supremacy, which declared Elizabeth the Supreme Governor of the Church of England, and the Act of Uniformity, which mandated the use of the English Prayer Book, established a church of the old and the new. On one hand there was remarkable continuity, in that the Settlement retained much of the medieval church in terms of the ministry and church structures. The 'threefold' order of ministry of deacons, priests (or presbyters) and bishops was continued. Geographic authorities called dioceses, with their cathedrals, headed by bishops and deans who had authority over the lesser clergy, were also retained, as was the most enduring structural component of the English church, the parochial system. The parish church remained, as it had for hundreds of years before, the focus of most people's spiritual and communal lives.

But there was real discontinuity as well. Despite Elizabeth's personal misgivings, clergy were allowed to marry, although the official position was that the celibate state was to be preferred but that marriage was better than scandal. Of greater significance in terms of its widespread impact on the lives of almost everyone, English was confirmed as the undisputed language of public worship. The Book of Common Prayer of 1559, a modified form of the 1552 Book of Common Prayer from her brother Edward's reign, provided almost exclusively the only Christian rites to be used in the English church. The Bible, which formed a considerable proportion of Prayer Book worship, was to be read only in English. The cause of the vernacular as a worthy medium for the worship of God and for hearing his word had won the day.

Figure 12 *pp. 40–1* Antonis van der Wyngaerde, 'View of Hampton Court Palace'. Ashmolean Museum, University of Oxford, WA.C.I.G.IV.9b.

The Puritan critique of the Church of England

Early in Elizabeth's reign, the greatest domestic criticisms of the Settlement came from English Roman Catholics, especially the bishops that the Queen had inherited from her sister Mary I. As the reign progressed, English Catholics were marginalized, silenced, or found ways of adapting and coexisting with the established church through performing sufficient outward acts of conformity to keep the authorities satisfied. By the 1570s, the key domestic theological debates were between different types of Protestants – essentially between those known as 'conformists', who on balance approved of the key characteristics of the Elizabethan Settlement, its Prayer Book and government by bishops, and those members of the Church of England who identified those same elements as irredeemably tainted by popery. This second group was known as Puritans, or, as they often styled themselves, 'the godly'.

In understanding these debates, it is vital to note that the disputes were almost entirely between members of the same church. 'Separatists' – that is, Protestants who found the Church of England so objectionable that they removed themselves from it entirely – were few and far between in this period. Indeed, the law provided no opt-out clause for membership of the Established Church: every English man, woman and child was an 'Anglican' in that sense, and Puritanism is rightly understood as one (though varied) theological strand within the *Ecclesia Anglicana*.

The two main areas of complaint for Puritans, therefore, concerned how the church worshipped and how the church was governed. In the case of the former, the Prayer Book was subject to some colourful and creative abuse. It was 'an unperfect book, culled and picked out of that popish dunghill, the mass book'. In the case of the latter, a church with a hierarchy of degrees between the clergy also smacked of popery:

> And as safely may we, by the warrant of God's word, subscribe to allow the dominion of the pope universally to reign over the church of God, as of an Archbishop over an whole province, or a Lord Bishop over a diocese, which containeth many shires and parishes. For the dominion that they exercise, the Archbishop above them, and they [the bishops] above the rest of their brethren, is unlawful and expressly forbidden by the word of God.[1]

Both the Prayer Book and episcopal government were, in the eyes of the Puritans, so infused and corrupted with popery that they were beyond redemption. The salvation of the Church of England lay in a purified liturgy along the lines of Zurich and Geneva and a presbyterian church polity with its ministerial parity created by the elimination of the top level of the clerical hierarchy.

At the same time as growing Puritan discontent within the Church of England, there was an increasing sense of a Catholic threat both internationally and at home. After twelve years on the throne pursuing an openly Protestant agenda, Pope Pius V finally excommunicated Elizabeth in 1570 – a belated attempt to support the Catholic uprising in the north in 1569. This sparked a series of anti-Catholic laws, given all the more urgency because the threats to assassinate the Queen following her excommunication were far from empty.

Against such a background, one might have thought that Puritans made the 'logical corollary' to growing national anti-Catholicism by campaigning for a more 'purified church'. Elizabeth's longest serving Archbishop of Canterbury did not see it like that. To John Whitgift (Archbishop from 1583 until his death in 1604) internal dissension and flagrant breaching of the church's discipline weakened the Church of England in the face of its Roman Catholic nemesis. Throughout the 1580s, Whitgift embarked on a hard-nosed and systematic attempt to enforce conformity on erring clergy, angering not only Puritan ministers but more importantly their powerful lay patrons. Opposed by some of the Queen's closest councillors, Whitgift's war against the Puritans should have failed despite enlisting equally ruthless lieutenants such as Richard Bancroft (who became Whitgift's successor at Canterbury in 1604). But the Presbyterians over-reached themselves. Increasingly the Puritans lost credibility, through a series of botched parliamentary initiatives to reform church government, an increasingly vitriolic publishing war culminating in the fatally backfiring series of satirical tracts against the bishops by one 'Martin Marprelate', and the tarnishing of the movement with the charge of separatism in the late 1580s. Men like Bancroft now had the perfect excuse to arrest and interrogate the leaders of the Presbyterian cause. By the 1590s, the public discourses of Puritanism had largely retreated into the rather torturous theological speculations represented by the work of one of its greatest sons, William Perkins. Perkins was more concerned with the mechanics of the mystery of salvation than the nuts and bolts of church polity. Changes were afoot for the conformists as well. Whitgift's intellectually pragmatic, if-it-ain't-broke-don't-fix-it, approach to episcopacy was being superseded by younger men like Bancroft who, taking a leaf out of the Presbyterian book, began to preach and publish that episcopacy, not Presbyterianism, was the form of church government authorized by divine law. The key issue at the heart of this theological dispute was whether there was a hierarchy in the ministry between presbyters and bishops (episcopacy) or an equality between all ordained ministers (Presbyterianism). By the time of James's accession to the English throne *iure divino* churchmen, asserting that episcopacy existed by divine law, were increasingly embedded in the ecclesiastical hierarchy.

To be fair, the collapse of the Puritan movement by the 1590s was not exclusively down to the miscalculations of the godly. At the grassroots the much maligned Prayer Book was winning the affection and loyalty of many ordinary parishioners by the 1580s. More dramatically, the defeat of the Spanish Armada in 1588 confirmed many in the view that England's 'Protestant wind' was clearly 'Protestant' enough for God.[2]

Supreme Governor of the Church of England

In 1603, Elizabeth also left to her successor a role which the Tudors had made uniquely their own – that of Supreme Governor of the Church of England. Simply to see the Supreme Governor as the 'lay head' of the church is to misunderstand its significance to contemporaries. Both Elizabeth and James understood themselves to be accountable to God for the good governance and well-being of the national church entrusted to their care. Many of their subjects may have thought that their sovereigns should be a bit more accountable to them or at least pay more attention to their advice. Elizabeth, however, bequeathed James a robust doctrine of the Royal Supremacy, one that he would exercise in an expansive way throughout his reign. In fact, upon entering adulthood, James VI had already proved himself a wily and effective monarch in matters not only of the Scottish state, but of the Scottish kirk (figure 13). During his minority in the 1560s and 1570s, Scottish ministers had pretty much had a free hand in the running of the Church of Scotland. From the mid-1580s, the adult James's tough interventionist approach with the kirk proved both highly confrontational and often highly successful. By contrast to their plain-speaking Scottish counterparts, the English bishops and clergy must have appeared positively obsequious, to say the least. Elizabeth may have been Deborah, the righteous Judge over Israel, but in his mind James was Solomon, the builder of the Temple and the wisest king in Christendom.[3]

The Millenary Petition of 1603

The accession of a new monarch in 1603 with solid Calvinist credentials, coming from a church which, while containing bishops, was seen as being truer to the Reformed principles of Geneva and Zurich, awakened many English Puritans out of their quietism. Indeed, there is something about a new reign which creates optimism from surprising quarters, as Roman Catholics and separatists also entertained the hope that James would lessen the degree of persecution and exclusion that they

had endured under Elizabeth. The bishops, on the other hand, were anxious. It was an exaggeration to say, as one critic did, that they feared 'the ruin of their estate',[4] but senior churchmen were not confident that they would find in James I such a bulwark against Puritanism as they had in the Queen. As it turned out, they were all wrong. James would prove an enthusiast for the maligned ceremonialism of the Prayer Book, claiming at the Hampton Court Conference that he had lived among Puritans since the age of ten but 'I may say of myself as Christ did of himself, Though I lived amongst them … I was never of them.'[5] Indeed, James would be no protector to papist or separatist; no advocate of the Puritan agenda for reform of the church; but as Supreme Governor, he would prove himself a friend to the church of the Elizabethan Settlement.

As James travelled south from Scotland to England in April 1603 he was presented with a petition claiming the support of a thousand English clergy and others – hence its name, the 'Millenary Petition'. The petition in fact carried no names and was probably manufactured in London, as most petitions of the period claiming to give voice to the grassroots were. It was a canny piece of prose. God, the petitioners were convinced, 'hath appointed your Highness our physician to heal these diseases' – a flattering allusion to James's own writings on kingship. The petition spoke carefully and deliberately in terms of the *abuses* of the current ecclesiastical status quo, skirting around direct criticism of the church settlement itself. The petitioners were 'neither factious men affecting a popular parity in the Church, nor … schismatics aiming at the dissolution of the state ecclesiastical'.[6]

The Millenary Petition's most important outcome, however, was the idea of a gathering to examine the state of the church. The very notion of being shut away in a theological 'talking shop' for several days would have appalled the learned but pragmatic Elizabeth. Her own piety, shaped by a childhood in which expressing the wrong opinion could have deadly consequences, made her dislike the terrier-like disputes of professional theologians. James, in contrast, loved – as much as he loved hunting – a good theological knockabout, provided he could assume the part of both umpire and player. He undertook both roles with verve at Hampton Court.[7]

Figure 13 King James I. After John de Critz the Elder (*c.*1552/3–1642). Bodleian Library, LP 82.

The Hampton Court Conference of 1604

Planned originally for November 1603 but delayed by an outbreak of plague, the gathering of divines and prominent laymen under the chairmanship of their new Supreme Governor took place over three days in mid-January 1604. We are dependent largely on four independent accounts of the Conference (plus some letters, including one by the King), varying in length, and none free from bias. By far the most substantial was *The Summe and Substance* produced by William Barlow, Dean of Chester, through the encouragement of Whitgift and Bancroft. Barlow maintained that his account was intended as a corrective against 'some partial, some untrue, some slanderous' accounts. 'What is here set down', he said, 'for the truth thereof shall be satisfied'.[8] In fact, Barlow was providing 'spin' on the Conference to show maximum unity between the King and the bishops. When Barlow invited Robert Cecil to be the dedicatee for his tract, the King's minister wisely asked to see it first and then avoided contact with Barlow until after *The Summe and Substance* was published. Barlow did have his reward, however, being promoted to the See of Rochester in 1606.[9]

Accounts of the Conference tend to refer to 'parties', but that is somewhat misleading. Attendees were not representatives sent by constituencies. Invitations came from the Privy Council and those flying the Puritan flag were outgunned both in numbers and in firepower. The four Puritan 'plaintiffs', as Barlow called them, were Thomas Sparke, who had been a disappointment to his own side at the earlier Lambeth conference in 1584 over Prayer Book subscription; Laurence Chaderton, the first Master of the Puritan foundation of Emmanuel College, Cambridge; and the Suffolk minister John Knewstubb. Head and shoulders above them all was the fourth, a man respected for his learning even by his theological opponents: John Rainolds, President of the humanist foundation of Corpus Christi College, Oxford, who had exchanged his post as Dean of Lincoln for that of President of Corpus in 1598. John Gauden, a seventeenth-century biographer of the college's most famous divine, Richard Hooker, remarked that John Jewel, John Rainolds and Richard Hooker made a 'triumviri of the little Colledge, those three men of Renown in whose names it justly glories'. Gauden added that Rainolds was the 'onley Atlas on that side' – that is, the Puritan side. This remark is patently untrue, but nonetheless Rainolds was by far the most substantial theologian at Hampton Court to argue the Puritan case.[10]

Indeed not all the bishops present were as ferociously anti-Puritan as Whitgift and Bancroft. Henry Robinson of Carlisle was perhaps Rainolds's oldest friend. Bishops Rudd (St David's), Babington

(Worcester) and Matthew (Durham) were sympathetic to moderate Puritans, preferring them inside the tent, rather than outside of it. Rainolds probably owed his preferment as Dean of Lincoln to Whitgift himself and dedicated an unpublished work 'A Defence of the English Liturgy against Robert Browne' – a notorious separatist – to the Archbishop. These networks of friendship and patronage warn us against easy models of polarization. There was real theological diversity represented at the Conference, but in many ways it was a gathering of centrist groupings and resembled, in the words of Patrick Collinson, more of a 'round table' than a debating chamber. Further, the Conference was completely ad hoc. It had no real precedent, no agreed procedures or constitutional standing – all of which gave the King enormous freedom in the chair. Whatever was agreed would require royal or parliamentary authority to bring about.[11]

On the first day, 14 January, the King met with the bishops, deans and members of the Privy Council, to discuss matters of church ceremonialism raised in the Millenary Petition. Dudley Carlton, later Viscount Dorchester, reported that the King "made a speach with great respect to them [the bishops] and theyr calling, and told them he sent not for them as persons accused, but as men of choise by whom he sought to receive instruction".[12] The King took some bishops down a notch or two but largely supported the lawful ceremonies of the church, apart from his opposition to emergency baptism by midwives and laymen allowed by the Prayer Book.[13]

Two days later, the Conference met again and this time the 'Puritan Four', led by Rainolds, were admitted. This was the key day of the Conference. Presumably, in order to dampen any suggestion that the Archbishop's performance was under scrutiny, Whitgift was absent. Bancroft, however, was there to give the Puritan cause the thumping he believed it deserved. He received a royal rebuke for his tone but James did not interrupt his anti-Puritan tirade. The floor then went to the godly Rainolds: his thankless task was to present to the King a wide-ranging set of grievances without sounding too aggrieved. Doctrinal issues such as predestination were raised, but James made it clear that he would entertain no revision to the Thirty-nine Articles that defined the doctrine of the Church of England, however 'soft' the Puritans thought the Articles to be on this subject. Rainolds then presented the standard list of Puritan complaints: subscription to the Prayer Book, particular ceremonies of the liturgy, poor Sabbath observance, and the lack of a preaching ministry for every parish. The King was not completely dismissive of his concerns but it became painfully clear to Rainolds that the key theological weapon in the Puritan critique of the church, the taint of popery, had no traction with James. The King remarked that 'by this argument we might renounce the Trinity, and all that is holy, because it was abused in popery' and, turning directly to Rainolds, added, 'they used to wear hose and shoes in popery, therefore you shall now go barefoot'. The final royal blow for Rainolds and his party followed his suggestion that a synod of bishops and presbyters be established to determine controversial issues in the church. According to Barlow, this resulted in James's most famous remark of his reign – 'no bishop, no king' – as he stormed from the room.[14] Two days later, the Puritan representatives were admitted to the King's presence and assured of his sympathy with their concern for abuses in the church, whilst also receiving a royal exhortation to obey their bishops.[15]

Such painful humiliation for Rainolds at the hands of 'Solomon' is redeemed for the modern reader by what is now considered his greatest contribution at Hampton Court. It was Rainolds, amidst his long list of complaints about the condition of the Church of England, who suggested that a new translation of the Bible was needed. Perhaps buoyed up by the fact that his previous proposition concerning better observance of the Sabbath had received 'general and unanimous assent', he went on to plead for a new translation. The translations from the time of Henry VIII and Edward VI were 'corrupt and not answerable to the truth of the original'. James leapt on this suggestion with alacrity as the sort of scholarly project that appealed to him. The King had 'urged … earnestly, and with many reasons', including the 'glory the performing thereof should bring to this Church', the suggestion for a new translation of the Bible made at the General Assembly meeting in Fife in 1601, but without success.[16] Further, the, to his mind, odious Geneva Bible with its disagreeable marginal notes would be supplanted by a new version with royal authority and free of objectionable commentary. And, not unimportantly, it would give the fractious churchmen a project to coalesce around and a shared sense of purpose. In assessing the Hampton Court Conference, therefore, the humiliated Rainolds emerges as the actor responsible for its greatest long-term achievement. And what might appear a victory for bishops may also, with hindsight, be seen as a missed opportunity for addressing abuses in the church – a failure that contributed to the cataclysmic and tragic events of the civil wars of the 1640s.[17]

Developments in university education

Although the immediate origin of the King James Bible lies in the events of 1604, it would not have been possible without the revolution in learning that had been under way for a century and was typified by the founding of Rainolds's college, Corpus Christi, at Oxford in 1517 (figures 14 and 15). The twin aims of its founder Richard Fox, Bishop of Winchester, were the advancement of humanistic learning (the study of Latin and Greek) alongside the traditional curriculum, and the institution of a stricter regime of academic discipline than prevailed generally in the University at that time. Fox established three public lecturers, in Humanity (i.e. Latin), Greek and Divinity (theology), thereby formalizing the teaching of Greek in English universities; the first equivalent Greek appointment at Cambridge was made in 1530.[18] The official arrival of Greek in Oxford was greeted with consternation by some because it represented a challenge to the traditional modes of theological discourse: following the preaching of an anti-Greek sermon in the University Church in 1518, the noted humanist Sir Thomas More intervened in the controversy with a 'Letter to Oxford' denouncing the resistance to the coming of Greek. The Greek curriculum delivered by Fox's lecturer taught grammar, rhetoric and poetry. A large proportion of the college's members were required to attend the lectures, thereby gaining a familiarity with Greek authors including Aristotle, Sophocles and Homer – all of whom were later to be cited in their deliberations by the Bible translators who were the inheritors of this educational legacy.

Not only the substance but also the style of sixteenth-century education contributed to the working methods of the KJB translators. At the heart of the colleges' working lives were their libraries, which were supplemented by the fellows' own personal collections (figure 16). The colleges' book-buying was dominated by theology, in particular editions of the works of the Latin and Greek Church Fathers; copies of the medical writer Galen, of Homer, Plato and Aristotle, and works of reference and language-learning such as commentaries, lexicons and thesauruses were also purchased, along with texts of civil law and scientific books in some colleges. Gifts were frequently made by fellows and former fellows. Another useful method of enhancing a collection was to buy the library of a learned man upon his death: the largest single amount spent by an Oxford college in the sixteenth century was £120, paid by Magdalen for the library of Bishop John Jewel.[19] At Corpus, Bishop Fox provided 97 volumes for his new library; by 1589, the library contained 478 volumes, including an unrivalled holding of Greek manuscripts from the collection of William Grocyn.[20]

Apart from attending lectures (typically given in the college hall) and studying in libraries, a student worked under the scrutiny of a tutor, in whose chambers he lodged. Tutors assumed domestic and financial responsibility for their young charges, who generally entered a college at about fifteen. Tutors also read to their students, instructed them, supervised their work and exercised disciplinary oversight. Students at Oxford in the second half of the sixteenth century typically studied the

Figure 14 Corpus Christi
College, Oxford. Photograph
© Tim Rawle.

traditional disciplines of logic, grammar and rhetoric, alongside newer subjects such as history (figure 17). Mathematics, natural philosophy, medical science and modern languages such as Italian were also studied. Language exercises in Latin and Greek, including of course translation, played an important role in students' lives, as did the traditional practice of disputation, in which participants defended and attacked a set proposition or question. As humanist influence spread, the practice of declamation (delivering a rhetorical speech) also became a regular feature of university education. A student's reading life would be dominated by classical authors – the Latin poets (Virgil, Ovid), playwrights (Terence, Plautus) and rhetoricians (Cicero, Quintilian); Greek poets and playwrights (Homer, Euripides); Plutarch and Sallust in history, Plato and Aristotle in philosophy. Humanist editions for all these would have been used, and a humanist Greek grammar, dictionary and New Testament would have been constantly to hand. Christianity underpinned all of these activities, both intellectually and practically. A high proportion of the undergraduates at Oxford and Cambridge would have been destined for the church, and their lives were still structured by a liturgical regime inherited from the Middle Ages: both before and after the Reformation the collegiate day began at 4 or 5 a.m. in the college chapel with prayer and readings from the Bible.[21] Two Cambridge colleges, Emmanuel and Sidney Sussex, were expressly Puritan foundations intended for the training up of godly preachers; Laurence Chaderton, one of the four Puritan delegates to the Hampton Court Conference in 1604, was at the time Master of Emmanuel and became a figurehead for beleaguered Puritan clerics in the early years of James's reign.

The study of ancient languages and of the Bible were self-evidently intertwined pursuits that illuminated one another. As described so eloquently in Miles Smith and Thomas Bilson's preface to the KJB, scripture was the bedrock upon which all human endeavour and aspiration was founded: 'Happie is the man that delighteth in Scripture, and thrise happie that meditateth in it day and night.' Such total and personal immersion in the Scriptures – the translators use the energetic verbs 'searching' and 'studying' – necessitated a vernacular Bible with a sure foundation in textual scholarship. So the KJB translators ask, as Erasmus, Tyndale and the Wycliffite translators before them had all done, 'But how shall men meditate in that, which they cannot understand? How shall they understand that which is kept close in an unknowen tongue?' In this context, Bible translation is far more than an academic or ecclesiastical enterprise. It is, rather, a transformative engagement in the life of individuals and of society: 'translation it is that openeth the window, to let in the light' wrote Smith and Bilson.[22]

Figure 15 The Tower Room, part of the original President's Lodgings at Corpus Christi College, Oxford. Photograph © Tim Rawle.

This combination of ecclesiastical politics, humanist scholarship and reformed commitment to the vernacular Bible shaped the lives and work of the KJB translators. The academic world in which most of them lived and moved as they worked on the translation was typically high-minded, close-knit, self-regulating and self-scrutinising, whilst being also at times, no doubt, claustrophobic and faction-ridden. This was no less true of the Jacobean church. Nevertheless, the individual and collective endeavour of Bible translation was in many ways the natural extension – indeed, fulfilment – of the training in languages, textual scrutiny, translation and disputation that the translators had received in their youth and had themselves delivered to others. To the founders of the humanist colleges of Oxford and Cambridge, such as Bishop Fox, there could have been no higher calling than that to which their successors were summoned in 1604.

Figure 16 *pp. 56–7* The Chained Library of Hereford Cathedral. The books in college libraries would also have been secured in this manner, with a chain attached at one end to the front of the book and at the other to a rod running along the bottom of each shelf. Miles Smith, member of the first Oxford company of translators, left some of his annotated books to Hereford Cathedral. © The Dean and Chapter of Hereford and the Hereford Mappa Mundi Trust.

Figure 17 *above* Arts End of Duke Humfrey's Library (1488), the oldest part of the Bodleian Library, Oxford. Engraving by David Loggan (1675).

Notes

1. Both quotations are from 'A view of popish abuses yet remaining in the English church, for which the godly Ministers have refused to subscribe' from *An Admonition to Parliament* (1572) in H.C. Porter, *Puritanism in Tudor England* (Columbia, S.C., 1971), pp. 123, 131. Judith Maltby is grateful to Jane Freeman and Diarmaid MacCulloch for their comments.

2. Diarmaid MacCulloch, *The Later Reformation in England 1547–1603* (London, 1990), pp. 44–61; Peter Lake, *Anglicans and Puritans? Presbyterian and Conformist Thought from Whitgift to Hooker* (London, 1988), pp. 88–139; Judith Maltby, *Prayer Book and People in Elizabethan and Early Stuart England* (Cambridge, 1998), pp. 31–82. The magisterial study of Elizabethan Presbyterianism remains Patrick Collinson, *The Elizabethan Puritan Movement* (London, 1967).

3. Jenny Wormald, 'James VI and I: Two Kings or One?', *History* 68 (1983), 187–209, at pp. 196–8.

4. David Calderwood, *The True History of the Church of Scotland*, ed. T. Thomson and D. Laing (Edinburgh, 1849), cited in Patrick Collinson, 'The Jacobean

Religious Settlement: The Hampton Court Conference', in Howard Tomlinson (ed.), *Before the English Civil War* (London, 1983), p. 28.

5. William Barlow, *The Sum and Substance of the Conference*, in Edward Cardwell, *A History of the Conferences* (Oxford, 1841), p. 199.

6. 'The Millenary Petition', in J.P. Kenyon, *The Stuart Constitution* (Cambridge, 1966), pp. 134, 132; Collinson, 'The Jacobean Religious Settlement', pp. 30–33; Frederick Shriver, 'Hampton Court Revisited: James I and the Puritans', *Journal of Ecclesiastical History* 33 (1983), 48–71, at pp. 50–51.

7. Shriver, 'Hampton Court Revisited', p. 50.

8. Barlow, *The Sum and Substance*, p. 169.

9. Collinson, 'The Jacobean Religious Settlement', pp. 36–7; Shriver, 'Hampton Court Revisited', pp. 64–5; C.S. Knight, 'William Barlow', *Oxford Dictionary of National Biography* (*ODNB*).

10. Collinson, 'The Jacobean Religious Settlement', pp. 38, 33; Shriver, 'Hampton Court Revisited', pp. 57–8. For Chaderton, see Arnold Hunt, 'Laurence Chaderton and the Hampton Court Conference', in Susan Wabuda and Caroline Litzenberger (eds), *Belief and Practice in Reformation England: A Tribute to Patrick Collinson from His Students* (Aldershot, 1998). John Gauden, *The Life and Death of Mr Richard Hooker* (London, 1661), pp. 10–11.

11. Collinson, 'The Jacobean Religious Settlement', pp. 39, 34; Shriver, 'Hampton Court Revisited', p. 58.

12. Cited in Shriver, 'Hampton Court Revisited', p. 59.

13. Ibid., p. 58.

14. Barlow, *The Sum and Substance*, pp. 199–204.

15. Shriver, 'Hampton Court Revisited', p. 61.

16. John Spottiswoode, *History of the Church of Scotland*, ed. M. Napier and M. Russell, 3 vols (London, 1847–51), Vol. III, pp. 98–9. Spottiswoode was Archbishop of St Andrews from 1615 to his death in 1639; his *History* was first published in 1655.

17. Barlow, *The Sum and Substance*, pp. 187–8.

18. James McConica (ed.), *The History of the University of Oxford*, Vol. III: *The Collegiate University* (Oxford, 1986), pp. 17–29.

19. See N.R. Ker, 'The Provision of Books', in ibid., pp. 441–77, at p. 451.

20. J.R. Liddell, 'The Library of Corpus Christi College, Oxford in the Sixteenth Century', *The Library*, 4th series, 18 (1938), 385–416.

21. On collegiate life, see James McConica, 'The Collegiate Society', in McConica (ed.), *The Collegiate University*, pp. 645–732; and Victor Morgan and Christopher Brooke, 'Tutors and Students', in Victor Morgan, *A History of the University of Cambridge*, Vol. II: *1546–1750* (Cambridge, 2004), pp. 314–42.

22. 'The Translators to the Reader', in Alfred W. Pollard (ed.), *Records of the English Bible* (London, 1911), pp. 340–77, at pp. 347–9.

Figures 18–19 The University
Church of St Mary, Oxford.
In the Middle Ages St Mary's
served as the seat of the
University's government and
housed its library; in the
sixteenth and early seventeeth
centuries academic disputations
were still held there.
Photograph © Tim Rawle.

Figure 20 *pp. 62–3* Ralph
Agas, map of the city of
Oxford, 1578.

3

The Oxford Translators

Julian Reid

I T HAS OFTEN BEEN OBSERVED that the success of the King James translation is particularly remarkable, considering that it was the work of a committee – in fact, the work of six separate committees. A team of about fifty translators – the exact number is disputed – was drawn almost exclusively from the universities of Oxford and Cambridge, and divided into six companies, two each meeting in Cambridge, Oxford and Westminster. Each company was set its own group of texts from either the Old or the New Testament. At Oxford the first company, headed by John Harding, President of Magdalen College and Regius Professor of Hebrew, was appointed to translate the Old Testament prophets. The Oxford New Testament company was to translate the four Gospels, the Acts of the Apostles and the book of Revelation, under the direction of the Dean of Christ Church, Thomas Ravis. These official appointments notwithstanding, the companies actually met in Merton and Corpus Christi Colleges, in the lodgings of their respective heads, Henry Savile and John Rainolds (figures 21 and 22).

Socially, the translators came from varied backgrounds, some the sons of urban tradesmen, others the offspring of country gentlemen, or provincial artisans. The origins of some are entirely obscure. While all were members of the Church of England, they represented widely differing opinions on the essentials of doctrine and church discipline – salvation, justification, the wearing of vestments, the use of ritual, and so on, reflecting the tensions that existed within the Jacobean church. Academically, however, the translators inhabited the same world. An early education in Latin, the international language of scholarship, was followed by admission to university in their early to mid-teens to study for a Bachelor's, then perhaps a Master's, degree, encompassing a broad curriculum of Latin and Greek authors (including prose, poetry, drama, history and philosophy), mathematics and astronomy. They were expected to be able to compose in Greek and Latin, to translate into and out of those languages with ease, and to teach, debate and converse in those languages as if they were their native tongues. Educated in a wide range of literary genres, they were acutely attuned not only to the meaning but also to the harmony, rhythm and cadence of the written and spoken word. Several of the translators taught themselves the biblical languages of Hebrew, Syriac and Aramaic, although these were

Figure 21 *pp. 64–5* Henry Savile, Warden of Merton College, Oxford, 1585–1622. Hieronymus Custodis (1594). © The Weiss Gallery, London.

Figure 22 *right* The monument to John Rainolds in the chapel at Corpus Christi College, Oxford. Photograph © Tim Rawle.

not officially part of the curriculum, and many went on to hold official teaching posts within the University and their individual colleges. For the ablest, election to a college fellowship provided the chance to study for higher degrees, culminating in the doctorate of divinity, the ultimate goal for an ambitious scholar. On considering individual lives, one is struck by their youth and precocity.

John Rainolds – First Oxford Company

Of all the Oxford translators, it is perhaps John Rainolds who epitomises a certain preconception of the translators – learned, stern and puritanical. His life typifies the academic experience of many of the translators, while exemplifying the changes to which they were subjected during this theologically most volatile of centuries. Rainolds was born in 1549, a younger son of a prosperous Devonshire family of Catholic sympathies. A career at Oriel College, to which he was admitted at the age of eight, appears to have been interrupted, perhaps as a result of the religious conflicts affecting both country and university. In 1558 an uncle, Thomas Rainolds, was deprived of the wardenship of Merton College for his Catholic beliefs and died in prison. John Rainolds was subsequently awarded a scholarship at Corpus Christi College, to which he was admitted in 1563.

Two weeks after his seventeenth birthday, Rainolds was admitted probationary fellow of his college, the appointment being formally recorded in the college's admission register.[1] Only six weeks earlier he had witnessed a significant event in the life of the University. In early September, Elizabeth I had visited, hearing speeches, attending academic disputations, and witnessing dramatic performances in the hall of Christ Church. By her visit, Elizabeth bestowed her approval on the University, but also clearly demonstrated that she was keeping a watchful eye on its members. Who can tell whether, at sixteen, Rainolds appreciated the significance of the occasion, but he played his part, contributing to a collection of celebratory verses in Latin, Greek and Hebrew by members of Corpus Christi.[2] He also played an even more public part, taking the female role of Hippolyta in a performance of Richard Edwards's *Palamon and Arcyte*, one of several plays performed during the Queen's visit.

After graduating B.A. in 1568, Rainolds was made a full fellow of Corpus Christi. At its foundation in 1517, the college had been revolutionary in including classical Greek as a central subject of the curriculum. Rainolds graduated M.A. in July 1572 and his skill in Greek was rewarded by his being appointed Greek lecturer, a post he held for the next six years. Among the texts on which he lectured was Aristotle's *Rhetoric* – a core text of the Arts curriculum – for which two series of lecture notes survive together with his lecture copy of the printed edition.[3] The notes are executed in Rainolds's microscopically small but exquisitely painstaking handwriting.

It was during this time – we do not know when exactly – that Rainolds severed his connection with Rome and embraced a reformed Christianity. His family's experience is illustrative of the confessional cross-currents which at the time ran alike through colleges and families. Two of Rainolds's brothers, Jerome and Edmund, also held fellowships at Corpus Christi, from which they were ejected in 1566 and 1568 respectively for holding Catholic beliefs. Another brother, William, had apparently accepted the Elizabethan reforms, but in 1572 he resigned his fellowship at New College, was received into the Catholic Church and ordained priest. He was appointed Professor of Scriptures and Hebrew at the English College in Rheims; in effect, a Catholic university in exile. During preparation of the Catholic translation of the New Testament published at Rheims in 1582, he was sometimes called upon to answer criticisms emanating from Protestant scholars in England – his younger brother, fellow of Corpus Christi, being among them.

Rainolds was ordained in 1576, and was awarded his doctorate in divinity in 1585. It is in his doctoral robes that he appears in a portrait that hangs in Corpus Christi College, the sleeveless scarlet habit that distinguished the Doctor of Divinity contrasting with a black cassock-like gown. The atmosphere within the college, however, was not harmonious. There may have been a residual sympathy for Catholicism among some of the fellows, and in 1588 he resigned his fellowship and migrated to the more congenial Queen's College.

Although he was a gifted scholar, Rainolds's Puritan opinions barred his path to promotion. In May 1589 the Queen refused to approve his election to the Regius Chair of Theology and Thomas Holland, later one of Rainolds's fellow translators, was appointed in his stead. Significantly, in spite of holding the Greek readership at Corpus Christi, and his proven abilities in Hebrew, Rainolds was never offered either of the Regius Chairs in those languages. Elizabeth may have thought that she had safely promoted him out of harm's way when, in 1593, Rainolds accepted the office of Dean of Lincoln. But he dragged his heels in Oxford and was not installed in office until 1598. By this time William Cole, the President of Corpus Christi, had been persuaded to exchange office, and by the middle of December Cole was Dean of

Lincoln and Rainolds President of Corpus Christi. As a symbol of his office, Rainolds was invested with the founder's ring. At his death in 1528, Richard Fox, the founder of Corpus Christi, had left his episcopal ring – a gold band, enamelled with green and set with a large blue sapphire – to John Claymond, the first President. Claymond in turn left it to his successor, from whom it has passed to all successive presidents of the college.

The King James Bible was the culmination of Rainolds's life's work – the final justification of his hard-won scholarship, and of his journey from Rome to Geneva. Indeed, as noted in the previous chapter, the inception of the new translation has been attributed to him. Whereas Elizabeth had kept Rainolds at arm's length, James invited him to the Hampton Court Conference in early 1604, as a member of the Puritan delegation. As we have seen, according to the account of the conference written by another delegate, William Barlow, it was Rainolds who suggested a new translation to replace the officially approved but unsatisfactory Bishops' Bible.[4]

The first Oxford company of which Rainolds was a member was allotted the task of translating the Old Testament prophets. Although John Harding of Magdalen College officially headed the company, according to the Oxford historian Anthony Wood the translators met in Rainolds's lodgings once a week, 'and there as 'tis said perfected the work, notwithstanding the said Doctor, who had the chief hand in it, was all the while sorely afflicted with the gout'.[5] It may have been out of consideration for Rainolds's crippling affliction that the translators met at Corpus Christi rather than at Magdalen. Henry Hindley, the Vice-President of Corpus Christi, also recorded that

> Not long after he was set on work with the rest of such Doctors as were joined with him in translating the Prophets, his eyesight began sensibly to fail... During the work of the Translation (which before his death was almost brought to an end) though he was diverse times rudely troubled with his diseases of the Gout both in hands and feet, and of the colic, yet even in extremities he failed not to be present ever on the translating days with the rest, yea even in his last sickness too, though at length he grew so weak that not able to go up a few stairs into a higher room where they met, nor to endure there either standing or sitting, he was carried thither by his men … and laid upon a pallet.

Rainolds died in his Lodgings on 21 May 1607, and was buried four days later in the college chapel.

Rainolds left a substantial library of over 2,000 volumes; while its content was predominantly theological, it also betrayed evidence of wider concerns. An interest in national affairs, represented by maps of

England and copies of John Norden's *Speculum Britanniae* and William Camden's *Britannia*, was off-set by works of international reference. His gallery was furnished with maps of Europe, Asia, Africa and America. Among the works he left to Corpus Christi were volumes of Theodore de Bry's *Descriptiones Americae*, while to Richard Bancroft, the Archbishop of Canterbury, he left accounts of India and Muscovy. It is with some justification that a contemporary was to write, 'He alone was a well-furnished library, full of all faculties, full of all studies, of all learning; the memory, the reading of that man, were near to a miracle.'[6]

Henry Savile – Second Oxford Company

The life of Henry Savile, who hosted the New Testament company in Merton College, parallels that of Rainolds in many respects. He too was born in 1549 into a provincial landowning family; in this case, in Yorkshire. He too was a younger son who was to carve an academic career for himself, rise to be head of a college, and to distinguish himself among the Bible translators. But they were of a very different temper. Savile was admitted to Brasenose College in 1561, aged twelve. He demonstrated proficiency in all the subjects of the curriculum, but his first love was mathematics and astronomy. In December 1565, still only sixteen, he was elected fellow of Merton College. Studying for the degree of M.A., he systematically worked his way through Euclid's *Elements*, before turning his attention to the *Almagest* of the Greek astronomer Ptolemy. Immersing himself in the original Greek text he discovered many imperfections in the existing translations. As a result, he began his own translation of Ptolemy into Latin. He translated about half the text, his manuscripts surviving in the Bodleian Library together with his printed edition of the *Almagest*, the margins filled with his comments and observations.[7] The printed edition included several early commentaries, which Savile translated as well, so that one can, for example, compare his annotated copy of Theon of Alexandria's commentary against his own manuscript translation.

At Merton, Savile was well placed to pursue his studies in astronomy. Its library housed not only copies of Euclid and Archimedes, but also Latin translations of works by Arabic scholars. Scientific instruments were provided for the use of fellows, which were added to by gifts from later fellows, so that by the late sixteenth century Merton boasted a fine collection of quadrants and astrolabes, with which Savile and his contemporaries could make celestial observations. During Savile's wardenship the college was left a particularly fine astrolabe made by the Flemish instrument maker Walter Arsenius, the bequest of former fellow John Woodward (figure 23).

In 1578 Savile commenced a four-year tour of Europe, making contacts with many important scholars and visiting some of its greatest libraries. He travelled as far east as Poland and south as far as Italy, by way of France, Germany and Bohemia. Upon his return his undoubted abilities were recognised by his appointment as Greek tutor to Elizabeth I – a connection that was to have significant impact on his career.

As fellow of Merton College, Savile was eligible for election as its Warden. Leaving nothing to chance, however, he used his proximity to the Queen to ensure his election in 1585, provoking the opposition of others in the college, who objected both to his arrogance and to such inter-ference in their affairs. Leonard Yate, elected fellow in 1593, later maintained that Savile was 'too much inflated with his learn-ing and riches', but since he was 'so great and a favourite to the Queen, that there was no dealing with him'.[8] Savile was appointed Provost of Eton College in 1595, once again through the Queen's influence: he held this post concurrently with the warden-ship of Merton for the rest of his life. He was not in holy orders, as required by Eton's statutes, but that was easily dispensed with by royal command. Savile was the only one of the translators not to be ordained.

The year before, Savile had himself painted by Hieronymus Custodis (figure 21) one of the foremost portrait painters in Elizabethan England. It is not the portrait one expects of a scholar. There is no surplice or academic cap here. Instead, here is the courtier, royal favourite and man of the world. His suit may be of sober black, but it is of fashionable cut, his cloak of damasked silk. An open book at his right hand, betokening scholarship, is balanced by the sword hanging at his waist, symbolising action. His brown eyes regard the observer with all the confidence of the age; he has all the air and swagger of Raleigh and Drake. Yet his looks belie his scholarship. He

ost end it eam hoc et similis theoremats, qᵒ supra demonstrabi-
mus totaq̃ interualla horarū dieꝫ respondere. nisi
statuamus à qbusuis terræ locis à meridie ad aqlōrē
.i. transuerso trium habitationum signa aqγ, qβγ in alia
maximorū mundi circulos plano
erecto ad horizōtas p aβγ. et ab
ipsis ad circū mundi π, copulatis
πα, πβ, πγ egitenus plano p
ipsa educti; et in sphæra mundi
max circtm efficere ξξηθ. et sta-
tuis in ipsis παρ, πβυ, πγξ, ad
rectos ipsis constituamus degtos suos
ξαθ, ξβχ, ηγλ, uel sectiones ξξηθ
et horizōtis circaqᵐp, ιυξ, puta
ad uertices. et qᵘ ξηθ, ξυχ circu
ferentie aqrales motu sint (uaᵃ q
supra terrā apparens, semp sint æqlia, uñ sex signa sit sep
conspicua, sex reliqᵘ nō conspicua, à quoniaꝙ puucto raptat excordia
ablata toi ξθ, reliqᵘ ξξ, reliqᵘ ōe æqlis, q̃e ξη æqlis ξξ
eode mo. et qᵘ ad α habitatione sup terrā est ξηθ, ad β ξβχ,
aωγ, transitus ab α adβ abscodes astra in ξξ. patefaciet aut
proportionabiliter ea quæ sint in θχ, qm arcus æqles sint. qᵘ
uero in γ habitatione p supra terrā e ηθλ occultabit a β adγ
transitus arcū ξθ, et reuelabit arcū χλ æqle? dicit igit nos
ex phænomenis. mõr uero quāto ad aqlōrē magis gredians
toto i proportionē, boreali stellarū plures apparet, austra
lium dispareξξ. et manifestū qde ut aqr ad βγ sic ξξ ad ξη, et θχ
ad χλ. uiₐ in distātijs totius quaqᵘuersus hac apparētū
αξ respondentia euenat, sequit uo ut sup ost edimus nullā ξξ
terra figurā nisi sphæricā: un in hac sola figura plana
horizont in uno puncto ipsā cōtingat, et si stellati sū furior
dmam proportionate apparetū et uo apparetū. possumus
aut et aliter ipsā ξξ sphæricā figurā demonstrare, et in
medio sitā uniuersi. summatᵉ ē enim in superficie terrā
trium habitationū puncta αβγ. sitq̃ meridianus à habitationis ξ in spha mundi dξξ. et sit habitationis βθχ et γ, λμω.
et summaturₑ eoₓ sectiones horaiōₓ ū et meridianᵒ ₓ, δξ, ηξₓ
λμ. et ad rectos. his angtos in planis meridianoₓ sit α αξ, θλ, γμα

may have deputed routine administration to others, but he wrote and published extensively throughout his life.[9] In 1591 came English translations of the *Histories* and *Agricola* of the Roman historian Tacitus, and in 1598 *Rerum Anglicarum Scriptores*, a collection of English chronicles and histories. By 1600 Savile was also at work preparing an edition of the works of St John Chrysostom, the fourth-century Archbishop of Constantinople. With a team of scholars, including John Bois and Andrew Downes, who also worked on the Bible translation, he compared and edited different versions of the texts, their work resulting in an eight-volume edition that appeared between 1610 and 1613. The earlier volumes made a direct contribution to the Bible translation, being consulted by the committee of revision in 1610 as it worked its way through the epistles.[10] As the last volume of Chrysostom appeared, so Savile also published an edition of Xenophon's *Cyropaedia*.

In the midst of all this, between 1604 and 1608 the second Oxford company met in Savile's lodgings, systematically comparing their individual translations of the Gospels, the Acts and the book of Revelation. On 13 February 1605 books were transferred from the college library to the lodgings for use by the translators, and the names of those who met there entered in the College Register.[11] The task must have been essentially complete by September 1608, when on the 13th the first stone was laid of a new quadrangle that was to be built on the gardens beneath the windows of the lodgings. Work would not have begun had 'this outstanding undertaking', as the Register calls it, still been in progress.[12]

Savile sealed his career in 1620 by establishing two professorships, one each in geometry and astronomy (figure 24). Ever one to set the standard, Savile himself gave the first series of lectures, on the first book of Euclid's *Elements*. The lectures were published the following year and were to be his last publication.[13] He died at Eton on 19 February 1622 and was buried in the college chapel. His tomb is marked with a simple stone, but at Merton he is celebrated by an extravagant monument. In keeping with his own estimate of his abilities, his bust is flanked by figures of Euclid, Ptolemy, Tacitus and Chrysostom, as if to say he is their equal and they have come to pay their last respects.

Figure 24 Savile's translation of Theon of Alexandria's commentary on Ptolemy's *Almagest*. Oxford, Bodleian Library, MS. Savile 26, fol. 32v.

John Spenser – Second Westminster Company and John Harmar – Second Oxford Company

John Spenser, a member of the second Westminster company, followed John Rainolds as both Greek reader and President of Corpus Christi College (figure 25). There, however, similarities end, as Spenser was in conformity with the Elizabethan church in contrast with Rainolds's Puritanism, and his life appears to have been one of relative peacefulness. It was not, however, entirely without contention. Spenser was born in Suffolk but educated at the Merchant Taylors' School in London. Ten years younger than Rainolds, he graduated B.A. in 1577. Less than eight months later, aged only nineteen and not yet holding a fellowship, he was elected to succeed Rainolds as Reader in Greek. Rainolds, however, judged him too young and inexperienced and campaigned to have the election overturned. The case was referred to the Bishop of Winchester, the college's Visitor – its external arbiter in the event of disputes – but the Bishop confirmed Spenser's appointment.

Figure 25 John Spenser, President of Corpus Christi College, Oxford, 1607–14. From his monument in Corpus Christi College chapel. Photograph © Tim Rawle.

Spenser occupied the readership for ten years, after which he held a number of parochial appointments in Essex, Hertfordshire and London, and served as a chaplain to James I. He continued his studies in theology, and was awarded his doctorate in 1602. On 9 June 1607 he was installed as President of Corpus Christi, following the death of Rainolds three weeks earlier. Little can be said of his seven years in office beyond the observation of his biographer that they seem to have been 'peaceful and uneventful'.[14] Spenser's own religious opinions favoured the middle way outlined by his contemporary Richard Hooker in *Of the Lawes of Ecclesiastical Politie*. Spenser held Hooker in great respect, and after the latter's death set to editing the *Ecclesiastical Politie* for publication. It appeared in 1604, Spenser writing an introduction, in which he lamented 'this unhappy controversy about the received ceremonies and discipline of the Church of England' which had 'rent the body of the church into divers parts, and divided her people into divers sects'.[15]

At his death Spenser left part of his library to Corpus Christi, including his copy of the tragedies of Sophocles from which he had lectured (figure 26). The plays of *Ajax* and *Oedipus Tyrranus* in particular are interlined with items of Latin vocabulary, while the margins are annotated with comments, giving us an idea of how the plays were perceived in the late sixteenth century and their moral lessons adduced. They demonstrate the grasp of Greek language and literature attained by Jacobean scholars, but the role of classical texts in the translation

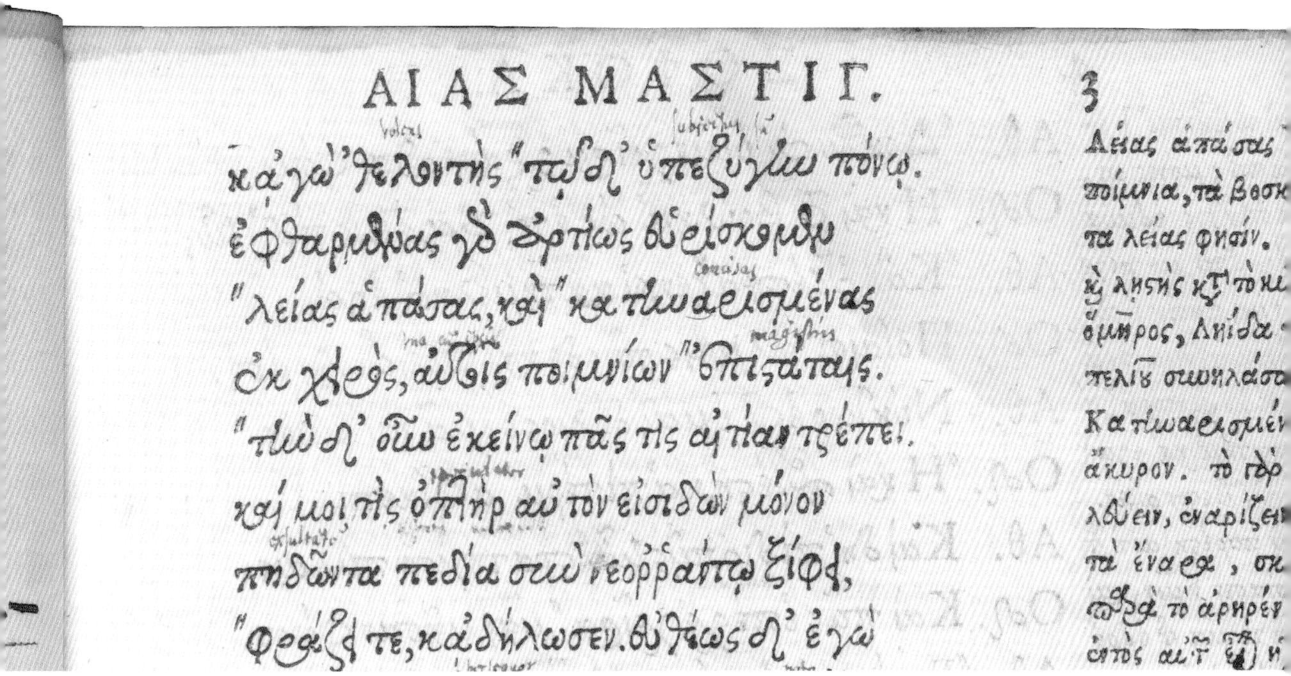

ΑΙΑΣ ΜΑΣΤΙΓ.

of the Bible went even further. The King James translators examined classical texts minutely for usage and nuance to elucidate the meaning of the sacred text. In his notes of the revision of the epistles, John Bois recorded the many sources the revisers examined: not only Christian commentators such as St Augustine and St John Chrysostom, but also more than a dozen classical authors, including Plato, Aristotle and Homer.[16]

John Harmar was Spenser's senior by three or four years. He was born in Newbury, Berkshire, although his parentage is unknown. After schooling at Winchester College he proceeded to New College, Oxford, where he graduated B.A. in 1577 – the same year as Spenser – and was elected to a fellowship. Like Savile, he spent some time travelling in Europe, attending lectures by Theodore Beza in Geneva. In March 1585 he was made Regius Professor of Greek, the university readership in Greek established by Henry VIII. In 1586 he produced an edition of six sermons of St John Chrysostom, which was the first book in Greek to be printed in Oxford.[17] His interest in Chrysostom persisted, and in 1590 he produced an edition of a further twenty-two Chrysostom sermons from manuscripts in the library of New College.

Harmar was appointed to translate the Gospels, Acts and Revelation with the second Oxford company, and is identified in the Merton College Register as one of those who met in the Warden's Lodgings for that purpose in February 1605.[18] Given his place in this company, and his

Figure 26 Sophocles' *Ajax* annotated by John Spenser, formerly Greek reader at Corpus Christi College. *Sophoclis Tragoediae Septem*, (Paris, 1568), p. 3. Corpus Christi College, Oxford O5.13.

interest in Chrysostom, it seems likely that he also assisted Savile, Bois and Downes in preparing the edition of Chrysostom's works. By a twist of fate, Harmar's career paralleled that of Savile in one more feature. In 1595, the same year Savile was appointed Provost of Eton College, Harmar was made Warden of Winchester College. At his death in 1613 his library was dispersed. Many of his books went to Winchester College, including Bibles in Dutch, French, Italian and Spanish – precisely the vernacular language editions distinguished in the Preface to the King James Bible.[19] His copy of Immanuel Tremellius's edition of the New Testament in Greek and Syriac, an essential tool for the King James translators, was left to the library of Winchester Cathedral.[20] Among other books left to Robert Harmar, possibly a nephew, were a copy of the Septuagint and a Hebrew Bible.[21]

George Abbot – Second Oxford Company

Perhaps the most successful of the translators in terms of professional advancement, and also the most controversial, was George Abbot (figure 27). Born in 1562 to Maurice Abbot, a Surrey clothworker, he received his earliest education at Guildford Grammar School. At sixteen he proceeded to Balliol College, where he took his Bachelor's degree in 1582. A fellowship at Balliol followed, where he dedicated himself to the study of theology, eventually taking his doctorate in 1597. This year was to be an *annus mirabilis* when, aged just thirty-five, Abbot was also appointed Master of University College. Though a small college, it had the distinction of being the oldest college in the University. Indeed, it claimed to have been founded by no less a person than King Alfred. Abbot spent thirteen years at University College, and it was while he was there that he joined Savile and the rest of the second Oxford company to work on the New Testament.[22]

Abbot's star was in the ascendant. In 1600 he was appointed Dean of Winchester (a post he held alongside the mastership of University College), he was one of the delegates to the Hampton Court Conference in January 1604, and he oversaw the visit of James I to the University of Oxford in 1605. In 1609 he was appointed Bishop of Coventry and Lichfield, but only seven weeks later he was appointed to the more senior diocese of London, following the death of its bishop, Thomas Ravis, another of the translators. Remarkably, less than fifteen months after first being consecrated bishop, Abbot was promoted higher still: in February 1611, he was elected Archbishop of Canterbury. Even at the time this remarkable feat of advancement was the subject of criticism. In June of the same year he was appointed to the King's privy council, providing him with political as well as religious influence.

Figure 27 George Abbot (1562–1633). Unknown artist, English School, seventeeth century. University College, Oxford. © The Master and Fellows of University College, Oxford.

In matters of religion Abbot was at once sincere and pragmatic. On matters of doctrine he was strictly Calvinist, and throughout his career a fierce opponent of Rome. But in discipline he was accommodating, maintaining the office of bishop as biblically authorised, and allowing 'seemely conformity' in matters of ceremony, within defined limits. He set an example by preaching regularly, and sought to establish good discipline throughout his dioceses, to ensure that worship was conducted properly, and congregations properly instructed. To the extremes of religious opinion, however, he was steadfastly opposed, and in pursuit of his own vision of religious orthodoxy he was prepared to use whatever means were approved by the state. In 1614 he urged the execution of imprisoned Catholic priests. Yet, when James I ordered the death sentence against two Protestants, Edward Wightman and Bartholomew Legate, for proposing opinions at the opposite extreme, Abbot approved that sentence too, condemning them as 'blasphemous heretikes'.

In the summer of 1621 a tragedy occurred that was to mark the rest of Abbot's life. Invited by Lord Zouche to consecrate a new chapel at his house in Hampshire, he also took the opportunity to go hunting. On 24 July he loosed a bolt from his crossbow, which struck the arm of his host's gamekeeper, Peter Hawkins, severing the artery. Within the hour he was dead. The incident was investigated by a royal commission and Abbot was exonerated on the grounds that Hawkins's death had been 'through his own fault' because Hawkins had previously been warned not to pass between the huntsmen and their quarry. Abbot settled an annual pension of £20 on Hawkins's widow, and until his own death did penance once a week on the day on which the accident occurred.[23]

With the death of James I in 1625 Abbot's influence waned. His particular brand of churchmanship did not appeal to Charles I, who was more sympathetic towards Rome. The two even came into direct confrontation, and between July 1627 and March 1628 Charles had Abbot banished to one of his estates in Kent, for refusing to license the publication of a sermon that the King had himself authorised. Abbot died on 4 August 1633, and was buried not in his cathedral, as one might expect, but in Guildford parish church, the church of his childhood. A prayer that concludes his will might be taken as an honest expression of his life's purpose, 'beseeching Almighty God to increase the number of his faithful' and 'to abate more and more daily the strength of antichrist and popery'.

During his life Abbot had produced a number of publications, largely sermons and religious polemics, most of which died with him. One book, however, was to outlive him. In 1599, while the young Master of University College, he had published an undergraduate text book, *A Briefe Description of the Whole World*, which was to serve as a gazetteer of all the known 'monarchies, empires and kingdomes' of the world, outlining their systems of government, forms of religion, and peculiar customs. It passed through numerous editions and imprints, being finally reprinted in 1636. The information it provides becomes less reliable the more remote the country – Abbot included South America – but even much closer to home his observations are not without ignorance or prejudice. The Irish he describes as 'naturally rude and superstitious' while the Scots 'do barbarously speake' English.[24]

Leonard Hutten – Second Oxford Company

In contrast with the life of George Abbot, that of Leonard Hutten was quiet and uncontroversial. His origins are unknown, although he was born about 1556 and educated at Westminster School. He was admitted to Christ Church in 1574 and remained at the college for the rest of his life. Graduating B.A. in 1578, he followed the steep academic path taken by many of his fellow translators, and finally achieved his doctorate in theology in 1600. During the same period he was successively appointed to a number of provincial parishes in Yorkshire, Dorset and Northamptonshire, which were presumably served by paid curates. He left some literary remains, such as a copy of the sermon he preached on the anniversary of the accession of Elizabeth I, and verses he contributed to a compendium celebrating the visit of King Christian IV of Denmark to Oxford in 1606.[25] More substantial is a play in Latin of a sort popular with academic audiences at the time. *Bellum Grammaticale…* (*The Grammatical Battle, or Civil War between Nouns and Verbs*), which was first performed at Christ Church in December 1581, is a comedy telling how the irregularities of Latin grammar arose from civil war between nouns and verbs. It was revived a decade later for a second visitation of the University by Elizabeth I in 1592. It was accompanied by performances of two more plays: *Ulysses Redux* and *Rivales*, both by William Gager, Hutten's contemporary at Westminster and Christ Church. It may simply have been polite flattery, but in a collection of epigrams on members of Christ Church, Gager wrote of Hutten: 'Whether a comedy is to be written or performed, you, Hutten, can rightly take first place.'[26]

Hutten's one work of religious controversy, *An Answere to a Certaine Treatise of the Crosse in Baptisme*, appeared in 1605 while he was engaged on the translation with the second Oxford company. Its argument, that the sign of the cross in baptism is not idolatrous but consistent with the usage of the early church, would not have met with John Rainolds's approval. But his interests were not limited to comedy, theology or the flattery of princes. He left two works of antiquarian interest in manuscript, both now unfortunately lost. One was on the history of the foundation of Christ Church, the other on the 'Antiquities of Oxford'. The latter, however, survived long enough for it to be published in 1720 by the Oxford antiquary Thomas Hearne. While Hutten perpetuated the tradition of the refoundation of the University by King Alfred, he also recorded invaluable information on the religious houses of pre-Reformation Oxford, as well as providing an account of the principal buildings of the city in his own day.[27] There is no known likeness of Hutten. After his death in 1632 he was buried in Christ Church cathedral, where part of the Latin inscription in his memory can be translated as 'a soul learned, straightforward, godly'.

Ralph Hutchinson – Second Westminster Company

A letter that survives in the archives of St John's College sheds light on the role of colleges as charitable institutions in the Elizabethan and Jacobean age and the place of patronage. Ralph Hutchinson, a future President of St John's, was born in London in about 1552; the exact date is unknown (figure 28). Like John Spenser and several other King James translators – Lancelot Andrewes (the head of the first Westminster company), Roger Andrewes, John Perne and Ralph Ravens among them – Hutchinson had his schooling at the Merchant Taylors' School. The school had only been founded in 1561 by Sir Thomas White, also the founder of St John's College. In 1568, Sir Thomas White's widow was to write to the fellows of St John's,

> for as much as Sir Thomas White, my most loving husband hath … appointed me the naming of the three next scholars to be admitted there, these shall be to let you to understand that … I do presently present and nominate unto you Ralph Hutchinson, son to John Hutchinson (whom ye all well know to be greatly charged with a great number of children, and some of them very towards in learning).[28]

Thus was Ralph Hutchinson first brought to the attentions of the fellows of St John's. He was formally admitted to the college two years later, and graduated B.A. in 1574. In 1579, following his graduation as M.A., he was appointed to the college's readership in rhetoric. The post does not appear to have been wholly congenial, as the following year an appeal was made to the Visitor to deprive him of his post, for neglect of his duties. It is reassuring that even future translators of the KJB suffered basic human weaknesses. But he was clearly not incorrigible as he subsequently held the posts of medical fellow and Vice President. Abiding by college regulations, he surrendered his fellowship in 1586 in order to marry. Four years later he was to return to St John's as its President, the only senior member of the college who was allowed to marry. In 1604 Hutchinson was appointed one of the second Westminster company to work on the epistles alongside John Spenser, the only other Oxford scholar in the company. They must have made many journeys on horseback between Oxford and Westminster to attend the translating meetings, perhaps travelling together for greater safety, comparing notes as they went. The joint responsibilities of college head and translator may have proved too much. In any event, Hutchinson died in January 1606, aged only fifty-four. He was survived by nine children, emulating the example of his father.

Richard Mulcaster and the Merchant Taylors' School

Hutchinson was a product of the Merchant Taylors' School in London. Some of the schools attended by the translators had been long established: Winchester College, attended by John Harmar, was founded in 1382, and Westminster School, attended by four of the translators, traced its origins to the early thirteenth century. Merchant Taylors', in contrast, had only been founded in 1561, yet educated eight of the fifty or so men who contributed to the King James translation. The success of the school was attributable to its first master, Richard Mulcaster, who was appointed in the year of its foundation and served there for twenty-five years. He later served twelve years as the High Master of St Paul's School. Although born in Carlisle, Cumberland, he had received his own schooling at Eton College before proceeding to King's College, Cambridge, in 1548 at the age of sixteen. He later transferred to Oxford, where he graduated M.A. from Christ Church in 1556.

From surviving accounts, Mulcaster was skilled in Latin and Greek, which he duly imparted to his pupils. Remarkably, Hebrew was also taught at the school, although by a separate tutor. Language and literature were not restricted to the classroom and the pages of books. He encouraged the boys to act, and they gave several performances before the court of Elizabeth I, just as Rainolds and Hutten were to do at Oxford. He inspired respect among his pupils: translator Lancelot Andrewes reportedly kept a portrait of him in his study. His most famous pupils were the poet Edmund Spenser, author of *The Shepheardes Calender* and *The Faerie Queene*, and the dramatist Thomas Kyd, author

Figure 28 Ralph Hutchinson, President of St John's College, Oxford, 1590–1606. From his monument in St John's College chapel. Photograph © Tim Rawle.

Figure 29 The tomb of James Montague at Bath Abbey. Montague was Dean of Worcester and member of the second Oxford company. He became Bishop of Bath and Wells. © Angelo Hornak/Bath Abbey.

of *The Spanish Tragedy*. Mulcaster was also the author of an ambitious, and unfinished, treatise on the state of education in England in his time, together with suggestions for its reform. This appeared in two volumes as *Positions Concerning the Training up of Children* and *The First Part of the Elementarie*. Remarkably for an academic work, it was written in English, but that was simply to promote his thesis that Englishmen should be taught in their own language. To support this, he recommended the publication of a standard grammar and dictionary, together with a standardisation of the spelling system. For teaching in the vernacular he argued with great passion, 'I love Rome, but London better, I favour Italy, but England more, I honour Latin, but worship English.' It is perhaps his most famous statement, but he developed his theme along the lines 'I do not think that any language is better able to utter all arguments, either with more pith or greater plainness, as our English tongue is.'

We recognise the skill of Edmund Spenser and Thomas Kyd because we are at home with the genres of poetry and drama, in a way that we are no longer attuned to listening to sermons or analysing the language and phrasing of biblical prose. But it may be that, by his conventional

teaching of the literature of ancient Greece and Rome, combined with a revolutionary advocacy of the English tongue, through his pupils Richard Mulcaster made his own unique contribution to the making of the King James Bible.

Figure 30 The Breakfast Room in the former Warden's Lodgings, Merton College, Oxford. As one of the principal private rooms of the Lodgings, it has been identified as the room where the second Oxford company worked. Photograph © Tim Rawle.

Notes

1. Corpus Christi College, Oxford, Archives B/1/3/1.
2. Corpus Christi College, Oxford, MS. 280, ff.180v–181r.
3. Bodleian Library, Auct. S 2.29.
4. William Barlow, *Summe and Substance of the Conference Which it Pleased his Excellent Majestie to Have with the Lords, Bishops and other of His… Clergie… at Hampton Court* (London, 1604), p. 45.
5. Anthony Wood, *Athenae Oxonienses: an exact history of all the writers and bishops who have had their education in the University of Oxford…* (London, 1691).
6. Philip Wynter (ed.), *The Works of the Right Reverend Joseph Hall*, 10 vols, (London, 1863), Vol. VI, pp. 149–50.
7. Bodleian Library, Savile W 14.
8. Andrew Clark (ed.), *'Brief Lives,' chiefly of Contemporaries, set down by John Aubrey, between the Years 1669 & 1696*, 2 vols (Oxford, 1898), Vol. II, p. 214.
9. 'Henry Savile', *ODNB*.
10. Ward Allen (ed. and trans.), *Translating for King James* (Nashville, Tenn., 1969), p. 9.
11. J.R.L. Highfield (ed.), *Registrum Annalium Collegii Mertonensis, 1603–1660* (Woodbridge, 2006), p. 28.
12. Ibid., pp. 49–50.
13. Henry Savile, *Praelectiones Tresdecim in principium elementorum Euclidis* (Oxford, 1621).
14. 'Stephen Wright', *ODNB*.
15. Richard Hooker, *Of the Lawes of Ecclesiasticall Politie*, ed. John Spenser (London, 1604).
16. Allen, *Translating for King James*, pp. 55 and 94.
17. John Harmar (ed.), *D. Ioannis Chrysostomi Archiepiscopi Constantinopolitani, homiliae sex…* (Oxford, 1586).
18. Highfield, *Registrum*, p. 28.
19. David Daiches, *The King James Version of the English Bible* (Chicago, 1941), p. 171.
20. Immanuel Tremellius (ed.), *He Kaine Diatheke/Novum Testamentum – Est autem interpretatio Syriaca Noui Testamenti, Hebraeis typis descripta* (Geneva, 1569).
21. Will of John Harmar, 1613: The National Archives, PRO, PROB 11/123.
22. Highfield, *Registrum*, p. 28.
23. Olga S. Opfell, *The King James Bible Translators* (Jefferson, N.C., 1982), p. 84. Adam Nicolson, *Power and Glory: Jacobean England and the Making of the King James Bible* (London, 2003), p. 156, gives the interval as once a month.
24. George Abbot, *A Briefe Description of the Whole Worlde wherein is particularly described all the Monarchies, Empires and Kingdomes of the same* (London, 1599); Robin Darwall-Smith, *A History of University College Oxford* (Oxford, 2008), p. 122.
25. Bodleian Library MS. Rawlinson C.79, f.140; British Library, Royal MS. 12 A LXIV.
26. Dana Sutton (ed.), *Leonard Hutten's Comedy 'Bellum Grammaticale'*, a hypertext critical edition, revised version 2008: www.philological.bham.ac.uk/bellum/intro.html.
27. Leonard Hutten, *De Antiquitatibus Oxoniensis*, published in Thomas Hearne (ed.), *Textus Roffensis* (Oxford, 1720).
28. St John's College Archives, MUN LII.16.

Figure 31 The Old Library at Merton College, Oxford. Books were borrowed from here for the translators. Photograph © Tim Rawle.

ÆTATIS SVÆ 64 s

M
Bis

4

Materials and Methods

Gareth Lloyd Jones,
Helen Moore and Julian Reid

Apocalipse

= wth the particular
bookes by them un
dertaken

ford *

{ m^r. Savile
{ D^r. Perrin
{ D^r. Ravens
{ m^r. Harmer.

{ D^r. Duport
{ D^r. Branthwaight
{ D^r. Radcliff

Cambridg

{ m^r. Ward Eman:
{ m^r. Downes
{ m^r. Boys
{ m^r. Ward Regall.

The Prayer of
manasses & the
rest of the Apochri
pha.

The Rules to be observed in Translation.

1 The ordinary Bible read in the church comonly call'd the Bishops Bib
to be followed, & as little Altred as the Truth of the originall will
mitt.

2 The Names of the Prophetts & holy writers wth the other Names i
the Text to be retayned as neere as may be accordinly as the vulga
used.

3 The old Eccliasticall wordes to be kept (viz) as the word Church
to be translated Congregation

4 When a word hath diverse significations. that to be kept wch h
bene most comonly used by the most of the Ancient ffathers, being
agreeable to the propriety of the place & the Analogie of faith

5 The Division of Chapters to be Altred either not at all. or as lit
as may be if necessity doth require.

6 No marginall Notes at all to be affixed. but only for the Explana
tion of Hebrew or Greeke wordes, wch cannot without some circu
locution so breifly & fitly be explened in the Text.

7 Such quotations of places to be marginally sett downe as sha
serve for fitt reference of one Scripture to another.

8 Every particular man of each company to take the same chapter
chapters & haveing amended & translated them severally by him
self where he thinkes good all to meet together, conferr w^t
have done, & agree for their part w^t. shall stand.

9. As one company hath dispatched any one booke in this manner th
sha

2.

shall send it to the rest to be considred of seriously & iudiciously,
for his Maiesty is very carefull in this point.

If any company upon the review of the Booke so sent shall doubt   10
or differ upon any place & withall send their Reasons: to w.ch if
they consent not. the diffrence to be compounded at the generall meeting, w.ch is to be of the cheife Parsons of each company at the end
of the worke.

when any place of especiall Obscurity is doubted of, letters to be   11
directed by Autority to any man in the Land for his iudgment
on such a Place.

letters to be sent from Every Bishop to the rest of his cleargie   12
admonishing them of the Translation in hand. & to move & charge
as many as being skilfull in the Tongues have taken paines
in that kinde. to send his particular observations to the Company
ether at westminster, Cambridg, or Oxford.

The directors in Each Company to be the Deanes of westminster   13
& chester for that place, & the kings professors in the Hebrew
& Greeke in each university,

These Translations to be used when they agree   ⎰ Tindalls
better with the Text then the Bishops Bible   ⎱ Matthewes   14.
                                                    Couerdalls
                                                    whitchurch
                                                    Geneva.

An Order agreed upon for translation of the Bible.

	Deane of westminster	Pentateuch
	Deane of Paules	
westminster	Dr. Saravia.	
	Dr. Clark	
	Dr. Lenfeild	
	Dr. Teigh	The story from
	Mr. Burleigh Stretford	Ioshua to the first
	Mr. King Sussex	booke of Chron: ex
	Mr. Thomson Clare	clusive.
	Mr. Bedwell	
	Mr. Livelie	From the history of
	Dr. Richardson	the Chron: with the
	Mr. Chaderton	rest of the story
Cambrydge	Mr. Dillingham	& the hagiographa
	Mr. Harrison	(viz) Iob. Psal: Pro:
	Mr. Andrewes	Cantic: Ecclesiastes
	Mr. Spalding	
	Mr. Bing	
	Dr. Harding	
	Dr. Reinolds	The foure greater
	Dr. Holland	Prophetts with the Co
Oxford	Dr. Kilby	mentari: & the
	Mr. Smith Hereford	lesser Prophetts.
	Mr. Brett	
	Mr. Faireclowe	

The places & persons agreed upon for the Hebrew with the particular Bookes by them undertaken.

	Deane of Chester	The Epies of
westminster	Dr. Hutchenson	st. Paul.
	Dr. Spencer	
	Mr. Fenton	
	Mr. Rabbitt	The canonicall
	Mr. Sanderson	Epies
	Mr. Dakins	
Ox	Deane of Christchurch	The 4 Gospells
	Deane of winchester	
	Deane of worcester	
	Deane of windsore	

The places & Persons agreed upon for the Greek.

FOLLOWING THE 1604 HAMPTON COURT CONFERENCE, six companies comprising 'certain learned men', as King James called them, were established to work on the new translation. There were two companies in each of Oxford, Cambridge and Westminster (figure 32).[1] Accounts differ, but it is likely that between 47 and 54 translators were recruited, almost exclusively from the universities of Oxford and Cambridge. The first Westminster company worked on Genesis–2 Kings under the direction of Lancelot Andrewes; the first Cambridge company, headed by Edward Lively, took Chronicles–Ecclesiastes; and the first Oxford company, led by John Harding, Isaiah–Malachi. The director of the second Oxford company was Thomas Ravis, and it worked on the Gospels, Acts and Revelation; the second Westminster company, led by William Barlow, translated the New Testament epistles; and the second Cambridge company, whose director was John Duport, worked on the Apocrypha.

The Rules of Translation

The translators' work was governed by a set of Rules specifying how they should go about their task. These Rules were drawn up by Bishop Richard Bancroft, ostensibly with input from the King, and they survive in several manuscripts, for example MS. Harley 750 in the British Library (figures 33 and 34). The Rules address three main issues: the use of earlier translations of the Bible; the appearance and language of the new translation; and the organisation of the companies' work. In the first category, it was laid down that the translators should follow the text of the Bishops' Bible of 1568 wherever possible, substituting the words of another translation, such as Coverdale or Geneva, where it was deemed 'to agree better with the text' (i.e. the original Hebrew and Greek) than the Bishops' Bible. The established chapter divisions, as employed in English from the Wycliffite Bible onwards, were also to be retained, but there were to be none of the contentious and discursive marginal notes typical of the Geneva Bible that were so disliked by the King. So far as language was concerned, the Rules specified that the new translation should retain the familiar English forms of biblical names and 'the old ecclesiastical words', such as 'Church' rather than

Figure 32 *pp. 86–7* Miles Smith, member of the first Oxford company, and author of the translators' Preface to the 1611 King James Bible. © The Governing Body of Christ Church, Oxford.

Figure 33 *p. 88–9* The Rules for the Translators, from British Library MS. Harley 750 fols.1v-2r. © British Library Board MS. Harley 750.

Figure 34 *left* The list of translators, from Britsh Library MS. Harley 750, fol. 1r. © British Library Board MS. Harley 750.

'Congregation'; this rule was intended to remove the new translation, as far as was possible, from the arena of Puritan controversy. In terms of organisation, the Rules laid down that individual members of the companies should work on the allotted text, and then confer and reach collective agreement. The Rules stipulated that the agreed text was then to have been circulated for comment to the other companies, who were to send any comments and alterations, with reasons, back to the originating committee. (Experts differ, however, on whether such cross-company consultation actually took place.) In addition, for particular points of contention the judgement of any learned man in the land could be sought, and the opinions of clergy deemed sufficiently learned were to be canvassed by the bishops. The final stage of the translation was the 'General Meeting', at which any outstanding differences of opinion were to be resolved.[2] The demands of the undertaking at a logistical and administrative level, let alone an intellectual one, were astonishing for an age in which Oxford and Cambridge were each separated from London by two days' riding on horseback.

These Rules being established, the first stage of the translation took place between 1604 and 1608. As dictated by the Rules, these four years would have been spent in individual and small group work on sections of the text, collective revision by the company of this work, group translation, and scrutiny of the finished translation by another company. By 1608, King James was anxious to see the project come to fruition, and he called in the work of the companies to the General Meeting at Stationers' Hall in London. Accounts of the membership of this final meeting differ: the Rules state that two members of the Oxford, Cambridge and Westminster companies should be selected to attend; this could mean twelve or, as suggested elsewhere, six. The General Meeting spent the years 1609 and 1610 in review and revision, perhaps as described thus by the polymath John Selden:

> That part of the Bible was given to him who was most excellent in such a Tongue (as the *Apochrypha* to *Andrew Downs*) and then they met together, and one read the Translation, the rest holding in their Hands some Bible, either of the learned Tongues, or *French*, *Spanish*, *Italian*, &c. If they found any Fault they spoke, if not, he read on.[3]

The final stages of the translation were overseen by Thomas Bilson, Bishop of Winchester, and Miles Smith, who became Bishop of Gloucester in 1612; they were also the authors of the 1611 Preface to the published translation.

Hebrew fountains and Greek streams

At the core of the translators' activity were the Greek and Hebrew texts, described in the 1611 Preface using a traditional water metaphor as 'Hebrew fountains and Greek streams'.[4] These texts were used by the translators alongside the polyglot bibles and commentaries against which they scrutinised their copies of the Bishops' Bible. For the New Testament, they would probably have used one of the editions of Erasmus's Greek New Testament printed in Paris by Robert Estienne, known as 'Stephanus'; the third Stephanus edition of 1550 was the first to include variant readings from different manuscripts and it became the basis of future editions of the Greek New Testament until the nineteenth century; Tremellius's Latin Bible of 1579 was also used for both Old and New Testaments. Erasmus's work in editing the Greek New Testament was inspired by the scholarship of the fifteenth-century Italian humanist Lorenzo Valla. Valla had attempted to assess the accuracy of the Latin Vulgate translation of the Bible by studying Greek manuscripts of the New Testament; on reading Valla's annotations (*Adnotationes*), Erasmus became convinced of the need for a reliable edition of the Greek New Testament and from 1511 onwards he began to examine, collate, emend and annotate manuscript witnesses to the New Testament text. The work was groundbreaking and controversial in its treatment of the scriptures as material documents to which humanistic principles of analysis and textual criticism could and should be applied. Although with the benefit of hindsight it is evident that Erasmus did not choose the best available manuscripts as the basis of his Greek text, and that some of his conjectures were misplaced, his edition still served as the bedrock of New Testament scholarship for hundreds of years. The first edition of Erasmus's Greek New Testament was published in 1516 with the title *Novum Instrumentum*, an 'instrumentum' being a document outlining the terms of an agreement; this refers to the covenants or 'testamenta' of Judaism and Christianity. Erasmus's methods were outlined in the notes that accompanied his text. His intentions were to identify textual corruption and restore the original meanings; to illuminate obscure or ambiguous passages; to correct inaccuracies in the Latin translation; and to compare the New Testament quotations from the Septuagint (the Greek translation of the Old Testament) with the Hebrew originals.[5] The first edition of Erasmus's New Testament printed the Greek text alongside a corrected version of the Vulgate's Latin, but subsequent editions printed Erasmus's own translation (with the Vulgate re-included from the fourth edition of 1527).

The translators possessed notable ability in oriental languages as well as Latin and Greek. Lancelot Andrewes, who led the first

Westminster company, became proficient in Latin, Greek and Hebrew at Merchant Taylors' School, and while studying at Pembroke College, Cambridge focused his attention upon Chaldee (that is, Aramaic), Syriac and Arabic as well as reputedly mastering fifteen modern languages. Andrewes was also a master of English prose style, whose ability in his sermons to 'squeeze' the 'juice of meaning' from words (as described by T.S. Eliot) has been admired down the centuries. William Bedwell, a contemporary of Andrewes at Pembroke and a member of the same translating company, was at the time England's leading Arabist; his lifetime's work was the writing of an Arabic–Latin dictionary. Not the least of the achievements represented by the King James Bible project was the gathering together in common cause of the country's most able scholars of these relatively new disciplines. Although there was no formal university provision at Oxford in Arabic until 1636, when Archbishop Laud established a professorship (first held by Edward Pococke of Corpus), Arabic was highly valued for its role in communicating Greek culture to the West. Syriac and Aramaic likewise were vital for the understanding of the Hebrew scriptures and the writings of the early Christian church.

Those gifted in Hebrew among the translators are almost too many to number. The first Oxford company, tasked with the translation of Isaiah to Malachi, included Thomas Holland, Regius Professor of Theology at Oxford and a notable Hebraist, and Miles Smith (one of the few translators recruited from outside the universities), who was reputed to be as familiar with Chaldee, Syriac and Arabic as with his mother tongue; the annotated books he left to Hereford Cathedral also reveal his remarkable command of scriptural and rabbinic Hebrew.

Hebraic studies had been rediscovered in England during the sixteenth century. On his return to Italy in 1551 the Florentine scholar Petrucchio Ubaldini reported that in England 'the rich cause their sons and daughters to learn Latin, Greek and Hebrew, for since this storm of heresy has invaded the land they hold it useful to read the Scriptures in their original tongues'.[6] This may not have been entirely true, but nevertheless a powerful impetus for the rediscovery of Hebrew came from humanistic and Protestant circles on the Continent. The German savant Johann Reuchlin (d. 1522) was acclaimed as the promoter and protector of Semitic studies. His emphasis on philology was adopted by Sanctes Pagninus and Sebastian Münster, whose chief contribution was to integrate rabbinic influence into Christian biblical scholarship on a far greater scale than anyone had done hitherto. The study of Hebrew philology, which the first Protestants regarded as part of the science of theology, was adopted by learned Englishmen, who laid durable foundations for the growth of Hebrew learning in England.

The rediscovery of antiquity associated with Renaissance humanism underlined the importance of Hebrew for biblical study. John Rainolds wrote to a friend on 4 July 1577 urging him to persevere with his Hebrew studies:

> I wish that you also joyne Hebrew to your Greek, though peradventure you have once began it and given it over. For in that you may follow me … who my selfe, when I was first Master of Arts, began the study of it, and being weary left it: the next year perceiving the necessary use of it, I set againe upon it, and I thanke God, since continued a student in it. Wherefore the Word of God, and that, if it may be, out of the very wel-spring, not out of the brooks of translations (if I may so tearme them) must be diligently read…[7]

Knowledge of the language not only enabled English Protestant scholars to read the Bible in the original, it also led them to appreciate the exegetical comments of post-biblical Jewish scholars. In many cases of textual difficulty the Ancient Greek and Latin versions offered no acceptable solution. This made the contribution of medieval rabbis towards understanding the Bible all the more valuable in an age when detailed grammatical commentaries on the text were still scarce.

The translation of scripture was not the only motive for learning Hebrew. In their efforts to maintain a distinct position against Catholic dogma, Protestants insisted that Hebrew should be part of the equipment of their disputants in confessional battles with Roman Catholics. Furthermore, they discovered that medieval Jewish commentaries could be consulted with profit in doctrinal debates because the rabbinic exposition of key passages supported their own interpretation. In disputed cases they utilized the opinions of the rabbis to add weight to their own cause.

The first recognized teacher of Hebrew in Tudor England was Robert Wakefield, who was appointed to a lectureship at St John's College, Cambridge, in 1523. He moved to Oxford in 1530, where he remained for the rest of his life.[8] By the mid-1540s the creation of Regius Chairs had put Hebrew teaching on a sound financial basis at both universities. Another crucial factor was the development of collegiate instruction. As their wealth increased through endowments and benefactions, individual colleges were able to provide the institutional framework necessary for the expansion of the new learning by appointing lecturers. By the end of the century several other colleges had followed the example of St John's, Cambridge, and instituted Hebrew lectureships to supplement university teaching.

The libraries

By 1600 a handful of schools were providing their senior pupils with the necessary groundwork. Like Lancelot Andrewes, Thomas Harrison of the first Cambridge company began to study Hebrew at Merchant Taylors' School and by the mid-1570s boys in the seventh form of Westminster School were expected to attend a Hebrew lesson between 4 and 5 p.m. each day. Private households too made their contribution. While the scholarly remains of the Tudor gentry are not abundant, the fact that some prominent lay people studied the language indicates that the Hebrew Bible was not regarded solely as the province of scholarly theologians. Access to Hebrew books was not difficult: inventories and catalogues demonstrate that by the end of the sixteenth century there was, in addition to Hebrew bibles and rabbinic commentaries, a wide range of grammars and dictionaries on the market.

No single record tells us exactly which sources were used by any one of the translating companies, but by putting together the evidence from a variety of records we can begin to understand the breadth of scholarship that was available to them. The Merton College Register – the record of decisions of the governing body – is tantalising in promising much. The entry for 4 September 1604 records that 'certain reverend men appointed by the King's Majesty to translate the first part of the New Testament, jointly received the following books from our common library.' The fellow maintaining the Register, however, sadly failed to enter the list. The Register provides other clues to the contents of Merton College library because it was used to record the acquisition of books by donation, bequest and purchase, and the loan of books to fellows. In March 1576, Master John Chamber withdrew from the library a Greek thesaurus in four volumes, while in October 1583 the college received several books from the estate of William Marshall, including a copy of the *Enarrationes in Evangelia* of Theophylact of Ochrid, a *Thesaurus Linguae Sanctae* – presumably that of the Italian scholar Sanctes Pagninus – and Otto Brunfels's *Annotationes... in Quatuor Evangelia et Acta Apostolorum*. In the spring of 1591 Thomas Savile, Henry Savile's younger brother and friend of John Rainolds, returned from the Continent with books purchased in Frankfurt, including a Talmud, a Greek thesaurus and a Greek–Latin testament, 'of the latest edition'.[10]

Donation inscriptions in the front of books are also revealing. Henry Savile himself gave to the library a copy of Pagninus's *Thesaurus Linguae Sanctae* (Lyons, 1575) and a copy of Immanuel Tremellius's *Grammatica Chaldaea et Syra* (1569). Other gifts and bequests included Sebastian Münster's *Dictionarium Hebraicum* (Basel, 1535), and Guillaume Budé's

Figure 35 *Sacra Biblia: Hebraice, Graece et Latine, cum annotationibus Francisci Vatabli,* (Heidelberg, 1599), formerly belonging to John Rainolds. Opened at the story of Jonah and the whale, p. 606. Corpus Christi College, Oxford Z.11.4.

[Latin column 1]

Iehouam Deum cæli h timeo, qui fecit mare & aridam.

10 Timuerunt itaque viri illi timore ingenti, & dixerunt e ei, Cur hoc fecisti? sciebant enim viri illi quòd à facie Iehouæ h fugeret: nam indicauerat eis.

11 Dixeruntque ad eum, Quid faciemus tibi, h vt sileat mare à nobis? nam mare h ibat & intumescebat.

12 h Quibus dixit, Tollite me, & proiicite me in mare, h & silebit mare h à vobis : h scio enim ego quòd propter me tempestas magna hæc superuenit vobis.

13 h Nitebantur autem remis viri illi h vt reducerent *nauem* ad aridam, sed non valuerunt: quia mare h ibat, h & intumescebat super eos.

14 Clamauerunt itaque ad Iehouam, & dixerunt, Quæsumus Iehoua ne obsecro pereamus h propter animam viri istius, h neque h ponas super nos sanguinem innocentem : tu enim Iehoua, h sicut voluisti, fecisti.

15 Tulerunt ergo Ionam, & proiecerunt eum in mare: h constititque mare ab h ira sua.

16 Timuerunt autem viri illi timore ingenti Iehouam, h & immolauerunt hostiam Iehouæ, h voueruntque vota.

CAPVT II.

1 PRæparauerat autem Iehouah piscem grandé, h vt deglutiret Ionam, & fuit Ionáh h in ventre piscis tribus diebus & tribus noctibus.

2 Et orauit Ionáh ad Iehouam Deum suum h de ventre piscis.

3 Dixitque, Clamaui h ex afflictione mea ad Iehouam, h & exaudiuit me: h de ventre inferni h clamaui, & exaudisti vocem meam.

4 Proiecisti autem me in profundum, *quod est* h in medium marium, & *ceu* flumé circundedit me: omnes vndæ tuæ & fluctus tui super me transierunt.

5 h Ego verò dicebam, h Proiectus sum e cóspectu oculorum tuorum: veruntamen h addam respicere ad templum sanctitatis tuæ.

[Latin column 2]

cæli ego timeo, qui fecit mare & aridam.

10 Et timuerunt viri timore magno, & dixerunt ei, Quid hoc fecisti, cognouerunt enim viri quòd à facie Domini fugeret: quia indicauerat eis.

11 Et dixerunt ad eum, Quid faciemus tibi, & cessabit mare à nobis quia mare ibat, & intumescebat.

12 Et dixit ad eos, Tollite me, & mittite in mare, & cessabit mare à vobis : scio enim ego quoniam propter me tempestas hæc grandis super vos.

13 Et remigabant viri, vt reuerterentur ad aridam, & non valebant: quia mare ibat, & intumescebat super eos.

14 Et clamauerunt ad Dominum, & dixerunt, Quæsumus Domine, ne pereamus in anima viri istius, & ne des super nos sanguinem innocentem: quia tu Domine, sicut voluisti, fecisti.

15 Et tulerunt Ionam, & miserunt eum in mare: & stetit mare à feruore suo.

16 Et timuerunt viri timore magno Dominum & immolauerunt hostias Domino, & & vouerunt vota.

CAPVT II.

1 ET præparauit Dominus piscem grandem, vt deglutiret Ionam: || & erat Ionas in ventre piscis tribus diebus & tribus noctibus.

2 Et orauit Ionas ad Dominum Deum suum de ventre piscis.

3 Et dixit, ||Clamaui de tribulatione mea ad Dominum, & exaudiuit me: de ventre inferi clamaui: & exaudisti vocem meam.

4 Et proiecisti me in profundum in corde maris, & flumen circundedit me: omnes gurgites tui & fluctus tui super me transierunt.

5 Et ego dixi, Abiectus sum à te, veruntamen rursus videbo templum sanctum tuum.

[Footnotes]

9 Timeo,]Id est colo. nam timor Domini, verus est ipsius cultus.

11 Vt sileat, &c.] Heb. Vt mari pacato ac tranquillo fruamur, siue tranquillú nobis fiat mare quod silens dicitur, nam mare iratum edit sonum vehementem. ¶Ibat &intumesc.]ibat, & tumultuabatur.i. subinde magis ac magis commouebatur. agitabatur. magis, siue magis fiebat tempestas.

12 Et silebit, &c.]i.& tranquillum fiet vobis mare.

13 Nitebantur autem remis]Ad verbum, Et foderunt .sub. in mari remis. Propriè significat fodere: sed quia qui remigant, videntur quasi fodere in aqua, accipitur & pro remos agere, id est navigare. ¶Et intumescebat] & tumultuabatur, vt paulo antè, versu 11.

14 Propter animam viri ist.] i. quod priuauerimus eum vita, fueritmúsque causa mortis huius. coniicientes eum in mare. Alii, propter animam, exponunt propter culpam [siue peccatum]hominis istius. ¶Neque ponas, &c.] Ionas erat illis innocens: non enim læserat eos, neque quidpiã damni acceperant ab eo. ¶Sicut voluisti, fec.] Præt. Heb. pro præf. sicut vis & liberata agis.

15 Constititque, &c.]conquieuitque mare à furore suo. id est ab agitatione & commotione sua.

16 Et immolauerunt, &c.]Singul. Heb. pro plur. & antecedens pro re-

latiuo. & immolauerunt illi hostias, animo scilicet ac deliberatione id est statuerunt apud se & decreuerunt se immolaturos hostias in honorem Domini, quum primum scilicet reuerti possent in Ierusalem. ¶Voueruntque vota.] Iub. ipsi Deo cuius Ionas se dicebat Prophetam. nam vistanto miraculo fuerunt conuersi ad Dominum.q.d. obtulerunt in honorem Domini plurima dona.

IN CAPVT II.

3 Ex afflictione mea]ex quo fuit tribulatio mihi.i. in tribulatione positus, ¶Et exaudiuit me]Hoc dicit quòd perstitisset illæsus & cooperie & mente in ventre illius piscis. ¶De ventre inferni]Seipsum sequenti versu declarat.i de vasto barathro. hoc est de ventre illius ceti immanis, qui similis erat barathro. ¶Clamaui,]vociferatus sum.

5 Proiectus sum, &c.] Phrasis Hebræa, pro, putabam me proiectum à te. vel, quando proiectus sui in mare, fere defondeb animum. putabam enim me mortuum. ¶Addam respicere, &c.] Loquendi modus Hebraicum, pro, spero me adhuc aspecturum templum sanctum tuum quod in Ierusalem, quum videam me permanere viuum & illæsum in ventre ceti.

משנה תורה

הוא ספר היד שחיבר הרב הגדול רבינו משה בן הרב רבי מיימון הספרדי זצ"ל:

עם הפירוש עזרא ועם הסמ"ג ועם ההגהות מיימוניות נדפס מחדש מוגה ומדוייק ברוב העיון מתוך ספרים קדמונים נמצאים בדפוס וכתיבת יד מעויינים ומוגהים מחכמים גדולים אנשי שם ע"י הגאון ראש הגולה מהרר דוד פיצינשטון ז"ל ונעם העתקות של הרב גדול בחורה מהרר עזריאל דיינה זל:

עוד הסכמנו לחבר קונטרס קנקנית שיחלוק לספרים יסמנו וכו דמוכים ונביאלי עולם גם כתחדש על הכלבבים בתחלה חיבר וכו קומות שיחבר הכולנם אל שהוא עקר וגדול לזה הספכר גם זה לעשותה זה הקטבנות אשר השיג הרמב"ם ז"ל על היחבור הזה למען יהיה שלה בתבלית השלבמות לא יוכל כל כו עוד הסכמנו כו יואת מקום יהדיים בטובקים יזמון כל דין בכ"לין בחזיה סין מוטורי ויחזשו ככך גם בכל מקום יזמון על דגלו לאחומות בחוזה דף כמוא עד כדפם עצו קמיפתחות שנדפסו לפנים ולא כתפשעו בגליות אלו שה הכריחות מא"ד לימבוא כל דין בקלות:

גם הסכמנו לכדפים בהזרובה מה שבתב בע"לין חכם וחום ואם הזכבר כדוואה הרב רך מאיר מוסמו לנקרים סבתב חלבו בלשון החייויוי אשר כדכם מהרב הכנ"לחדין והבכם רואו בין הקק"מיות גהליעולם הספר מוענבר עם מבמים ושבליים קדושים ורמוקים ייצנוו בחת שלא לחדעמום תוך הספר בסתא ואולו לא יבדקו להדוכ למתי תורה כ"אשר יבנבו חינין הסקמות כסת מוענג לך דה אך אימה הפכמנות להפם כנ"ן כל כדם ולעשות כסכן קיש ואיש:

פה ונציאה

בבית כן ווסק בית טליון מארקו אנטוניו יוסטיניאן כצליחו ס' לב"ק תקת מוסלת הספרית ילך הגדל והסא הלבחיתם תחן:

Lexicon Graeco–Latinum (Geneva, 1554). An even earlier record, an inventory of the library compiled in 1556, reveals editions of many of the early Church Fathers, both Greek and Roman, including John Chrysostom, Basil, Jerome and Ambrose. But pride of place was given to the Complutensian Polyglot Bible of 1517–22 sponsored by Cardinal Jiménez at Alcalá in Spain, which printed parallel Hebrew, Greek and Latin texts of the Bible. It is listed first in the inventory, and is still preserved in the library.[11]

For the translators who met at Corpus Christi College, working on the Old Testament prophets, we are even more fortunate as to our sources. In the January following John Rainolds's death in 1607, Henry Hindley, Vice President of the college, wrote an account of Rainolds's final months, including his contribution to the translation. He recorded, 'The translation I am sure cost him largely for there was no book which might be useful but he provided.'[12] This claim would appear to be no exaggeration as the probate inventory compiled after Rainolds's death reveals a personal library of over 2,000 volumes, while a more detailed inventory preserved in the Bodleian Library provides enough information to identify many of the titles, undoubtedly consulted by the translators.[13] That many were concerned with biblical languages and scholarship, and were left to fellow translators, only serves to confirm this conclusion.

The inventory runs to over one hundred pages, with four pages recording the bequest of a hundred books to the library of Corpus Christi College. These included a *Sacra Biblia: Hebraice, Graece et Latine* (1599), with copies of the annotations of François Vatable (figure 35). This sixteenth-century French scholar published nothing during his own life but Robert Estienne, one of his pupils, reproduced Vatable's lecture notes in his own edition of the Bible between 1539 and 1545, and they were frequently reprinted in subsequent editions. Other bibles left to Corpus Christi included a Hebrew bible printed in Venice, unquestionably one of the editions by Daniel Bomberg, and a copy of Immanuel Tremellius's Syriac New Testament with his own Latin translation, printed in Geneva in 1569. The importance of Tremellius to the translators is witnessed by the fellow copy of the 1569 New Testament owned by John Harmar, and Tremellius's 1575 edition of the complete bible owned by John Spenser.[14] Rainolds left a further Hebrew Bible to Thomas James, Bodley's Librarian, and a copy of Sebastian Münster's Hebrew and Latin Old Testament to William Bennion of All Souls College.

Rainolds's bequests to his fellow translators are also revealing. The translators valued the scholarship of Jewish commentators concerning their own scripture and religious law, and in Rainolds's bequests we

Figure 36 *Mishneh Torah,* Moses Maimonides (Venice, 1550). Title page with *ex testamento* inscription of John Rainolds, 1607. Corpus Christi College, Oxford Z.47.8.

find examples of the works of Maimonides (Rabbi Moses ben Maimon), Nachmanides (Rabbi Moses ben Nachman), David Kimchi, Joseph ben Gorion and Joseph Karo, among others (figure 36).

Peter Thacher, a student of Corpus Christi, was the recipient of Theophylact of Ochrid's commentaries on Habakkuk, Jonah, Nahum and Hosea, while Henry Mason, Chaplain of Corpus Christi, received 'Ribera in Prophetas minores': the *Commentaria in duodecim prophetas minores* of Francisco de Ribera. That Ribera was a Spanish Jesuit did not automatically disqualify his scholarship, although his opinions would have been balanced by those of the Swiss Protestant Rudolph Gwalter, whose *In Prophetas Duodecim, quos vocant minores* was also to be found in Rainolds's library and ended up in the hands of William Cape of Queen's College.

Miles Smith, who at the time of the translation was a canon of Hereford, joined Rainolds in his lodgings at Corpus Christi to work on the prophets. His surviving books in Hereford Cathedral library also reveal the tools of the biblical translator: a copy of David Kimchi's *Sefer Michlol*, comprising a Hebrew grammar and dictionary printed in Venice by Daniel Bomberg (1545 and 1529 respectively); a second Hebrew dictionary, printed in Basle (1599); Elia Levita's *Lexicon Chaldaicum* printed by Paul Fagius in 1560; and Old Testament Hebrew texts printed by Bomberg and Estienne, with accompanying rabbinic commentaries, including those of Ibn Ezra, Rashi and Kimchi on the twelve minor prophets.[15]

At first glance we might wonder what the works of the sixteenth-century Italian naturalist Ulisse Aldrovandi were doing in a predominantly theological library, until we recollect that many creatures find their place in scripture – the sparrow alone upon the house top, the pelican of the wilderness, the worm that smote Jonah's gourd, and the flies, lice and locusts that plagued the Egyptians. Rainolds owned copies of both his *Ornithologiae* (Bologna, 1599–1600), and (figure 37) *De Animalibus Insectis* (Bologna, 1602). The works of Aldrovandi include the traditions surrounding the natural world preserved in classical literature, but to these he added modern principles of scholarship, such as close observation of animals and their native habitats. The level of observation is revealed in the meticulous engravings that illustrate his works. At the same time he incorporated linguistic scholarship and in the *Synonima* that accompany each creature he cites its name in different languages, including Greek and Hebrew.

Rainolds was not alone in possessing such modern works of natural history. In 1605 Merton College received a substantial bequest from the estate of former fellow John Chamber, including books for the library. Among these were copies of Conrad Gesner's *Historia Animalium* and

Figure 37 John Rainolds's copy of Aldrovandi's *De Animalibus Insectis* (Bologna, 1602), showing locusts and grasshoppers. Aldrovandi recorded the names of insects in various ancient languages, helping the translators to identify insects mentioned in scripture. Corpus Christi College Library N.8.5

A verô viridi,& fubalbido variat.Tibia ac pediculi inftar ferræ dentati , dilutè puniceâ funt.
Alæ media fui parte vltra extremam aluum in longum protenduntur,quaternæ. Harum bi-
næ fuperiores fufco , & balio maculofæ. Inferiores ex fufco argenti fplendore micant, ac à
volatus officio ceffante infecto, minimè vt illæ fimplæ funt , fed decuplo rugarum ordine in
fe complicatæ,quomodo mantilia extergendis manibus dicata , & puerorum illæ ex charta
laternæ viæ duces, multiplici plicarum ferie fibi mutuo incumbentium componi folent;
quas cùm ad volatum explicat,in trium digitorum latitudinem diftenfas eft intueri.

Secûda Tabula duodecim habet Locuftarum diuerfas fpecies. Prima è maiorum genere
dorfû habet colore ochræ nigris minutis pûctis fiue guttulis confperfo. Alarû tegmen viri-
defcit,& eiufdê coloris & magnitudinispunctulis notatur. Caput,pectus & aluus itê pedes
viridi ochroq; variat. Aluus in aduncû aculeû orhræ colore definit; capite Perlis fimilis eft.
Antênas habet mirê lôgitudinis, & tenuitatis,rubicûdas fubrutilas. Nu.2.Locufta capite &
antennis Cochleâ fiue Domiportâ æmulatur.Capite,nifi oculi id proderêt,carere videretur.

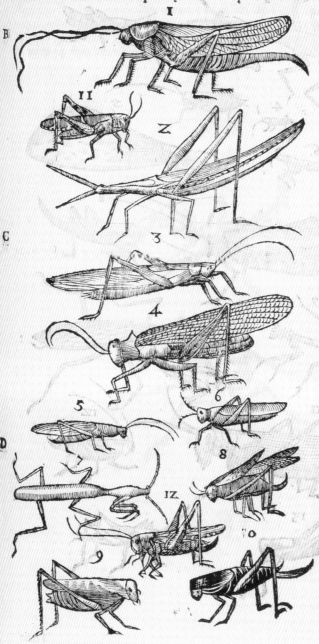

Antênæ craffæ funt,& craf
fa quoq; admodû femora
pofteriorum pedum.Alas
habet corpore protenfio-
res.Vndiq; concolor fibi.
Color eft cinereo flaue-
fcês.Num.3.Locufta eft è
genere vulgarium, vnico-
lor,viridis,præter antênas
quæ lutefcunt.Quarta tri-
color Locufta vocari po-
teft. Vulgo Frate hoc eft
monachus nominatur, nô
ob colorû diuerfitatê , fed
quòd cucullata eft.Caput
collû cucullatum , pectus,
& femora pofteriorum pe
dû funt viridia. Tibiæ verô eorundê pedum fangui
nei planè coloris: cætera
omnia cinerea. Antennæ
exiles,furfû erectæ.Quinta
ex aculeatarû fiue cauda-
tarû genere , vbiq; vnico-
lor,viridis.Num.6.exatro
cinerea,vndiq;fibi conco-
lor eft. Septima ἄπτρος,
Bruchus dici poteft, fœtû
illius maximæ,quæ primo
loco in prima tabula fpe-
ctatur,effe puto: nam etiâ
gibbofa eft, & priores pedes, è pectoris initio è gib
bi feu tuberculi regione ,
producit, & viridis eft to-
ta.Num.8.ea videtur, cu-
ius defcriptionê fupra de-
dimus ex authore de natu
ra rerum: nam aculeum
habet pro cauda,vt ille lo
quitur , & tota viridis eft,
caput equino capiti fimi-
le. Tales Hollandi, vt au-
dio Corenmefenvocât.Ta
les ego propriè legitimas

Icones Animalium Quadrupedum, originally published in the 1550s. Gesner had pioneered the close observation of the natural world so successfully practised by Aldrovandi. Savile ensured that the volumes of Gesner were secured for his own use, at a cost of £7. It seems too much of a coincidence that Savile would make such an acquisition just when he was engaged on the Bible translation.[16]

With the refounding of the university library by Sir Thomas Bodley in 1602 another resource was put at the disposal of the scholars who would come to work on the King James project. Within a year, at least five of them – George Abbot, Thomas Holland, John Perne, John Rainolds and Richard Kilby – were registered as readers.[17] Whatever might be lacking in their private or college libraries might be found there. In 1605 Thomas James, Bodley's first librarian, published a catalogue of the library, revealing the riches available to the translators: bibles, concordances, grammars, and commentaries rabbinic, patristic and contemporary.[18]

Finally, the notes compiled by John Bois of the work done at the General Meeting in 1610 provide substantial evidence of works used by the translators, and the way they were utilised. Precisely the same sorts of books found at Merton, in the Bodleian Library and in the libraries of John Rainolds and Miles Smith were used by the revision committee. Dictionaries and thesauruses of Greek words and phrases were examined for meaning and nuance, including the lexicon of obscure Greek words compiled by the fifth-century grammarian Hesychius of Alexandria. Church Fathers, early and late, were scrutinised for their interpretation of the epistles. John Chrysostom in particular was appealed to, and where volumes had already been published, it was the Eton edition masterminded by Henry Savile that was consulted. Theophylact of Ochrid was once again consulted, and reference made to Theodoret of Cyrrhus, a fifth-century Syrian theologian whose works included commentaries on the epistles. Other authorities from the ninth and tenth centuries, in the persons of Photius, Patriarch of Constantinople, and Arethas, Archbishop of Caesarea, informed the translators' deliberations. Arethas's works included a commentary on the book of Revelation.

As might be expected of such a modern piece of scholarship as the KJB, many of the great European scholars of the sixteenth century are represented among the books the translators used, such as Erasmus, Guillaume Budé, Theodore Beza, Joseph Scaliger, Isaac Casaubon and Girolamo Zanchi. Perhaps less expected is the recourse the translators made to classical literature, to the poets, historians and philosophers of classical antiquity: Homer and Pindar; Xenophon, Thucydides and Polybius; Aristotle and Plato.[19]

It is remarkable how far biblical scholarship had come in the century prior to the publication of the King James Bible. Aldus Manutius had only started printing classical Greek texts in 1494, and Erasmus's Greek New Testament had only appeared in 1516. The next hundred years had seen the publication of grammars and dictionaries, increasingly accurate texts of scripture in the original languages, and manifold commentaries from the early days of the church onwards. The translators' grasp of their sources may not always have been perfect, but we can only be awed by the breadth of their learning and the comprehensiveness of the resources available to them.

Preparing the text

Three key documents bear witness to the process whereby the KJB was translated. The first is a 1602 copy of the Bishops' Bible, now in the Bodleian Library, that at the time of its purchase was described as 'a large Bible wherein is written downe all the Alterations of the last Translacion' (figure 38).[20] At the beginning of the translation work, forty copies of the Bishops' Bible were distributed to the companies to act as the basis of the new translation, as described in Rule 1. These Bibles were originally unbound, and so were handled as loose sheets. The Bodleian 1602 Bible is a bound copy that contains some of the sheets on which manuscript revisions to the Old and New Testaments were marked; it is the only surviving witness to the use made by the companies of these Bishops' Bibles and it refers to the work of four companies. The annotations made to the Old Testament reflect a late stage of revision – either as sent to the General Meeting in 1610, or as agreed at that meeting – and cover Genesis to Isaiah 4; the first four chapters of Jeremiah, Ezekiel and Daniel; and Hosea to Malachi inclusive.[21] The New Testament annotations relate to the work undertaken by the second Oxford company of translators and were made by three scribes, who handled respectively Matthew and John 17; Mark and Luke 1–18; and Luke 19–24 and John 18–21. These New Testament annotations comprise three stages of revision that probably took place over the period 1607 to 1610, perhaps after review by the other companies as described in the Rules. The annotations in the Bodleian 1602 Bible do not, however, represent the final text of the KJB as it was printed: further revisions were undertaken subsequently.[22]

The second material witness to the making of the translation is a manuscript deposited in Lambeth Palace Library in the seventeenth century, Lambeth Palace MS. 98. This manuscript is entitled 'An English translation of the Epistles' (with the first four words added in a different hand), and contains the letters of Paul, James, Peter, John

28 But Jesus turning backe vnto them, sayd, Yee daughters of Hierusalem, weepe not for me, but weepe for your selues, and for your children.

29 For behold, the dayes are comming, in the which they shall say, Happie are the barren, and the wombes that neuer bare, & the paps which neuer gaue sucke.

30 Then shall they beginne to say to the mountaines, * Fall on vs, and to the hilles, Couer vs.

31 For if they doe these things in a moist tree, what shall be done in the drie?

32 * And there were other two euill doers, led with him, to be put to death.

33 * And after that they were come to the place which is called Caluarie, there they crucified him, and the euill doers, one on the right hand, and the other on the left.

34 Then sayd Jesus, Father, forgiue them, for they wote not what they doe: And they parted his raiment, and cast lots.

35 And the people stoode beholding, and the rulers mocked him with them, saying, He saued other men, let him saue himselfe, if hee be verie Christ, the chosen of God.

36 The souldiers also mocked him, comming to him, and offering him vineger,

37 And saying, If thou bee the king of the Jewes, saue thy selfe.

38 And a superscription was written ouer him with letters of Greeke, and Latin, and Hebrewe, THIS IS THE KING OF THE IEWES.

39 And one of the euill doers, which were hanged, railed on him, saying, If thou be Christ, saue thy selfe and vs.

40 But the other answering, rebuked him, saying, Fearest thou not God, seeing thou art in the same damnation?

41 And we truely are righteously punished, for we receiue according to our deeds, but this man hath done nothing amisse.

42 And he sayd vnto Jesus, Lord, remember me when thou commest into thy kingdome.

43 And Jesus said vnto him, Verely I say vnto thee, to day shalt thou be with me in paradise.

44 And it was about the sixt houre, and there was a darkenesse ouer all the earth, vntill the ninth houre.

45 And the Sunne was darkened, and the vaile of the temple was rent, euen thorow the middes.

46 And when Jesus had cried with a loude voice, hee sayd, * Father, into thy hands I will commend my spirit: And when he thus had said, he gaue vp the ghost.

47 When the Centurion saw what was done, he glorified God, saying, Verely this was a righteous man.

48 And all the people that came together to that sight, when they sawe the things which were done, smote their breasts, and returned.

49 And all his acquaintance, and the women that followed him from Galilee, stood afarre off, beholding these things.

50 * And beholde, there was a man named Joseph, a counseller, and hee was a good man, and a iust,

51 (The same had not consented to the counsell and deed of them) which was of Arimathea,

a citie of the Jewes, which same also waited for the kingdome of God.

52 He went vnto Pilate, and begged the body of Jesus.

53 And when he had taken it downe, he wrapped it in a linnen cloth, and layd it in a sepulchre that was hewen in stone, wherein neuer man before was layd.

54 And that day was the preparing of the Sabboth, and the Sabboth drew on.

55 The women that followed after, which had come with him from Galilee, beheld the sepulchre, and how his body was layd.

56 And they returned, and prepared sweete odours and ointments, but rested the Sabboth day, according to the commandement.

The xxiiij. Chapter.

13 Christ appeareth to the two disciples that went to Emaus.

BUT vpon the * first day of the Sabboths, very early in the morning, they came vnto the sepulchre, bringing the sweete odours, which they had prepared, and other women with them.

2 And they found the stone rolled away from the sepulchre.

3 And they went in, but found not the bodie of the Lord Jesu.

4 And it came to passe, as they were amazed thereat, beholde, two men stood by them in shining garments.

5 And as they were afraid, and bowed downe their faces to the earth, they sayde vnto them, Why seeke ye the liuing among the dead?

6 He is not here, but is risen: * Remember how he spake vnto you when he was yet in Galilee,

7 Saying, The Sonne of man must bee deliuered into the hands of sinfull men, and be crucified, and the third day rise,

8 And they remembred his words,

9 And returned from the sepulchre, and told all these things vnto those eleuen, and to all the remnant.

10 It was Marie Magdalene, and Joanna, & Marie Jacobi, & other that were with them, which told these things vnto the Apostles.

11 And their words seemed to them fayned things, neither beleeued they them.

12 * Then arose Peter, and ranne vnto the sepulchre, and when he had looked in, hee sawe the linnen clothes layd by themselues, and departed, wondring in himselfe at that which was come to passe.

13 * And behold, two of them went that same day to a village called Emaus, which was from Hierusalem about threescore furlongs.

14 And they talked together of all these things that had come to passe,

15 And it came to passe, that while they communed together, and reasoned, Jesus himselfe drew neere, and went with them.

16 But their eyes were holden, that they should not know him.

17 And he sayd vnto them, What manner of communications are these that yee haue one to another as ye walke, and are sad?

18 And the one of them, whose name was Cleophas, answering, sayd vnto him, Art thou

onely

Center marginal references (left column)

Esa.2.19.
osee.10.8.
apo.16.16.

Mat.22.38.

Mat.27.38.
mar.15.27.
iohn 19.18.

Psal.30.6.

Mat.27.25.
mar.15.43.
iohn 19.38.

Right marginal notes

a That is, the first day of the weeke.
Mar.16.1.
iohn 20.21.

Mat.17.23.
mar.9.31.
luke.9.22.

Iohn 10.6.

The Gospel on the Munday in Easter weeke.
Mar.16.12.
b That is, 7. miles and an halfe.

onely a ſtranger in Hieruſalem, and haſt not knowen the thinges which are come to paſſe there in theſe dayes?

19 He ſaide vnto them, What things? And they ſaid vnto him, Of Ieſus of Nazareth, which was a Prophet, mightie in deede & word before God and all the people,

20 And how the high Prieſts and our rulers deliuered him to bee condemned to death, and haue crucified him.

21 But we truſted that it had bene he which ſhould haue redeemed Iſrael: and as touching all theſe things, to day is euen the third day ſince they were done,

22 Yea, and certaine women alſo of our companie made vs aſtonied, which came early vnto the ſepulchre,

23 And when they found not his body, they came, ſaying that they had ſeene a viſion of Angels, which ſay that he was aliue.

24 And certaine of them which were with vs, went to the ſepulchre, and found it euen ſo as the woman had ſayde, but him they ſaw not.

25 And he ſaide vnto them, O fooles, and ſlow of heart, to beleeue all that the Prophets haue ſpoken:

26 Ought not Chriſt to haue ſuffered theſe things, and to enter into his glory?

27 And he began at Moſes, and all the Prophets, and throughly interpreted vnto them in all the Scriptures, thoſe things which were written of himſelfe.

28 And they drewe nigh vnto the village, which they went vnto, and he made as though he would haue gone further.

29 And they conſtrained him, ſaying, Abide with vs, for it draweth toward night, and the day is farre paſſed: And he went in to tarie with them.

30 And it came to paſſe, as he ſate at meate with them, he tooke bread, and bleſſed it, and brake, and gaue to them.

31 And their eyes were opened, & they knew him, and he vaniſhed out of their ſight.

32 And they ſaid one vnto another, Did not our hearts burne within vs, while hee talked with vs by the way, and opened to vs the Scriptures?

33 And they roſe vp the ſame houre, and returned againe to Hieruſalem, and found the eleuen gathered together, and them that were with them,

34 Saying, The Lord is riſen indeede, and hath appeared to Simon.

35 And they tolde what things were done in the way, and how he was knowen of them in the breaking of the bread.

36 And as they thus ſpake, Ieſus himſelfe ſtood in the mids of them, and ſaith vnto them, Peace be vnto you.

37 But they were abaſhed and afraide, and ſuppoſed that they had ſeene a ſpirit.

38 And hee ſayde vnto them, Why are yee troubled, and why doe thoughts ariſe in your heartes?

39 Behold my hands and my feete, that it is euen I my ſelfe: handle me and ſee, for a ſpirit hath not fleſh and bones, as ye ſee me haue.

40 And when he had thus ſpoken, he ſhewed them his hands and his feete.

41 And while they yet beleeued not for ioy, and wondered, he ſaid vnto them, Haue ye here any meate?

42 And they offered him a piece of a broyled fiſh, and of an hony combe.

43 And he tooke it, and did eate before them.

44 And he ſaide vnto them, Theſe are the wordes which I ſpake vnto you, while I was yet with you, that all muſt needes be fulfilled which were written of me in the law of Moſes, and in the Prophets, and in the Pſalmes.

45 Then opened he their || wits, that they might vnderſtand the Scriptures.

46 And ſaid vnto them, Thus it is written, and thus it behoued Chriſt to ſuffer, and to riſe from death the third day:

47 And that repentance and remiſſion of ſins ſhould be preached in his Name among all nations, and muſt begin at Hieruſalem.

48 And ye are witneſſes of theſe things.

49 *And beholde, I will ſend the promiſe of my father vpon you: But tarie ye in the citie of Hieruſalem, vntill yee be endued with power from on high.

50 And he led them out into Bethanie, and lift vp his hands, and bleſſed them.

51 *And it came to paſſe, as he bleſſed them, he departed from them, and was caried vp into heauen.

52 And when they had worſhipped him, they returned to Hieruſalem, with great ioy:

53 And were continually in the Temple, praiſing and lauding God. Amen.

Here endeth the Goſpell by Saint Luke.

The Goſpel on the tueſday in Eaſterweeke. Mar.16.14. ioh. 20.19.

Ioh.15.26. acts.1.4.

Mar.10.19. acts.1.9.

The thirteenth chapter.

1 Though I speake with the tongues
of men and of angels, and have not charity,
I am become sounding brasse, or a tinck-
ling tymball.

2 And though I have the gift of prophesye, and understand all secrets, and all
knowledge, and though I have all fayth,
so that I remove mounteynes, and have
not charity, I am nothinge.

3 And though I bestowe all my goods
to feede the poore, and though I give my
bodye that I be burned, and have not
charity, it profiteth me nothinge.

4 Charity suffereth long, and
is kynde, Charity envyeth not, Charity
doth not frowardly, swelleth not

5 Doth no unseemly thinges, seeketh
not her owne, is not easily provoked,
thinketh no evill.

6 Rejoyeth not in iniquity, but
rejoyeth in the truth.

7 Beareth all thinges, beleeveth all
thinges, hopeth all thinges, endureth all thinges

8 Charity never fayleth, but whether there be prophesyes, they shall fayle,
whether there be tongues, they shall cease,
whether there be knowledge, it shall ba-
nish away.

9 For we knowe in part, and we
prophesye in part.

10 But when that which is perfect
is come, then that which is in part, shall be
come away.

11 When I was a childe, I spake
as a childe, I understoode as a childe, I
thought as a childe: but when I became
a man, I put away childish thinges.

12 For now we see through a
glasse darkly): but then shall we see
face to face. Now I knowe in part:
but then shall I knowe even as also
I am knowen.

13 And now abideth fayth, hope,
charity, these three, but the greatest of
these is charity.

is not insolent
or rash.

with the truth

and Jude. This section of the translation was the work of the second Westminster company, headed by William Barlow, whose account of the conference at Hampton Court Palace was recorded in the *Summe and Substance*. MS. 98 represents the work of the translators in its first stage, and it was probably copied for the purpose of reviewing the translation. Each page is ruled with red lines into four columns. The central two columns fill most of the page, with margins to the left and right edges, and the top and bottom of the page. Only the left margin and centre left column are used, leaving the right half of the page blank, presumably for annotations. The manuscript is copied in a neat secretary hand, with clear chapter divisions and each verse starting on a new line (figure 39). Although the number of each verse is recorded, the space for the translation is sometimes left blank; this suggests that MS. 98 was to be used in conjunction with a copy of the Bishops' Bible, which was presumably to be followed for these missing verses.[23] There are three kinds of marginal annotation in MS. 98: alternative English translations, preceded by 'or'; literal Greek meanings for idiomatic English words, preceded by 'Gr.' and alternative readings of the originals, indicated by 'Some copies read'.[24] The particular significance of MS. 98 lies in the insight it provides into the multiple processes of revision that characterised the translation. Within the text of the Epistles, the KJB makes 6,261 revisions to the Bishops' Bible. MS. 98 proposes 4,131 revisions, of which 844 were rejected and 3,287 accepted into the KJB. In addition, another 1,765 revisions that do not appear in MS. 98 were incorporated into the 1611 text.[25] The multilayered work of consultation, comparison, revision and creation that characterises the translation of the KJB can be seen in the MS. 98 reading for 1 Cor. 13:4: 'Charity suffereth long and is kynde charitye envyeth not charity doth not frowardly swelleth not.' The KJB translation reads: 'Charity suffereth long, and is kind; charity envieth not; charity vaunteth not itself, is not puffed up.' The translators must have pored over the choice of words for these verses. They adopted from MS. 98 the new reading 'kynde', replacing 'curteous' in the Bishops' Bible, but the old-fashioned adverb 'frowardly' (from the Bishops' Bible, and beyond that Tyndale) evidently did not please, being replaced in the KJB with the original and memorable phrase 'vaunteth not itself'. 'Swelleth not' (again inherited from Tyndale) did not find favour either; instead the Geneva and Douai–Rheims rendering 'is not puffed up' becomes adopted into the final version. The translators' sustained and detailed meditation on the range of English idioms from which they could choose here is further attested by the KJB marginal note, 'Or, is not rash', itself abbreviated from MS. 98's original marginal note, 'Or, is not insolent or rash'.[26]

Figure 38 *pp. 104–5* The annotated Bodleian Bishops' Bible of 1602, showing Luke 23–24. Oxford, Bodleian Library, Bib. Eng. 1602 b.1, fols. 429v and 430r.

Figure 39 *left* A manuscript translation of the New Testament epistles, showing I Corinthians 13. Lambeth MS. 98, fol. 57. Lambeth Palace Library.

After the six companies had finished their work, the General Meeting comprising twelve (or, in some accounts, six) translators delegated from the companies met at Stationers' Hall in London.[27] The review process probably took place over nine months in 1610. One of the members of the final review committee was John Bois of the second Cambridge company, which translated the Apocrypha. Bois made notes concerning points of interest arising from the meeting's discussion; a record of these notes survives in a seventeenth-century copy-of-a-copy made by the theologian and antiquarian William Fulman of Corpus Christi College, Oxford. Fulman left his papers to Corpus, and it was among these that Bois's notes were rediscovered in the 1950s.[28] Bois's notes are in Latin, and relate to the General Meeting's discussion of the Epistles and Revelation; they reflect his own scholarly interest in points of linguistic detail, and make frequent reference to the opinions of his former Cambridge tutor and Regius Professor of Greek, Andrew Downes, also a member of this review committee. Bois's notes constitute ample proof of the pair's renowned learning in Greek, and provide a fascinating insight into the process of revision that shaped the final text of the KJB, although they do not account for all of the changes that took place in these final stages of the translation. As well as recording the translators' intricate scholarly debates, Bois's notes also reveal a degree of attention to matters of English idiom and some concern with the style and register of the translation. The English phrasing of Hebrews 13:8 generated some discussion, for example, with Downes suggesting that the literal rendering ('Jesus Christ yesterday and today the same and unto the ages') would be more 'semnoteros' ('majestic') if rearranged as 'yesterday, and to day the same, and for ever'. The ultimate translation, however – 'Jesus Christ the same yesterday, and to day, and for ever' – differs again by placing 'same' earlier in order to enhance the grammatical parallelism (figure 40).[29]

The evidence concerning the methods employed by the translators and the materials they consulted is scattered across a diverse range of sources, some of which – notably the annotated 1602 Bishops' Bible – have as yet been only partially studied. As an enterprise, the translation was grounded in the linguistic and textual skills nurtured in the Elizabethan schools and universities, whilst drawing at the same time on the encyclopaedic knowledge possessed by the translators in areas such as natural history and classical literature. Most importantly, the combination of individual literary brilliance such as that manifested by Lancelot Andrewes, collective endeavour, and diligent oversight succeeded in producing a translation that blended the established tradition of English Bible translation with the new insights gained by a century of scholarly advances.

Figure 40 John Bois's notes of the deliberations of the General Meeting on the epistles of St Paul, London, 1610. Corpus Christi College, Oxford MS. 312, fol. 73v.

Ἔχωμεν χάριν] Gr. schol. Let us give thanks, εὐχαρισθ-
μεν. pro λατρεύωμεν, legunt λατρεύομεν.

Cap. 13. 3. as being yourselves also subject to adversity] A.D. ὡς
κỳ αὐτοὶ ἄνθρωποι ὄντες. Al. ὡς κỳ αὐτοὶ συγκακουχουμενοι.
ad verbum, as being yourselves also in a body.

Ibid. v. 5. with things present.

Ibid. v. 8. yesterday, and to day the same, and forever] AD.
Si hoc modo verba collocentur, σεμνότερος erit ὁ λογος. A.D.

Ibid. v. 15. the fruit [or, sacrifice. A.D.] of our lips etc.

Ibid. v. 18. to behave ourselves as is meet.

Ibid. v. 21. or, disposing of you, or, working with you as
it pleaseth him.

In Epistolam Jacobi.

Cap. 1. 1. ἐν τῇ διασπορᾷ] i.e. διασπαρεῖσι, διασπαρμύναις.
Deut. 28. 25. κỳ ἔση διασπορᾷ [vel, ἐν διασπορᾷ] ἐν πά-
σαις ταῖς βασιλείαις τῆς γῆς.   Greeting, or, wisheth
prosperity.

Ibid. v. 3. τὸ δοκίμιον τῆς πίστεως] i.e. ἡ θλῖψις, ὁ πει-
ρασμος. Quid intersit autem inter δοκίμιον et δοκι-
μήν, quaere apud Bezam in Rom. 5. 1. ut in hunc lo-
cum, ubi docet δοκίμιον esse causam τῆς δοκιμῆς.

Ibid. v. 4. or, failing in nothing.

Ibid. v. 5. or, without twitting, or, hitting in the teeth.

Ibid. v. 8. or, A wavering minded man.

Ibid. v. 11. or, the goodlynesse, sightlynesse of the appearance.

Ibid. v. 15. Suggestio, Delectatio, Consensus, Actus, quatuor
gradus peccati.

Ibid. v. 17. παραλλαγὴ] i.e. ne minima quidem variatio
aut mutatio. παραλλάττειν enim significat, aliquantu-
lum discrepare, et inquit Budaeus, κατά τι μὲν ὁμοι-
ῦσθαι, κατά τι δὲ διαφέρειν.

.ut

Cap. 2. 2. your Synagogue. quia ἡ συναγωγή non solet in Sacris
literis nisi de sacris caetibus et conventibus intelligi.
                                                    Ibid. v. 4.

D. Rainolds sicknes & death.

D. Rainolds being in London about Colledge affaires in Michaelmas t[erm]
tooke such a cold, as deprived him of his voice for one weeke, [though] [the] [ill] helpe
breedd in him a Cough, w[hi]ch left him not till his death. At lo[ng]
worke w[i]th y[e] rest of such Doctors [as] were joyned w[i]th him in trans[lation]
sight begunne sensibly to faile, so much, that he was not able at
our [chappell on] such festivall dayes as our Founder designed him
being altered sundry tymes both in y[e] Chapter and [some] prayers, w[h]en
y[e] Epiphanie was twelmonth [as] being unwilling to passe y[t] dutie ob-
red presently after y[e] Absolution to send y[e] booke to our Viceprin[cipal]
to performe it. During y[e] worke of y[e] Translation (w[hi]ch
most brought to an ende) though [he] was divers tymes greivously
y[e] Gout both in [hands] and feete, and of y[e] Colicke, yet even in [the]
he present ever on y[e] translating dayes w[i]th y[e] rest, yea even [he]
[leng]th he grew so weake that not able to goe by a few stairs into [the]
[n]ow to endure here either standing or sitting he was caryed hither
[the] translators [at] [his] [own] lodging to him to worke [as] [he] was no [otherwise]
[n]or at least [a] weeke togither, [upon] his pallett. Thus continued he [to]
[his] death, w[hen] he was forced to keepe his bedd.

    This disease was Cough of y[e] longues, ingendred, [as] I thinke, b[y]
but finally grew on worke w[i]th more strength) about y[e] 17 of Ma[rch]
[b]y one of our Tenants to follow some timber for reparations of
[th]ine some 8 myles of Oxford, and [he] being appointed for that
[in] readines & to meet him at y[e] place, y[e] day appointed (w[hi]ch [was]
[y]e 17[th] of March) proved very cold, & to my remembrance, tempes[t]
[h]e returned home [the] same night, and y[e] next morning came not down
[as] before, being ill affected w[i]th his former dayes worke, & [his]
[n]e. [After] his tyme he [kept] in his [chamber]

Notes

1. From King James's letter attempting to secure financial provision for the translators via ecclesiastical livings, as circulated by the Bishop of London, Richard Bancroft; cited in Alfred W. Pollard (ed.), *Records of the English Bible: The Documents Relating to the Translation and Publication of the Bible in English, 1525–1611* (London, 1911), p. 331.

2. Transcriptions of the Rules for the translators are given in ibid., pp. 53–5, and David Norton, *A Textual History of the King James Bible* (Cambridge, 2005), pp. 7–8.

3. John Selden, *Table Talk* (London, 1689), p. 3.

4. From the Preface of the Translators (1611); cited in Pollard (ed.), *Records of the English Bible*, p. 353.

5. Jerry H. Bentley, *Humanists and Holy Writ: New Testament Scholarship in the Renaissance* (Princeton, N.J., 1983), pp. 112–93 on Erasmus; here pp. 121–2.

6. Cited by Charlotte Carmichael Stopes, *Shakespeare's Environment* (London, 1914), p. 302.

7. John Rainolds, *A Letter of Dr Reinolds to his Friend, Concerning his Advice for the Studie of Divinitie* (London, 1613), sigs A5v–A6r.

8. Gareth Lloyd Jones (ed.), *Robert Wakefield: On the Three Languages* [1524], (Binghamton, N.Y., 1989).

9. J.R.L. Highfield (ed.), *Registrum Annalium Collegii Mertonensis, 1603–1660* (Woodbridge, 2006), p. 28.

10. J.M. Fletcher (ed.), *Registrum Annalium Collegii Mertonensis, 1567–1603* (Oxford, 1976), pp. 83, 163, 273.

11. Merton College Archives MCR 4277, membranes 8–9. The authors are indebted to Dr Julia Walworth for drawing this inventory to their attention and to Professor Rodney Thomson for sharing with them his as yet unpublished transcript.

12. Corpus Christi College, Oxford, MS. 303, f.123r.

13. Probate inventory: Corpus Christi College, Oxford, MS. 352; library inventory: Bodleian Library, MS. Wood D. 40.

14. Tremellius's 1569 New Testament recorded in John Harmar's will, 1613: The National Archives, PRO, PROB 11/123.

15. The authors are indebted to Nicholas Baker, former Librarian of Hereford Cathedral, for this information.

16. Merton College Archives, *Liber Rationarius Bursarium 1585–1633*, f.102v, MCR 3.1.

17. G.W. Wheeler, 'Readers in the Bodleian, Nov. 8, 1602–Nov. 7, 1603', *Bodleian Quarterly Record* 3 (1920–22), 212–17.

18. Thomas James, *Catalogus librorum bibliothecae publicae quam vir ornatissimus Thomas Bodleius…nuper instituit* (Oxford, 1605).

19. Ward Allen (ed. and trans.), *Translating for King James* (Nashville, Tenn., 1969).

20. William Dunn Macray, *Annals of the Bodleian Library*, 2nd edn (Oxford, 1890), p. 102.

21. Norton, *A Textual History*, p. 22.

22. Ward Allen and Edward C. Jacobs (eds), *The Coming of the King James Gospels: A Collation of the Translators' Work-in-Progress* (Fayetteville, N.C., 1995), p. 5.

23. Norton, *A Textual History*, p. 16.

Figure 41 *pp. 110–111* The former Warden's Lodgings at Merton College, where the second Oxford company met. Photograph © Tim Rawle.

Figure 42 Account of work on the translation in the President's Lodgings, Corpus Christi College, prior to the death of John Rainolds in May 1607. Corpus Christi College, Oxford MS. 303, fol. 123r.

24. Ward Allen (ed.), *Translating the New Testament Epistles, 1604–1611: A Manuscript from King James's Westminster Company* (Ann Arbor, Mich., 1977), p. xliii.

25. Allen (ed.), *Translating the New Testament Epistles*, p. xxi.

26. See p. 75 of Allen's edition of MS. 98 for this verse.

27. As reported to the Synod of Dort in 1618; see Pollard (ed.), *Records of the English Bible*, pp. 336–9. The alternative figure of six is given in the *Life* of the translator John Bois by his contemporary Anthony Walker, printed in 1779. See Allen (ed.), *Translating for King James*, pp. 139–40.

28. Allen (ed.), *Translating for King James*, comprises a photographic facsimile and translation of the notes. Another copy of the Bois notes, this time made from the original, exists in the British Library (MS. Harley 750, fos. 3r–16r); see David Norton, 'John Bois's Notes on the Revision of the King James Bible New Testament: A New Manuscript', *The Library*, 6th series, 18 (1996), 328–46.

29. Allen (ed.), *Translating for King James*, pp. 86–7; discussed by Gerald Hammond, *The Making of the English Bible* (Manchester, 1982), p. 182.

...chus est in superius...

...kinge. opponente Mro Lee in Theolog. disputationibus

...moratio Fundatoris. Et scrutinium celebratum

...ntur

...nieut in.

...uos mutuo acceperant è communj Bibliotheca Collegij

...ondsor. Et Wigorniensij) reducuntur ad

...i ipse Dnus Custos et D. Abbots Decanus Wintoniensij

...ndsor. Doctor Harmar Custos Collegij Wintoniensij

...Hutton sæpius multum operæ posuerunt in

...novj testamenti. ab ipsa Regia Maiestate

...ati.

MIDDLE EARTH

SEA

SEA OF...

M. CARMEL
Dabesheth
Acho
Iokneam
Marilah
Kattah
Naim
Endor
Briann'oth
Shimron
ZEBU...
Enhadah
Abez
Sarid
Chisloth
Wilderness
of Tabor
Chora...
Dor.
S
Tanaath
Ophrath
MANAS
Remeth
Beth pacin
Shunem
Daberoth
Abez
Ganeleth
Itchazinah
Cesaria straton
Kishon
Samuel...
ISSACHAR
Dalmi
Tapha nashna
Magdala
Gita hepheth
Arimathia
Hadadrimmon
Jezre
Valley
Machmethath
Tapluah
Nogdda
Nabeli
ynem
Beth shemesh
Tanaath
Taptuah
EPHRAIM
setrath
Samaria
Sharur
Arumah
Tinnath serath
R MONT
Shechem
Beth shean
Tagruth shebb
Linah
Zenurim
Loppe
Beth haron
Samuel
Sepulchre Azaroth
Lebonah
Shilah EPHRAI
Dothan
Zarthan
hosthita
Gashom
Imperio
Nebth
CARPENTERS
VALEI
Almon
Bethel
Bethshem
Kirsaim
Beth
Dei
DAN
Tarah
wildernes of Gibeon
Rekem
Misrot
Geba
Zebouth
Abelonim
Rakkon Shuren
Pispothech
Mahdd
Lesstah
Irpel
HIU
Aznaveth SALISMAH
Nazeth
Beth bazar
Piration
Ashdad
Cipris
Ichud
Askba
Adonai
Omri
Gibeon
Glach
Enon
Bet
Noeah
Gazarij
Elthekzk
Yadeth
Tar lath
Nebaler
Kertes
Valley of
Ekron
Jumes
Chepirah
Anoab
Ephraim
Athor
Askton
Timah
Altarkon
Cedon
Haif
Beth
Benck
Beth baccoris
BENIAMIN
Gilgal
JORDAN
PLAINA
Mixandrium
Beth
sheralzt
Unamah
Ashma
Noebh
Betzer
Kethyh
Samphinum
Vakei of
Badenten
Athrna
PLAINS of TABOR
JERUSALEM
M. OLIVIT
Debir
Beth phaet
Bethhaqla
Askalon
Ziphron
Tent of Dan
SHUAL
Iphah
LAPH
Bethania
Bahurim
Caleba
Hipshon
Abrahams
Rachels sepulchre
Bethsorem
garden
Gath
Helon
Yarmuth
Anab
Midlin
Toih
Dilean
Eleutheropolis
al-Ish
Aptha
Bethelem
Absolons
Nibshan
Ether
Gederah
Ascuth
Zelhsh
Iache
Magdala
Iokdam
Hadasha
Sodom
Shaarim
Huntah
Lachish
tent
Arab Libna
Wilder
Pizgah
Ziglag
Herodium
Sheba
Chezil
Dannah
Tapush
Elaken
Wildernes
of Hareth
Madach
Beth dag
Pekoth
Kormah
Adithaim
Hebron
Gilgh
of Ziph
Haluk
Migdal
Zenan
Sechadah
Gomorrah
Tochen
Ziph
Naamah
Istia
Tekoa
Wildernes of Tekoa
DEAD SEA
Peboth
Debir
Keriath
Mizphe
Iarvel
Cittie of salt
Ain
Achzib
Ashnah
Ismah
Beth arnoth
Lachish
Jarvel
Kain
Baaleth
IUDAH
Dumah Valei of
Asham
Wilderness of Iervel
Kain
Jagur
Gileah of
Majon
Engedin
Bethpallet
Majon
Maaleth Akra
Karysah
Zephathah
Carmel Rock of divisi on
Beth zur
Eder
Cliffs of Triz
Zeboin
MO
Hadiah
Ziph
Kinah
Kabzeel
The cave where in David cutt Saules lepp
NOW CALLED
THE
Kerioth
bim
Kerioth
Adallah
Kedsh
Admah
THE LAKE OF SODOM
Tamar
KADESH
Aerons sepulchre
M. HOR
MO
DIMON FLU.
Kadesh Barnea
WILDERNES OF EDOM
THE
Kadesh
Parez
Meribah
COUNTRIE OF TEMAN
Libnah
Risah
EDO
BIA

5

The 1611
King James Bible
and its
Cultural Politics

Hannibal Hamlin,
Judith Maltby
and Helen Moore

'B Y HIS MAJESTIES SPECIALL COMMANDEMENT': thus the 1611 first edition declared itself on its title page, which was engraved by the Antwerp artist Cornelius Boel and depicted Apostles and patriarchs. In the centre at the top of the page are Peter and James, flanked by Matthew and Mark; the title is represented as though engraved in stone, and features Moses and Aaron on either side. The Apostles Luke and John are seated at the bottom. Two well-known iconographical depictions of Christ, as the Lamb of God and the pelican who feeds her young with her own blood, are situated between the two pairs of Apostles at top and bottom (figure 44). The 1611 King James Bible was a work simultaneously of innovation ('Newly Translated out of the Originall tongues') and continuity ('with the former Translations diligently compared and revised'), possessing impeccable credentials that were attested not only by the reference to the King's commission, but also the description 'Appointed to be read in Churches'. Despite its later, popular designation as the 'Authorized Version', the KJB was never officially described as such (unlike the late sixteenth-century editions of the Bishops' Bible); the label 'authorized' started to be used for the KJB from 1620. This suggests that initially the Bishops' Bible and the KJB coexisted in churches, with the former being gradually replaced by the new translation.[1] Despite its reference to royalty and unlike previously 'appointed' or 'authorized' versions, the KJB title page invokes the monarch verbally rather than visually: the title pages of the Coverdale (1535), Great (1539) and Bishops' (1568) Bibles had all given the reigning monarch visual pride of place. The 1611 New Testament has its own title page, a woodcut depicting the twelve tribes of Israel and the Apostles that was borrowed from the Bishops' Bible (figure 45). From the second edition onwards, this woodcut was used for the general title page as well.[2]

The preliminary matter to the KJB includes a dedication to King James, the translators' preface, calendars and almanacs, and a list of the books of the Bible. Most copies also include a set of 'Genealogies of Holy Scripture' and a map of Canaan by the historian and cartographer John Speed (figures 46 and 47). Speed had been granted a privilege to include his genealogies in the Bible for ten years; ironically, they were probably based upon those he had compiled together with Hugh Broughton (published as *Genealogies Recorded in the Sacred Scriptures*,

Figure 44 The general title page of the 1611 King James Bible, engraved by Cornelius Boel. Oxford, Bodleian Library, Bib. Eng. 1611 b.1.

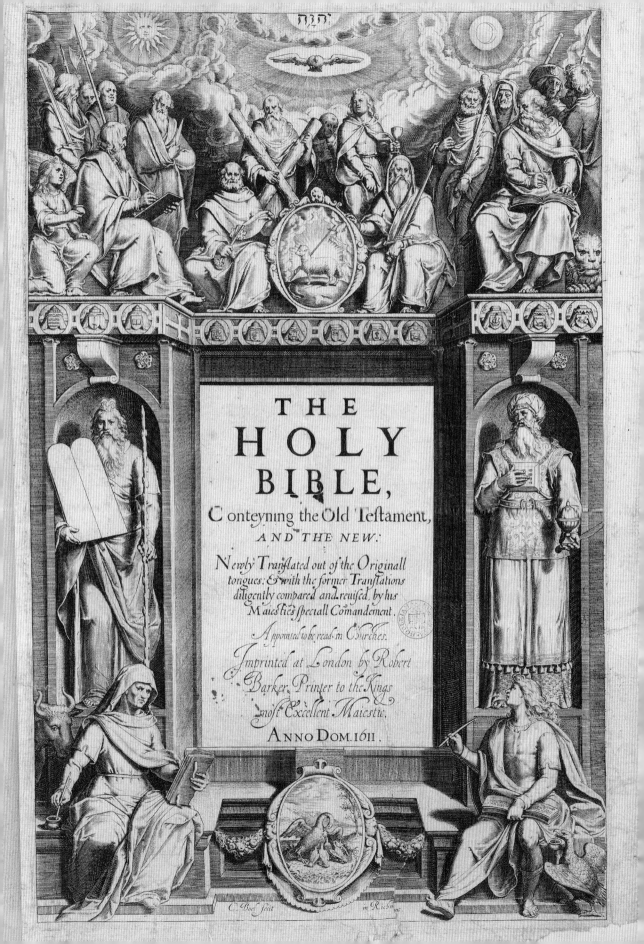

יהוה

THE HOLY BIBLE,

Conteyning the Old Testament,

AND THE NEW:

Newly Translated out of the Originall
tongues: & with the former Translations
diligently compared and reuised, by his
Maiesties speciall Comandement.

Appointed to be read in Churches.

Imprinted at London by Robert
Barker, Printer to the Kings
most Excellent Maiestie.

ANNO DOM. 1611.

C. Boel fecit in Richm.

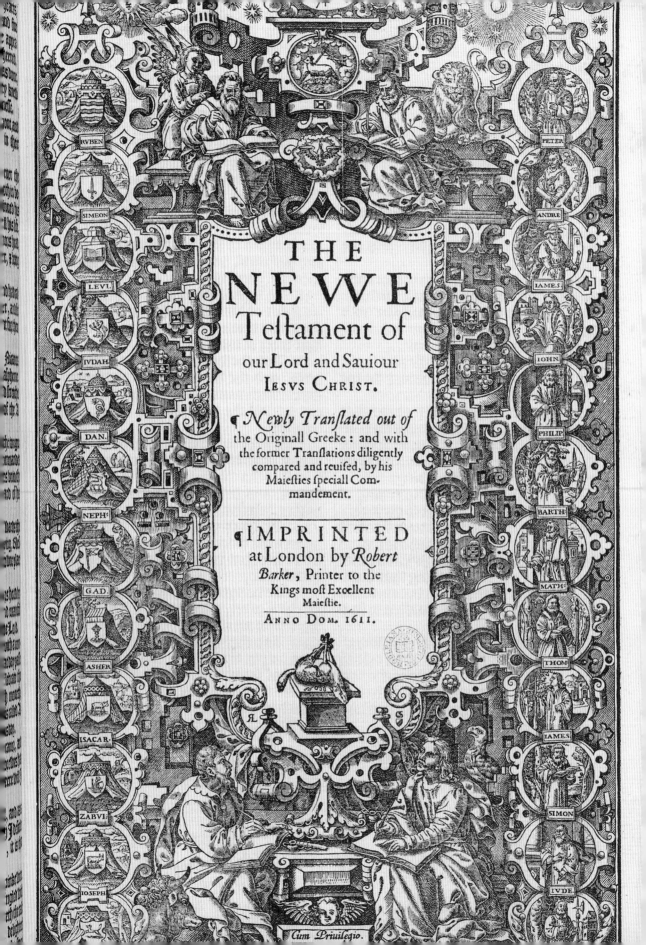

THE NEWE
Testament of
our Lord and Sauiour
Iesvs Christ.

¶ Newly Translated out of
the Originall Greeke : and with
the former Translations diligently
compared and reuised, by his
Maiesties speciall Com-
mandement.

¶ IMPRINTED
at London by *Robert*
Barker, Printer to the
Kings most Excellent
Maiestie.
Anno Dom. 1611.

1592), the arch-critic of the KJB who had not been invited to participate in the translation.[3] The large folio format, the layout of the text in double columns and the use of black letter type (with inserted words in small roman type) all hark back to the authorized Bibles of the sixteenth century, and present a stark contrast to the readable roman type and copious annotations of the Geneva and Douai–Rheims versions. Visually, text prevails: although ornaments and decorated capitals are used (some of the latter featuring mythological figures such as Pan and Daphne), there are no further illustrations beyond the preliminary matter (figures 48 and 49). The combined effect of size, paper quality and type is one of 'ecclesiastical splendour' that is also 'plain and formal'.[4] Very soon after its first printing the KJB also began to appear in smaller editions that were aimed at the market for private reading. The popular Geneva Bible, pre-eminent in this area, exerted a powerful influence on these editions: the octavo 1612 edition of the KJB was printed in roman type like the Geneva, and the 1613 black letter quarto included 'Two right profitable and fruitfull Concordances' by R.F.H. that had appeared frequently with quarto Geneva Bibles.

The early history of the printing of the KJB is full of quirks, oddities and some high drama. The KJB was printed by Robert Barker, the King's printer, who incurred considerable costs in purchasing the rights and printing the text. The world of Bible printing was competitive and cut-throat, and documentary evidence suggests that Barker was blighted by managerial, financial and legal problems that forced him to sell stock at reduced prices and to borrow heavily from other printers. Eventually Barker was imprisoned for debt in 1635; he died still in prison in 1645.[5]

Printing errors were a fact of life in the early modern printing house, but in the context of Bible printing they can become notorious. The 'She' Bible of 1613 (partly printed in 1611) was so called because Ruth 3:15 reads 'She went into the city' rather than the mistaken 'He...' of the first edition (it is sometimes therefore called the 'He Bible'). Worst of all was the 'Wicked' Bible of 1631, in which the seventh commandment in Exodus 20:14 reads 'Thou shalt commit adultery': when the mistake was discovered, all 1,000 copies were called in to be destroyed (surviving examples are therefore extremely rare), and the printers were fined £300[6] (figure 51).

Reactions to the KJB

The eminent historian Thomas Babington, Lord Macaulay described the English Bible (in 1828 undoubtedly the KJB) as 'a book which if everything else in our language should perish, would alone suffice to show the whole extent of its beauty and power'.[7] Such hyperbolic

Figure 45 *p. 120* The New Testament title page of the 1611 King James Bible. Oxford, Bodleian Library, Bib. Eng. 1611 b.1.

Figure 46 *p. 121* Engraving of Adam and Eve from the genealogies included in the preliminary matter of the 1611 King James Bible. Oxford, Bodleian Library, Bib. Eng. 1611 b.1.

accolades are routine. For the eighteenth-century English writer and actor Samuel Jackson Pratt, the KJB was simply 'the noblest composition in the universe', just as a century and a half later it was for the American literary scholar John Livingstone Lowes 'the noblest monument of English prose'.[8] Even the crusty journalist and author of *The American Language*, H.L. Mencken, professed that the KJB was 'unquestionably the most beautiful book in the world'.[9] Charles Allen Dinsmore thought it 'finer and nobler literature than the Scriptures in their original tongues'.[10] Yet when the KJB first appeared in 1611, it seems barely to have been noticed, let alone recognised as a masterpiece of style. In one of the few early responses to the new English Bible, the Hebraist Broughton stated that the 'ill done' translation should be burned.[11] Notable among modern dissenters from the collective praise is David Daniell, who regrets the regressive choice of the Bishops' Bible over the Geneva translation, and in particular the consequent diminution of the voice of Tyndale's translation.[12] Broughton's criticism may have been partly sour grapes, since he was notably excluded from the translation teams, but the polymath John Selden had no such axe to grind. In his *Table Talk* (published in 1689 but recorded during the two decades before his death in 1654), Selden expressed his sense of the oddity of the KJB's style:

> There is no book so translated as the Bible. For the purpose, if I translate a *French* book into *English*, I turn it into *English* phrase and not into *French* English. [*Il fait froid*] I say 'tis cold, not it makes cold; but the Bible is rather translated into *English* Words than into *English* phrase. The *Hebraisms* are kept, and the Phrase of that Language is kept: As for Example, [He uncovered her Shame] which is well enough, so long as Scholars have to do with it; but when it comes among the Common People, Lord what Gear do they make of it![13]

Faced with so strange a story in the KJB's reception history, the modern reader interested in assessing its style or literary value may well be confused. Is it a glorious masterpiece of English prose or an awkward forcing of Hebraic square pegs into English round holes?

The truth seems to be both. The fifty-odd translators of the KJB were immensely learned, but, with the possible exception of Lancelot Andrewes, not especially rich in literary gifts, at least based on their sermons and other writings. But then they were not concerned with producing a 'literary' work, but rather an English Bible that rendered the Hebrew and Greek as accurately and literally as possible, based on the best knowledge then available. (This is one reason why the myth of Shakespeare being called in as a consultant is absurd; as Ben Jonson remarked, he had 'small Latin and less Greek', and presumably

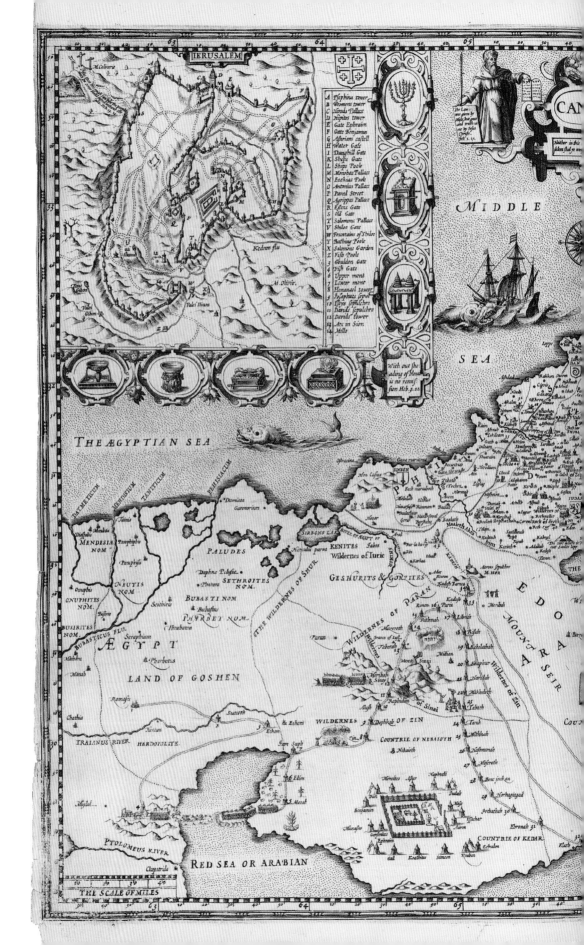

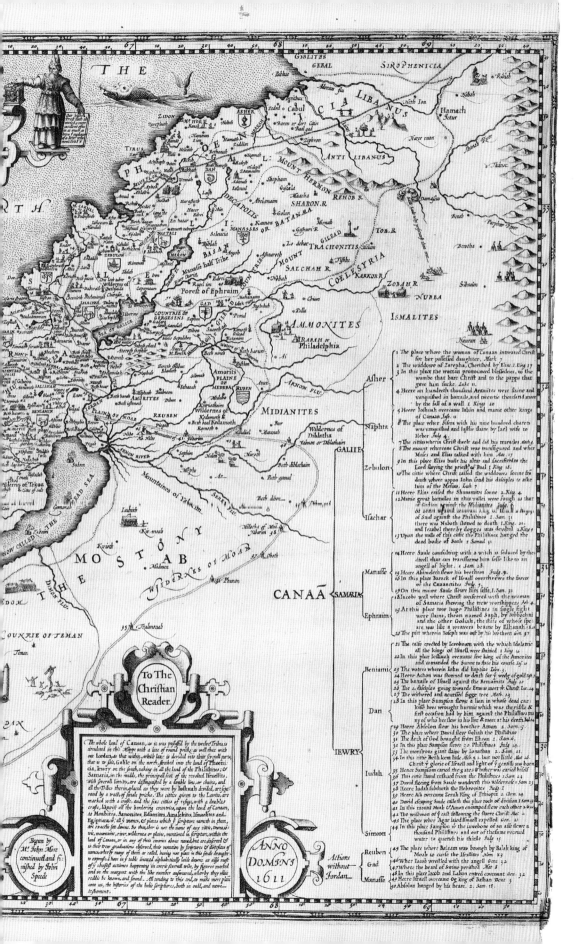

THE
FIRST BOOKE
OF MOSES,
called GENESIS.

CHAP. I.

1 The creation of Heauen and Earth, 3 of the light, 6 of the firmament, 9 of the earth separated from the waters, 11 and made fruitfull, 14 of the Sunne, Moone, and Starres, 20 of fish and fowle, 24 of beasts and cattell, 26 of Man in the Image of God. 29 Also the appointment of food.

IN* the beginning God created the Heauen, and the Earth.

2 And the earth was without forme, and voyd, and darkenesse was vpon the face of the deepe: and the Spirit of God mooued vpon the face of the waters.

3 And God said,* Let there be light: and there was light.

4 And God saw the light, that it was good: and God diuded † the light from the darkenesse.

5 And God called the light, Day, and the darknesse he called Night: † and the euening and the morning were the first day.

6 ¶ And God said, * Let there be a † firmament in the midst of the waters: and let it diuide the waters from the waters.

7 And God made the firmament; and diuided the waters, which were vnder the firmament, from the waters, which were aboue the firmament: and it was so.

8 And God called the * firmament, Heauen: and the euening and the morning were the second day.

9 ¶ And God said,* Let the waters vnder the heauen be gathered together vnto one place, and let the dry land appeare: and it was so.

10 And God called the drie land, Earth, and the gathering together of the waters called hee, Seas: and God saw that it was good.

11 And God said, Let the Earth bring foorth † grasse, the herbe yeelding seed, and the fruit tree, yeelding fruit after his kinde, whose seed is in it selfe, vpon the earth: and it was so.

12 And the earth brought foorth grasse, and herbe yeelding seed after his kinde, and the tree yeelding fruit, whose seed was in it selfe, after his kinde : and God saw that it was good.

13 And the euening and the morning were the third day.

14 ¶ And God said, Let there bee * lights in the firmament of the heauen, to diuide † the day from the night: and let them be for signes and for seasons, and for dayes and yeeres.

15 And let them be for lights in the firmament of the heauen, to giue light vpon the earth: and it was so.

16 And God made two great lights: the greater light † to rule the day, and the lesser light to rule the night: he made the starres also.

17 And God set them in the firmament of the heauen, to giue light vpon the earth:

18 And to * rule ouer the day, and

A   ouer

no Aramaic or Syriac at all.) The translators worked from principles entirely opposite to those of many modern Bible translators, who aim for what Eugene Nida termed 'functional' or 'dynamic equivalence', what Selden called translating by phrase rather than word.[14] The Nida-inspired *Good News Bible* thus converted the words, idioms and syntax of the Hebrew and Greek texts into English equivalents that the translators felt captured the sense of the originals, but that even children and the uneducated could easily understand. The KJB translators, on the other hand, aimed at (in Nida's terms) 'formal equivalence', or, as Selden recognised, a word-for-word rendition, even if this resulted in non-idiomatic 'Hebrew' English. This approach was shared by all the early English Bible translators from William Tyndale to 1611. Even the Catholic Rheims translators (principally Gregory Martin) made the case for this approach in terms the KJB translators would have approved:

> Because this speach [John 2:3–4] is subject to divers senses, we keepe the wordes of our text, lest by turning it into any English phrase, we might straiten the holy Ghosts intention to some certaine sense either not intended, or not onely intended, and so take away the choise and indifferencie from the reader, whereof (in holy Scripture specially) al Translatours must beware.[15]

Miles Smith, in 'The Translators to the Reader', the preface to the 1611 KJB, explained that 'we desire that the Scripture may speake like it selfe, as in the language of *Canaan*, that it may bee understood even of the very vulgar'.[16] It is striking that the KJB translators, like the *Good News* team, wanted the Bible to be understood by the 'very vulgar' or the common people; for Smith and his colleagues, however, this meant not mediating between the Hebrew original and the English reader, through paraphrase or 'dynamic equivalence', but presenting the reader with an English text that was as formally and literally identical to the Hebrew as possible.

Style and language

Many of the distinctive features of the KJB style are attributable to the translators' 'formal' approach, though many modern readers are unaware how much of the 'KJB style' – its characteristic diction, syntax, tone, rhythms – is taken from its predecessors, especially Tyndale, Miles Coverdale and the Geneva Bible. For example, one of the most famous features of biblical Hebrew is its parataxis. The Hebrew conjunction *waw* is coordinating, not subordinating, leaving to the reader all decisions about the relationship between consecutive clauses. Recognising this, the KJB translators used the coordinating conjunction 'and' with

Figure 47 *pp. 124–5* Map of Canaan by John Speed, included in the preliminary matter of the 1611 King James Bible. Oxford, Bodleian Library, Bib. Eng. 1611 b.1.

Figure 48 The opening of the book of Genesis in the 1611 King James Bible. Oxford, Bodleian Library, Bib. Eng. 1611 b.1.

far greater frequency than is normal in English, which tends towards the syntactic ('systematic arrangement') rather than paratactic ('placing side by side'). The contrast between the KJB and *The Good News Bible* is clear from the opening verses of Genesis:

> In the beginning, when God created the universe, the earth was formless and desolate. The raging ocean that covered everything was engulfed in total darkness, and the Spirit of God was moving over the water. Then God commanded, Let there be light and light appeared. God was pleased with what he saw. Then he separated the light from the darkness, and he named the light Day and the darkness Night. Evening passed and morning came – that was the first day. (*Good News*)

> In the beginning God created the heaven and the earth. And the earth was without form, and void; and darkness was upon the face of the deep. And the Spirit of God moved upon the face of the waters. And God said, Let there be light: and there was light. And God saw the light, that it was good: and God divided the light from the darkness. And God called the light Day, and the darkness he called Night. And the evening and the morning were the first day. (KJB)

The *Good News* translators no doubt felt that they were clarifying the syntax with coordinating conjunctions like 'then' and 'when', but they were actually making small but significant interpretative decisions that the KJB, like the original, left up to the reader. The KJB translators also left it to the reader to interpret the metaphors and ambiguities of the original, where modern translators again feel the need to interpret. In Thessalonians 4:4, for instance, Paul may be urging temperance ('each of you should learn to control his own body', New International Version) or he may be advising about marriage ('each one of you know how to take a wife for himself in holiness and honor', Revised Standard Version). Rather than offer an interpretation, choosing between these options, the KJB translators opt for ambiguity: 'that every one of you should know how to possess his vessel in sanctification and honour'. Elsewhere, 'vessel' is a metaphor for a person or the body (Psalm 31:12; Acts 9:15; 2 Timothy 2:21), but the woman is the 'weaker vessel' (1 Peter 3:7).

Even apart from the question of accuracy, however, the repeated and sometimes almost relentless 'ands' of the KJB are one feature of its distinctive style, its oddly (or grandly) Hebraic English. Another is the preference for 'noun + of + noun' constructions rather than the possessive apostrophe 's': 'the mountain of the house of the Lord', for instance, rather than the Lord's house's mountain (Micah 4:1), or the 'flower of the field' (Psalm 103:15) or the 'generations of Esau' (Genesis 36:1). Other Hebraisms include the use of 'even' to introduce

Figure 49 The opening of the Gospel of St Luke in the 1611 King James Bible. Oxford, Bodleian Library, Bib. Eng. 1611 b.1.

*Luk.24.
36.iohn 20.
19.
|| Or, toge-
ther.

*Mat.28.
19.

*Ioh.12.48

*Act.16.18

14. ¶ *Afterward he appeared vnto the eleuen, as they sate ||at meat, and vpbraided them with their vnbeliefe, and hardnesse of heart, because they beleeued not them, which had seene him after he was risen.

15. *And he said vnto them, Goe yee into all the world, and preach the Gospel to euery creature.

16. He that beleeueth and is baptized, shalbe saued, *but he that beleeueth not, shall be damned.

17. And these signes shal follow them that beleeue, *In my Name shall they cast out deuils, *they shall speake with new tongues,

18. *They shall take vp serpents, and if they drinke any deadly thing, it shall not hurt them, *they shall lay hands on the sicke, and they shall recouer.

19. ¶ So then after the Lord had spoken vnto them, he was receiued vp into heauen, *and sate on the right hand of God.

20. And they went foorth, and preached euery where, the Lord working with them, *and confirming the worde with signes following. Amen.

*Acts 2.4.

*Act.28.5.

*Act.28.8.

*Luk.24.
51.

*Heb.2.4.

¶The Gospel according to S.Luke.

CHAP. I.

1 The Preface of Luke to his whole Gospel. 5 The conception of Iohn the Baptist, 26 and of Christ. 39 The prophecie of Elizabeth, and of Mary, concerning Christ. 57 The natiuitie & circumcision of Iohn. 67 The prophesie of Zachary both of Christ, 76 and of Iohn.

Orasmuch as many haue taken in hande to set foorth in order a declaration of those things which are most surely beleeued among vs,

2. Euen as they deliuered them vnto vs, which from the beginning were eye-witnesses, & ministers of the word:

3. It seemed good to me also, hauing had perfect vnderstanding of things from the very first, to write vnto thee in order, most excellent Theophilus,

4. That thou mightest know the certainetie of those things wherein thou hast bene instructed.

5. ¶ There was in the dayes of Herode the king of Iudea, a certaine Priest, named Zacharias, of the course of Abia, and his wife was of the daughters of Aaron, and her name was Elizabeth.

6. And they were both righteous before God, walking in all the Commandements and ordinances of the Lord, blamelesse.

7. And they had no childe, because that Elizabeth was barren, and they both were now well strikē in yeeres.

8. And it came to passe, that while he executed the Priests office before God in the order of his course,

9. According to the custome of the Priests office, his lot was to burne incense when he went into the Temple of the Lord.

10. *And the whole multitude of the people were praying without, at the time of incense.

11. And there appeared vnto him an Angel of the Lord, standing on the right side of the Altar of incense.

12. And when Zacharias sawe him, hee was troubled, and feare fell vpon him.

13. But the Angel said vnto him, Feare not, Zacharias, for thy prayer is heard, and thy wife Elizabeth shall beare thee a sonne, and thou shalt call his name Iohn.

14. And thou shalt haue ioy and gladnesse, and many shall reioyce at his birth:

15. For he shall be great in the sight of the Lord, and shal drinke neither wine, nor strong drinke, and he shall bee filled with the holy Ghost, euen from his mothers wombe.

16. *And many of the children of Israel shall hee turne to the Lord their God.

*Exo.30.7.
leuit.16.17

*Malac.4.6

17 And

a parallel clause that extends the meaning of the preceding one ('For the day is near, even the day of the Lord is near, a cloudy day', Ezekiel 30:3); the use of 'thereof' as a possessive ('The leaves thereof were fair, and the fruit thereof much', Daniel 4:12); emphatic pronouns ('Know ye that the Lord, he is God', Psalm 100:3), sometimes with 'even' ('and she, even she herself said, "He is my brother"', Genesis 20:5); inverted object–subject–pronoun syntax ('as for his judgments, they have not known them', Psalm 147:20); and polyptoton, or the repetition of a word in different forms ('This now is bone of my bones and flesh of my flesh', Genesis 2:23, or 'with desire I have desired to eat', Luke 22:15).[17]

Actually, Hebrew writers generally loved repetition and exploited it far more than is normal in English, repeating not just words and phrases, as in the ritual formalism of the Creation story, but entire episodes or narrative patterns, as with the wells at which both Isaac and Jacob meet their wives (Genesis 24 and 29); the pattern is repeated even in the New Testament when Jesus meets the woman of Samaria (John 4). Modern readers may be inclined to think that these features of the KJB style are simply archaisms, which to some extent they are. But the features listed above are primarily idioms borrowed directly from Hebrew and, for the New Testament, a Hebraicized Greek (the notes of John Bois show the tendency of at least one influential KJB translator to work out the New Testament Greek by analogy with Old Testament Hebrew).[18] The New Testament writers themselves knew their scriptures (what for Christians eventually became the Old Testament) in the Greek of the Septuagint, which, since it was a translation of the Hebrew, naturally picked up characteristics of the original language.[19] Greek also shares some features with Hebrew, like the preference for parataxis.

What else, beyond its Hebraic features, characterizes the KJB style so admired in recent centuries? Despite the many shouts of praise, few of even the most ardent admirers of the KJB have explained why its style is so greatly to be admired. Even the political, literary and cultural luminaries who in 1979 protested to the Church of England's General Synod against the introduction of the New English Bible – as the *Guardian* described them, 'half the people one has ever heard of' – offered few specifics.[20] The most passionate acclaim for the literary grandeur of the KJB is often expressed in response to the publication of a major new Bible translation. The KJB translators themselves were aware of this phenomenon, as Smith remarks to the reader: 'was there never any thing projected, that savoured any way of newnesse or renewing, but the same endured many a storme of gaine-saying, or opposition?'[21] There are often legitimate reasons for favouring one translation over another, yet some of the heightened emotion must be attributed simply to the love of tradition, of the familiar, and the resistance to change.

Figure 50 Lancelot Andrewes, Dean of Westminster and Head of the first Westminster company. Unknown artist. Bodleian Library, LP 84.

Those who adulate the KJB usually have in mind its greatest moments, like Isaiah's 'Arise, shine, for thy light is come' (Isaiah 60:1) or Paul's 'For now we see through a glass, darkly' (1 Corinthians 13:12). They tend not to focus on the peculiar or impenetrable passages: 'Wherefore thus saith the Lord God, "Behold, I am against your pillows, wherewith ye there hunt the souls to make them fly, and I will tear them from your arms, and will let the souls go, even the souls that ye hunt to make them fly"' (Ezekiel 13:20); 'A man shall not take his father's wife, nor discover his father's skirt' (Deuteronomy 22:30). Those who celebrate the lofty nobility of the KJB are also not likely thinking of the many passages whose power lies in visceral detail or colloquial language: 'But Rabshakeh said, Hath my master … not sent me to the men that sit upon the wall, that they may eat their own dung, and drink their own piss with you?' (Isaiah 36:12); 'Meats for the belly, and the belly for meats: but God shall destroy both it and them' (1 Corinthians 6:13). Coverdale and Tyndale were ultimately responsible for many of the Anglo-Saxon colloquialisms in the KJB, and the language of these two passages was theirs, borrowed for the KJB. In other passages, however, the KJB translators favoured a more Latinate style: 'for all have sinned, and come short of the glory of God, being justified freely by his grace through the redemption that is in Jesus Christ: whom God hath set forth to be propitiation through faith in his blood, to declare his righteousness for the remission of sins that are past, through the forbearance of God' (Romans 3:23–25). 'Propitiation' and 'remission' are taken from the Rheims New Testament (1582), which adhered to the Latin Vulgate; Tyndale's renderings were, respectively, 'seat of mercy' and 'forgiveth' ('in that he forgiveth the sins that are passed'). Both these words had become familiar in theological language, however: 'remission of sin' was used often in the Book of Common Prayer, and 'propitiation' was regularly used in Thomas Norton's translation of John Calvin's *Institutes of the Christian Religion* and in John Foxe's *Actes and Monuments*. The KJB translators no doubt felt such diction was appropriate to Paul's theological subject matter. There is clearly not a single 'KJB style', but a variety of them. This is perhaps one of the strengths of the translation, but it is one which its advocates tend to ignore.

Variety is one of the essential features of good prose rhythm, however, as George Saintsbury recognized. In one of the few detailed analyses of the KJB style, Saintsbury suggested that the effectiveness of the KJB's rhythms lies in its simultaneously tending towards and yet ultimately resisting the regularity of metre.[22] The rhythms of biblical prose have a nearly metrical consistency, but enough variety is maintained to avoid monotony:

Figure 51 The 'Wicked Bible' of 1631, in which the seventh commandment was rendered as 'Thou shalt commit adultery' (Exodus 20:14). Oxford, Bodleian Library, Bib. Eng. 1631 f.1.

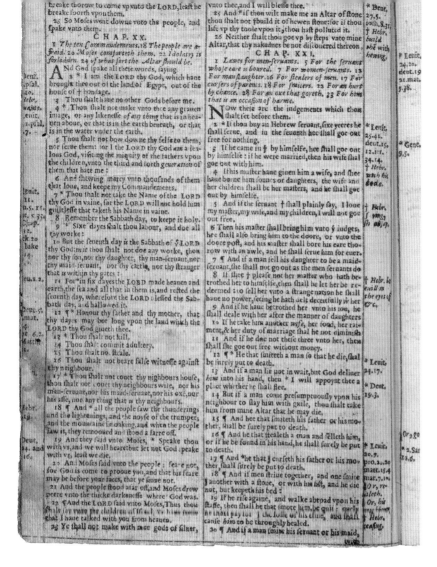

And there were in that same country shepherds abiding in the field, keeping watch over their flock by night. And lo, the angel of the Lord came upon them, and the glory of the Lord shone round about them, and they were sore afraid. (Luke 2:8–9)

The rhythm of these lines from the Nativity story is not metrical, but it is persistently rising, with a swing of often two (like a metrical anapest), sometimes one or three, unstressed syllables towards a stressed one ('and there *were*', '-ing in the *field*', 'keeping *watch*', 'of the *Lord*'). Elsewhere there are different rhythmic effects, but with a similar loose patterning. John's vision in Revelation 21:1 – 'And I saw a new heaven and a new earth: for the first heaven and the first earth were passed away, and there was no more sea' – works by a series of double stresses or spondees ('*new heav'n*', '*first earth*') that culminate in the triple stress of '*no more sea*'. Whether such effects were intended by the translators is impossible to know, but even if these scholars were not all great stylists, the writers of the original Hebrew and Greek texts (the Genesis authors, the Psalmists, Isaiah, John or Paul) often were. The translators were certainly attentive to the obvious parallelistic structures of Hebrew poetry, as in Psalms and Proverbs, or the repetitive rhetoric of Jesus' Sermon on the Mount (Matthew 5–7). Modern readers are generally astonished that great literature, as the KJB is supposed to be, can have been produced by a committee, let alone six committees. But why not? Perhaps in this case the literary skills of the whole group proved greater than the sum of its parts, especially given that they were also building on the shoulders of Tyndale, Coverdale and the Geneva Bible translators. As churchmen, moreover, the translators certainly understood, perhaps instinctively, the requirements of a language that was to be read aloud. Such language makes the KJB not only easy to read aloud, but also, as the Prayer Book collect puts it, to 'mark, learn, and inwardly digest'.[23] This is one reason why this translation has lodged in the ears and hearts of so many who have read it, and why, whatever its defects, so many are unwilling to let it go.

'Openly read': the Bible in church

The Bible in early modern England was not only read privately, but also heard. Domestic devotional practices of the period included reading the Bible out loud, an exercise which often brought together all the social elements of the household from the head of the house to the servants. The way most English people encountered the Bible, however, was when it was read aloud in public worship in parish churches: parish worship was, in the words of one historian, a 'soundscape'.[24] The Epistle Dedicatory to the KJB maintained that the aim of the translators was that 'God's holy Truth [will] be yet more and more known unto the people' professing the 'great hope that the Church of England shall reap good fruit thereby'. This goal was to be accomplished in no small part by the new translation's role in public worship.

The translators were not saying something new, but building on centuries of reading the Bible aloud in divine service as well as over half a century of doing so in the vernacular. In fact, the very process of translation for the KJB involved members of the various committees hearing verses read aloud.[25] The Preface to the 1559 Book of Common Prayer stated that the early Fathers of the church maintained 'that the people by the daily hearing of Holy Scripture read in the Church should continually profit more and more in the knowledge of God'. In contradiction to St Paul's injunction to have worship conducted in 'such a language spoken to the people … as they might understand and have profit by hearing the same', the Preface to the Book of Common

Prayer lamented that for many centuries after Latin had ceased to be the vernacular, the Bible was still read in that tongue 'so that they have heard with their ears only … and not been edified thereby'. [26] Richard Hooker, one of the most tenacious defenders of the Elizabethan Settlement, remarked: 'touching … the use of Scripture … openly read … [it brings about] inestimable good which the Church of God by that very mean hath reaped'.[27] Hooker went further than edification as a reason for reading the Scriptures aloud in public worship:

> I see not how we should possibly wish a proof more palpable, than this manifest received and everywhere continued custom of reading them publicly as the Scriptures. The reading therefore of the word of God, as the use hath ever been, in open audience, is the plainest evidence we have of the Church's Assent and Acknowledgement that it is his word.[28]

The practice of *reading* the Bible aloud and of *hearing* it read was the clearest evidence Hooker could provide for the Church's 'assent and acknowledgement' that it was God's word: the act had doctrinal as well as devotional significance.

Since the Reformation, the Bible's yokefellow in its role as a text for the public worship of God had been the Book of Common Prayer. Its Preface maintained that unlike the liturgical observances of the medieval church, which needed a small library to perform, 'curates shall need none other books for their public service but this book and the Bible'. Further, the Prayer Book directed, through tables of readings for the year, which parts of the Bible should be read in public services. The daily lectionary largely directed reading through a book of the Old and New Testaments in order, resulting in a large proportion of the Bible being read aloud in the course of a year. Lessons appointed for Communion on Sundays and holy days reflected the themes of the church year shaped around the events in the life of Christ or a saint's day.[29]

A striking thing about worship in conformity to the Book of Common Prayer was the sheer amount of the Bible in English to which congregations were exposed. On Sunday, inhabitants of a 'conforming' parish (that is, one in which worship was conducted according to the Prayer Book) would hear read an Old and New Testament passage plus psalms in Morning Prayer, and then the epistle and gospel passages for the service of Ante-Communion or the full service, if Communion was taking place. Evening Prayer had the same structure as Morning Prayer. In other words, congregations were exposed to at least six passages of scripture per Sunday as well as a number of psalms. Psalm singing, often in a metrical translation, grew in popularity in parish churches after the Reformation. The Prayer Book itself reproduced the translation of the Henrician Great Bible for the epistle and gospel readings for the Communion service on Sundays and major holy days, and for the liturgical Psalter. During Elizabeth's reign, the translation for all the other public readings of the Bible came from either the official Bishops' Bible (1568) or the widely used, but unauthorized, Geneva Bible. It was this role the 1611 Bible was expected to fill. The KJB did not replace the Great Bible for the Communion readings until the revisions of the 1662 Book of Common Prayer.[30]

The structures provided by the Prayer Book therefore exposed the laity – whether they could read or not and whether they could afford their own Bible or not – to considerable portions of the scriptures Sunday by Sunday. This Reformation emphasis on hearing clearly what was said or sung in church necessitated some reorganization of internal church architecture and, from Elizabeth's reign onwards, the provision of new pulpits, reading desks and lecterns often with sounding boards to aid these new requirements.[31] By 1611, therefore, the laity had come to expect to be able to be active hearers of God's word 'openly read' in church.

Notes

1. David Norton, *A Textual History of the King James Bible* (Cambridge, 2005), p. 47; on the difference between 'appointed' and 'authorized', see Alfred W. Pollard (ed.), *Records of the English Bible* (London, 1911), pp. 58–60.
2. A.S. Herbert, *A Historical Catalogue of Printed Editions of the English Bible 1525–1961* (London, 1968), pp. 130–33, and Pollard (ed.), *Records*, p. 64.
3. 'John Speed', *ODNB*.
4. Norton, *A Textual History*, p. 47.
5. Graham Rees and Maria Wakeley, *Publishing, Politics and Culture: The King's Printers in the Reigns of James I and VI* (Oxford, 2009), pp. 12 and 74–5.
6. Details of the early KJB editions mentioned here can be found in Herbert, *Historical Catalogue*, pp. 135, 139 and 162.
7. 'John Dryden (January 1828)', *Miscellaneous Writings and Speeches of Lord Macaulay*, Vol. II; consulted in the online text prepared by Mike Alder and Sue Asscher (Project Gutenberg).
8. Cited in David Norton, *A History of the English Bible as Literature* (Cambridge, 2000), p. 401.
9. Cited in Gustavus Paine, *The Learned Men* (New York, 1959), p. viii.
10. *The English Bible as Literature* (London, 1931), cited in Norton, *A History*, p. 401.
11. Hugh Broughton, *A Censure of the Late Translation for our Churches* (Middleburg, 1611), n.pag.
12. David Daniell, *The Bible in English* (New Haven, Conn., and London, 2003), p. 442.
13. *The Table-Talk of John Selden* (London, 1890), p. 6.
14. Eugene Nida, *Toward a Science of Translating, with Special Reference to Principles and Procedures Involved in Bible Translating* (Leiden, 1964).

15. *The New Testament of Jesus Christ, translated faithfully into English, out of the authentical Latin* (Rheims, 1582), annotations to John 2:4.

16. 'The Translators to the Reader', in Daniell, *The Bible in English*, p. 793.

17. The best analysis of such Hebraisms is Gerald Hammond, *The Making of the English Bible* (Manchester, 1982).

18. Ibid., p. 183.

19. William Rosenau, *Hebraisms in the Authorized Version of the Bible* (Baltimore, 1903).

20. On the so-called 'Great Petition', see Derwent May, 'Letter from London', *The Hudson Review* 33 (1980), 166, 168, 170, 172, 174–6. Signatories included, according to another account, 'Foreign Secretary Lord Carrington and Home Secretary William Whitelaw, 28 Privy Councillors, the Chief of Defence Staff, High Court judges, Lord Olivier, Henry Moore, Glenda Jackson, Sir John Gielgud, Poet Laureate John Betjeman, editors, dukes, industrialists and professors of English beyond number' (*Globe and Mail* [Canada], 9 November 1979).

21. Daniel, *The Bible in English*, p. 775.

22. George Saintsbury, *A History of English Prose Rhythm* (London, 1912), p. 146.

23. Collect for the Second Sunday in Advent, The Book of Common Prayer (1549 and subsequently).

24. John Craig, 'Psalms, Groans and Dogwhippers: The Soundscape of Worship in the English Parish Church, 1547–1642', in Will Coster and Andrew Spicer (eds), *Sacred Space in Early Modern Europe* (Cambridge, 2005), pp. 104–23, at pp. 104–5.

25. Adam Nicolson, *God's Secretaries: The Making of the King James Bible* (New York, 2003), pp. 209–10.

26. John Booty (ed.), *The Book of Common Prayer 1559* (Charlottesville, Va., 2005), pp. 14–15.

27. Richard Hooker, *The Lawes of Ecclesiastical Polity*, 2 vols (London, 1907), Vol. II, p. 81.

28. Hooker, *Lawes*, Vol. II. pp. 81–2.

29. W.K. Lowther Clarke, *Liturgy and Worship: A Companion to the Prayer Books of the Anglican Communion* (London, 1932), pp. 296–7 and 312–13; Massey Hamilton Shepherd, Jr, *The Oxford American Prayer Book Commentary* (New York, 1955), pp. xi–xv; John Gibaut, 'The Daily Office', in Charles Hefling and Cynthia Shattuck (eds), *The Oxford Guide to the Book of Common Prayer: A Worldwide Survey* (Oxford, 2006), pp. 453–5; Leonel Mitchell, 'Sanctifying Time: The Calendar', in Hefling and Shattuck (eds), *The Oxford Guide*, pp. 476–8.

30. F.E. Brightman, *The English Rite*, 2 vols (London, 1915), Vol. I, pp. xlix–li, clxxiii–clxxvi, clxxxiii–clxxiv; David N. Griffith, *The Bibliography of the Book of Common Prayer 1549–1999* (London, 2002), p. 110.

31. James F. White, 'Prayer Book Architecture', in Hefling and Shattuck (eds), *The Oxford Guide*, pp. 108–10; G.W.O. Addleshaw and F. Etchells, *The Architectural Setting of Anglican Worship* (London, 1958), pp. 68–84.

6

Afterlives of the
King James Bible
1611–1769

Peter McCullough and
Valentine Cunningham

FOR ALL THE ADMIRATION HEAPED UPON the King James Bible in modern times, perhaps the greatest surprise when approaching the translation historically is the markedly lukewarm reception it received for the first fifty years after its publication in 1611.

The KJB was not an instant classic, much less a cultural icon, in the reign of its namesake nor for decades thereafter. Any project of this kind can expect to have its detractors. Perhaps to none of the translators' surprise, and certainly not to the King's, was the response of Hugh Broughton, one of England's leading Hebrew scholars. Broughton had petitioned Elizabeth and her counsellors repeatedly for a better authorised English translation of the Bible, to no avail. Unsurprisingly, he was furious when passed over by Bancroft and King James to serve as a translator. A difficult personality with awkward ties to Puritanism, Broughton had publicly and privately crossed swords with the younger Lancelot Andrewes on matters of Hebrew scholarship, and Andrewes's chairmanship of the Westminster committee responsible for Broughton's cherished Pentateuch and historical books of the Old Testament could only have poured salt in his wounds. Broughton lost no time in publishing *A Censure of the Late Translation for our Churches* in 1611 from the relatively safe distance of Middleburg (in the Netherlands). Not mincing his words, he opined that the new version 'will greeve me while I breathe. It is so ill done. Tell his Majestie that I had rather be rent in pieces with wilde horses, then any such translation, by my consent, should bee urged upon poore churches.'[1]

Other criticisms may have been milder than Broughton's, but they could be encountered everywhere. When the future Bishop of Lincoln, Robert Sanderson, happened into a country church with his Oxford tutor, the translator Richard Kilby of Lincoln College, they sat through a sermon by a young preacher who devoted 'a great part of the hour allowed for his Sermon in exceptions against the late Translation of several words (not expecting such a hearer as Dr *Kilbie*)'. Afterwards, Kilby told the unsuspecting preacher that as for the young man's objections, he and his fellow translators 'had considered all them, and found thirteen more considerable Reasons, why it was translated as now printed'. 'The Preacher', according to Izaak Walton, 'was so ingenious to say, He would not justifie himself'.[2]

But, outside Miles Smith's fulsome Preface to the KJB, the translators themselves showed a striking reticence about their accomplishment, and even some diffidence when it came to using it. When Kilby himself preached the funeral sermon for his fellow Oxford translator Thomas Holland (fellow of Exeter College and Regius Professor of Divinity) in 1612, his eulogy made no mention of work on the Bible as one of Holland's academic achievements. Many translators also found it difficult to let go their greater familiarity with earlier versions when preaching. So, if the 1611 version was read from the lectern, it was often not heard from the pulpit. Perhaps most strikingly, Lancelot Andrewes himself rarely quoted, in fifteen years of preaching after its appearance, the new version to which he had contributed so much. He opted instead for preaching from the Vulgate and from his own English translations based on the Geneva Bible. Andrewes's practice, though, is far from a repudiation of the importance of translation; on the contrary, it is an insistence upon it. Precisely because of his multilingual erudition and deep familiarity with the earliest available originals of versions of the Scriptures, he had no fond notions about there being a single 'correct' text or translation, especially when it came to the business of exegesis or interpretation. So, in his sermon for the opening of Parliament in 1621, the text he declared from the pulpit was in fact a collation of Vulgate (Latin), Septuagint (Greek), prayer book, Geneva, and Authorized versions of Psalm 82:1:[3]

> Deus stat in Syngagoga Deorum: In medio Deos judicabit.
> The *Greeke*, word for word, the same.
> [a] God *standeth in the Congregation of* Princes: [a] The *Psalter*
> [b] *or*, in the Assembly of the Godds, [b] The *Geneva*
> [c] *or*, of the Mightie, [c] The *New* Translation
> In the middst will He judge the Godds.

Andrewes and Kilby were, it must be acknowledged, men who had grown up on earlier translations like the Geneva, and had probably memorized most of it. A younger generation, however, would come of age with the Bible of King James, and for them it would be their scriptural default. A particularly dramatic example is that of John Donne, more famous now as a poet, but in his day as one of England's greatest preachers. Donne had grown up a Roman Catholic and thus presumably without rote memorising of the Geneva; his very young age and short time as a member of Hart Hall (Hertford College) was itself probably a strategy to avoid legal conformity to the Church of England. Once reconciled to the English church, he came late to ordained ministry at the behest of King James in 1615. Donne was, as much as the KJB, a royally 'authorised version' of Jacobean conformity. From his first extant

Bee wise as serpents but innocent as Dous.

Ætat 42.

LXXX.
SERMONS
PREACHED BY THAT LEAR.
NED AND REVEREND DIVINE
IOHN DONNE. Dʳ IN DIVINITIE
LATE DEANE OF Yᵉ CATHEDRALL
CHVRCH OF Sᵀ PAVLES
LONDON.

M. Merian Iun.

sermon, preached at court in the year of his ordination, Donne never deviated from use of the KJB, which he repeatedly and approvingly cited as 'our new translation'. In consequence, the appearance of 160 of his much admired and imitated sermons in three successive folios (1640, 1649, 1660) did much to engrain the authorised text in the nation's religious consciousness (figure 52).

This process of acculturation to the KJB would no doubt have continued with greater strength were it not for the religious dislocations of the Civil War and Commonwealth, and the effects (more mundane, but just as influential) of business disputes over printing rights to the Bible. But those decades and those problems once past, the KJB emerged with the Restoration of the Church of England and its monarchical governor in 1660 as the hallmark of English religious vocabulary that it has been ever since. Nothing proclaimed this fact more than the reissue in 1660 of King James's Bible, now under the sovereign patronage and promulgation of his grandson, Charles II. The engraved frontispiece of that edition even avoided the non-monarchical iconography of the 1611 title page, opting instead for an updated version of those of Henry VIII and Elizabeth I, which had emphatically displayed the monarch as the true patron of the Scriptures as authorised for use in English churches. In the 1660 frontispiece, Charles II, classicised to the point of unrecognisability, sits enthroned as a new Solomon, guarded by royal lions, and surrounded by Apostles and Patriarchs, in an unmistakable allusion to the early Tudors (figure 53).

Further changes at the Restoration ensured the currency of the KJB in the re-established Church of England, not least the incorporation into the new Book of Common Prayer (1662) of the lessons or 'propers' for Sunday and feast day communion services in the King James version. Between 1611 and their proscription by Parliament in 1645, all prayer books had printed those readings in their versions from the old Bishops' Bible. This perhaps startling fact underscores just how halting was the 1611 version's march towards prominence.

The text in music

The psalms used in the prayer book remained unchanged. The Coverdale or 'prayer book' psalter has in fact never been dislodged from the Book of Common Prayer. Psalms were, from the Tudor days of Sternhold and Hopkins's hugely popular metrical versions (different yet again from the prayer book), the mainstay of English church music. The 'prayer book' psalms continued after the Restoration to provide the texts of psalms set both as anthems and as chant, as did the 'prayer book' versions of the canticles for morning and evening prayer (such as

Figure 52 Engraved frontispiece to John Donne, *LXXX Sermons*, 1640. Oxford, Bodleian Library, Fol. Θ328.

Figure 53 *pp. 144–5 The Holy Bible* (1660), inscription and frontispiece of the copy owned by Charles II and presented to Nathaniel Crewe in 1674. Lincoln College Senior Library L.4.10.

Sacrum isthoc, & à manu,
Regiâ acceptum, Donum,
in Collegium nup.ᵉ ᵉ suum LINCOLNIENSE
munificè contulit Reverendus admodùm
in CHRISTO Pater ac Dominus, Dom.
NATHANAEL CREWE,
Episcopus DUNELMENSIS, Præfectus
sacri Conclavis Regii, et hujus Collegii
non ita pridem, Rector
dignißimus.

Anno Dom. 1674.

THE HOLY
BIBLE
Conteining the Bookes
of the Old & New
TESTAMENT.

CAMBRIDGE
Printed by John Field,
Printer to the Universitie.
And are to be Chorogra-
phically set forth by J. Ogilby.
1660

the Magnificat). But the updating of the 1662 prayer book to include proper lessons in the King James version did finally begin to insert King James texts into the elite, and culturally influential, musical repertoires of the Chapel Royal and English cathedrals. Many great biblical texts in English other than psalms had been set before the Restoration by leading composers, but even after 1611 they eschewed the King James version, as in the case of Orlando Gibbons's much-loved setting of John 1:19–23 (*This is the record of John*), which dates from 1611–21 and follows Geneva. The giant of Restoration music, Henry Purcell, is perhaps the first great English composer to give choral expression to the King James translations of biblical texts. His early and unforgettable setting of the Song of Solomon 2:10–12 (*My beloved spake*, before 1678) for small string ensemble, choir and soloists, exploits to the full the beauty of the authorised translation's evocation of love and spring.

But no musical work – and one is tempted to say that nothing of any kind – did more to ingrain the most loved passages of the KJB into the popular consciousness than Charles Jennens's libretto for Handel's *Messiah* (1741–42). The great oratorio was Jennens's brainchild, and to him should go the credit for its masterful textual fabric, almost exclusively from the KJB. A deeply conservative Anglican Nonjuror, Jennens, and his 'word book' for the *Messiah*, epitomized precisely the combination of Stuart conformity and royalism heralded by the title page of King Charles II's 1660 King James Bible. In fact, so insistent was Jennens on the licensed authority of sound preaching from the authorised Scriptures that he risked Handel's ire by insisting that he reinstate the tenor *arioso* 'How beautiful are the feet of them that preach the gospel of peace' and its linked chorus 'Their sound is gone out into all lands' (Romans 10:15, 18), which Handel had dropped from

Figure 54 The 'Tenbury Manuscript', 'How beautiful are the feet'. This was Handel's conducting copy and was used in all his performances of *Messiah*. Oxford, Bodleian Library, Bodl. MS. Tenbury 347, fols. 65v and 66r.

early performances.[4] As scored by Handel, the 'sacred oratorio' (as it was called in early performances) was an instant success. Its Oxford debut on 4 April 1749 – in the Sheldonian Theatre as part of the University's celebrations for the opening of the Radcliffe Camera – initiated an eighteenth-century craze for provincial performances, including many more in Oxford. Just as David Garrick made Shakespeare into a national cultural commodity 150 years after his death with the 1769 'Shakespeare Jubilee' at Stratford, so Jennens and Handel (if perhaps somewhat less commercially) did the same for the KJB 150 years after its appearance (figures 54 and 55).

The importance of authorisation

It was in the year of Garrick's Shakespeare Jubilee (1769) that the KJB received its crowning imprimatur of authority – its first revision since 1611. Benjamin Blayney, fellow and Vice Principal of Hertford College, made five significant categories of adjustments: increased italicised 'supplied readings'; newly corrected readings; modernised spellings; new marginal notes; and correction of 1611 printing errors. Copies of the first edition are exceedingly rare since most of the print run was lost in a London warehouse fire; but the Bodleian holds a precious copy which escaped the flames. And Blayney's work, immediately known as the 'Oxford Standard' Bible , would reinscribe Oxford yet again into the history of the KJB.

It did indeed take time for the KJB to become what it ended up as, namely the version of the English-speaking world, the one in the ears and imagination of every Protestant churchgoer of whatever denomination or sect; its words, metaphors, stories populating the English language so pervasively that everyone, churchgoer or not, thought and spoke the KJB whether they knew it or not; its linguistic and narrative material, stories and personae the occupying power of English literature, feeding poetry's lines, the novel's plots and characterisation, shaping life-writing, fictional and non-fictional.

The stuttering rise to this eminence had much to do with the KJB's combative Established Church origins and promotion (aimed at wiping out its sectarian rivals). There was much built-up affection for its English predecessors, especially the Geneva Bible (with its handy marginal commentary and other ancillary aids to reading: this was the favoured textbook of Puritans and sectaries, Baptists, Congregationalists, English Presbyterians, and

(9)

Who is the King of Glory?
The Lord strong and mighty, the Lord mighty in Battle.
  Lift up your Heads O ye Gates, and be ye lift up ye everlasting Doors, and the King of Glory shall come in.
  Who is the King of Glory?
  The Lord of Hosts : He is the King of Glory.

RECITATIVE.

Unto which of the Angels said he at any Time, Thou art my Son, this Day have I begotten thee?

CHORUS.

Let all the Angels of God worship him.

AIR.

Thou art gone up on high, thou hast led Captivity captive, and received Gifts for Men, yea for thine Enemies, that the Lord God might dwell among them.

CHORUS.

The Lord gave the Word; great was the Company of the Preachers.

DUETTO and CHORUS.

How beautiful are the Feet of him that bringeth glad Tidings, Tidings of Salvation! That saith unto Zion thy God reigneth! Break forth into Joy, thy God reigneth.
                    B   AIR.

their like, but not only them). Too, the learned liked to read in original tongues, Greek especially, but also Hebrew. Certainly, many Protestant Christians would not, in increasing numbers as the Dissenter-creating ecclesiastical disturbances of the 1660 Restoration of the Monarchy unfolded, be in the churches this version was 'Appointed' to be read in. Very many Protestant Christians were indeed among the 'self-conceited Brethren, who run their own ways, and give liking unto nothing but what is framed by themselves, and hammered on their anvil', whom the KJB 'Dedication' expects will 'malign' the version of Church and King. The KJB was the version for which, along with its liturgical companion The Book of Common Prayer, Charles I was stubbornly martyred and for whose restoration Charles II was enthroned – as his instant reinstallation of the KJB in 1660 showed, with the grotesque and aggressive monarchical iconography of its new title page. The Dissenters who were shut out by the 1662 Act of Uniformity at one point believed the rumour going round that their Geneva Bibles were to be confiscated (little Daniel Defoe, brought up in the London non-conforming 'gathered church' his parents attended, was set to making a shorthand copy – he dropped out after doing the first five books).

John Milton, as author of *Samson Agonistes*, *Paradise Lost* and *Paradise Regained*, not to mention his paraphrases of the Psalms, the greatest poetic redoer of the Bible there has ever been, ticks so many of the reluctant boxes: republican, regicide, enemy of established churches. He certainly owned a KJB (his 1612 edition is in the British Museum) and a Geneva text Bible, but seems to have preferred reading the Junius–Tremellius Latin Bible, and was steeped in the Greek and Hebrew originals (he used the *Biblia Sacra Polyglotta* (1657) with text in Greek, Hebrew, Aramaic, Arabic, Persian, Syrian, the Vulgate's Latin, and an interlinear Latin translation of the Hebrew Old Testament).[5] Like the Revd Dr John Donne before him and Dr Samuel Johnson after him (whose sermons are all based on KJB texts, but who 'read much' in his Greek New Testament, which was 'generally within reach'), scholarly Milton clearly did not favour any one version over another, but particularly not the KJB.[6] His great (Latin) *De Doctrina Christiana* illustrates its arguments with proof texts drawn from Junius–Tremellius with occasional Latinisings of his own where that didn't fit his line on predestination or angels or soul-death, and so on. All were obscured by the book's 1825 'translator', George IV's Historiographer Royal Charles Richard Sumner, who, assuming an English poet would naturally use the KJB, lazily jobbed in the KJB text at every point (occasionally indicating the KJB's misfit with Milton's point, but never realising the basic problem).[7] Symptomatically, when Milton directly borrows an English Bible line (in Adam's eating confession, *Paradise Lost*, X:37–143

Figure 55 *The Sacred Oratorio* (1749), showing 'How beautiful are the feet'. This 'word book' was produced for the Oxford debut of *Messiah*. Oxford, Bodleian Library, Vet. A4 e.128 (3).

(Book IX in the original ten-book version), 'She gave me of the tree and I did eat') – a quotation which, according to David Norton, doyen of Bible as Literature studies, makes the poem 'incandesce' – it's a sentence common both to Geneva and to the KJB.[8]

There was, of course, no fudging the ecclesiastical conformities that the KJB was authorising. And within a short time the loyal (Royalist, establishmentarian) Anglican poets were taking to it as the unique scriptural source for their reflections. The poems of George Herbert, most Anglican of Anglican parsons, are soaked in what two of his poems call 'The Holy Scriptures'. And those are never not the KJB. Many of Herbert's titles point to the KJB passages they're built on – ones prescribed in the Prayer Book for the festivals the poems are celebrating and accompanying. As, for example, 'Coloss.3.3. Our life is hid with Christ in God', from the epistle set for Easter Sunday (a particular favourite of Herbert's, according to the editor of the great recent edition).[9] The Bodleian manuscript of Herbert's poems (figure 56), was copied (around June 1633) from an original sent by Herbert to his old Cambridge friend, the Anglican deacon Nicholas Ferrar, a friend of Charles I, at the lay religious community of High Anglicans at Little Gidding, whose daily prayer vigil was entirely a Prayer Book affair. (The poem 'Little Gidding' by twentieth-century Anglican Royalist T.S. Eliot celebrates the Ferrar community as the holy place 'broken king' Charles came to 'at nightfall', seeking shelter in his escape from Oxford, 2 May 1646.) Nicholas Ferrar was said by his brother John to have read Herbert's manuscript over and over, kissing it again and again, saying it was 'most worthy to be in ye hands and hearts of all true Christian, that feared God and loved the Church of England' – a poetry of the KJB for Anglican Christians, the only 'true' ones.[10]

Figure 56 George Herbert, 'The Holy Scriptures 1' and '2'. Oxford, Bodleian Library, Bodl. MS. Tanner 307, p. 38v and p. 39r.

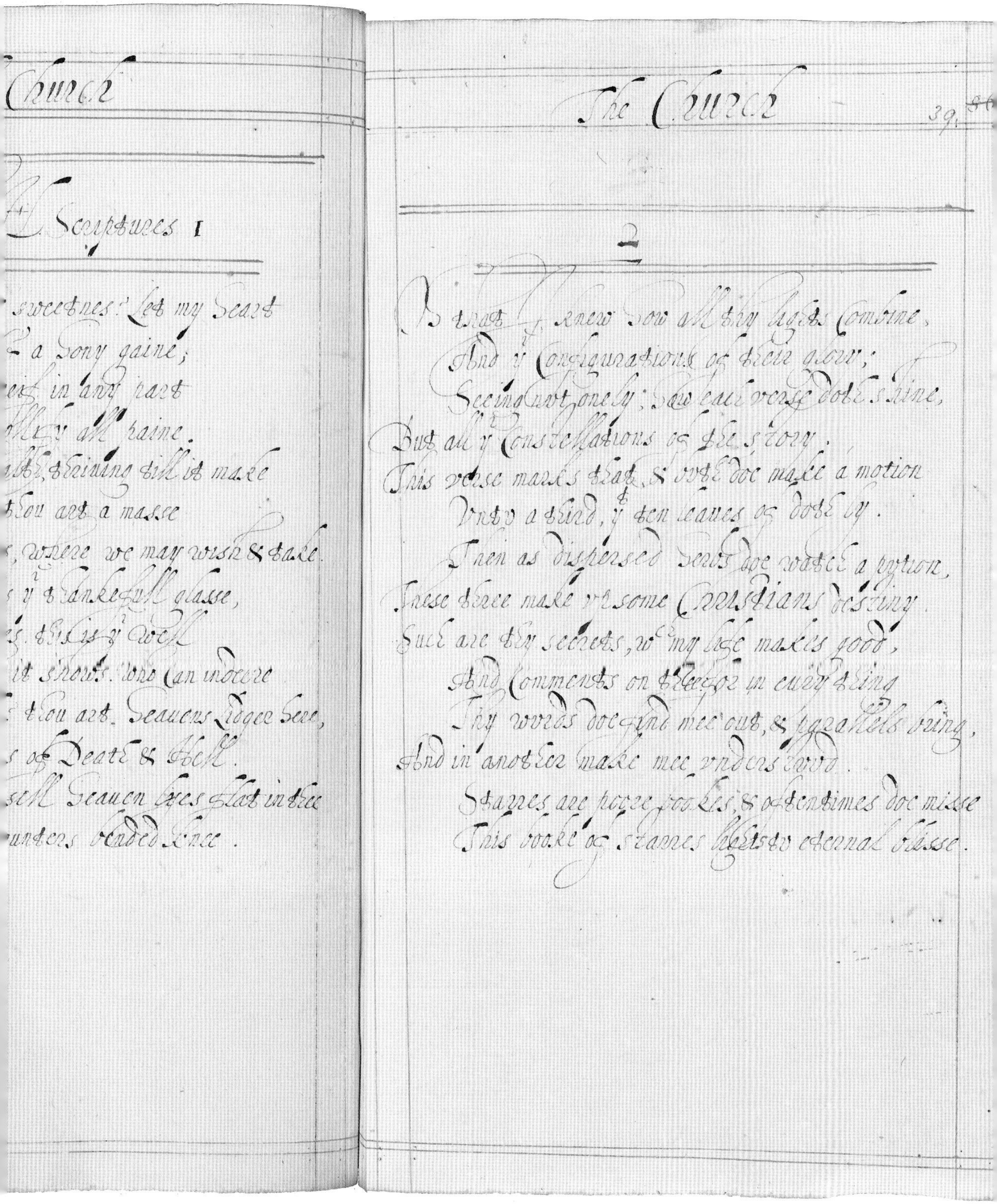

Church

H. Scriptures 1

sweetnes! Let my heart
a bony gaine;
in any part
all raine.
shining till it make
Thou art a masse
where we may wish & take
y thankfull glasse,
this y well
it shoots: who can indeere
Thou art heauens lidge here,
of Death & Hell.
sell heauen lyes flat in thee
unders ordered here.

2

Oh that I knew how all thy lights combine,
And y Configurations of their glorie:
Seeing not onely; how each verse doth shine,
But all y Constellations of the story.
This verse markes that, & both doe make a motion
Vnto a third, y ten leaues of doth ly.

Then as dispersed herbs doe watch a potion,
These three make vp some Christians destiny:
Such are thy secrets, wch my life makes good,
And comments on thee: for in euery thing
Thy words doe finde mee out, & parallells bring,
And in another make mee vnderstood.

Starres are poore bookes, & oftentimes doe misse
This booke of starres lights to eternal blisse.

Typically, the only Bible text in play in the greatly Bible-minded sacred poems of Royalist Anglo-Catholic Henry Vaughan is the KJB. Symptomatically, Vaughan's Preface to his *Silex Scintillans* volume (1655) – from which his 'To the Holy Bible' comes – praises Herbert as the 'blessed man' whose holy life and verse converted him from the ways of mere 'wit', and ends its KJB-packed encomium with a large amalgam of long KJB extracts. For their part, the highly biblicised Restoration poems produced by the then monarchist Anglican John Dryden – chief among them *Absalom and Achitophel* (1682), propping up Charles II as King David vexed by Absalom (illegitimate son Monmouth) and Achitophel (evil counsellor Buckingham) – are resolutely KJB in word and deed. Here was a politicising of KJB text and story backed by the propaganda of Dryden's *Religio Laici, or A Laymans Faith* (1682) and its Preface inveighing against the translations and versions of 'sectaries' and other ultra-Protestant 'fanatics' for being rooted in heretical Tyndale's version and the 'rigid opinions' brought in from Calvin's Geneva. '[N]ever since the Reformation has there wanted a text' of the sectaries' 'interpreting to authorise' rebellion and king-killing. The wonderful thing about the KJB, Dryden says, is not only that the 'laws divine' contained in 'that sacred volume' are *sufficient* and *clear* for their 'ordained' use, but that its style is 'majestic and divine'. It's the style which 'Speaks no less than God in every line'.[11] So, clarity of Established Church law and also stylistic majesty: unlike, we're meant to think, in the rival English versions.

Masters of English style

Already, then, in 1682, there was a certain kindling of the aesthetic enthusiasm for the KJB which would become the keynote of many modern literary-minded people who have no truck with Bible content – a stylistic eminence to the KJB (and its accompanying Prayer Book), which the self-styled Anglican constitutionalist the Revd Dr Jonathan Swift offered as linguistic example in his 1712 *Proposal for Correcting, Improving and Ascertaining the English Tongue*. The Prayer Book services have 'as great strains of true sublime Eloquence, as are any where to be found in our Language'. '[N]o translation our Country ever yet produced, hath come up to that of the *Old* and *New* Testament' in the KJB. 'I am persuaded that the Translators of the Bible were Masters of an English style much fitter for that Work' of keeping the English Language *simple* (plain and pure), than any other of 'our present Writings'.[12] It's a mark of the wicked seducer Lovelace in *Clarissa* (1748) (second novel of moralist Anglican printer and publisher Samuel Richardson – at one time intended for the Anglican ministry) that he prizes the KJB only for its 'beauty and noble simplicity' (Book VI, Letter CXX) and is untouched by its ethicity. Clarissa greatly offends him by her use of Bible passages as analogies for her melancholic plight as entrapped seducee. How dare she arrange her 'Collection of Scripture texts drawn up in array against me', he complains, rebutting point by point her 'Meditation' (one of four) on KJB extracts mainly from Job, beginning with 'O that my grief were thoroughly weighed, and my calamity laid in the balance together!' (Book V, Letter LXXI).

All Lovelace's sidekick John Belford can do in reporting Clarissa's awesome Biblicized grieving to Lovelace is tell how impressed he has been with the unexpected beauties of a KJB he recently found in a sick Uncle's closet ('style … truly easy, simple and natural'; 'an all-excelling collection of beauties'; far better than the beauties of 'Pagan authors', as a chance reading of Anthony Blackwall's *The Sacred Classics Defended and Illustrated* (1725, 1731) has confirmed). And that's a good realisation for scoffing wits and libertines to come to, but, so far as Richardson is concerned, it doesn't go nearly far enough in its ignoring of the Bible's *sanctions* and *sentiments*, which Belford mentions, but fails to connect with the put-on Clarissa's extensive personalisings of the text. Richardson's new medium of English prose fiction is happy to accept the KJB as linguistically fine, but what it's offering as more important still, and indeed generative for writing, is the ethicity, the religion, indeed the spirituality that the KJB-reading Clarissa is making her own.[13] Which had been from the start the assumption of the KJB poets Herbert and Vaughan – linguistic beauties, poeticity, yes, but secondary to the KJB's doctrines of necessarily personalisable faith ('*Your* life is hid with Christ in God', wrote St Paul in Colossians 3:3; '*Our* life is hid with Christ in God' in Herbert's version signalled the intensity of his and his poem's making the KJB text their very own): the KJB with life-altering personal moral point first and foremost. This is the assumption, of course, of the great eighteenth-century hymn-writers infected with the conversionist enthusiasms of the Evangelical Movement, Charles Wesley above all. But not only evangelical writers (and Richardson is that way inclined): dryly Christian ones, too; like the Revd Laurence Sterne, revving up the new textual self-consciousness of this still early-days medium of the English novel with ethical thrusts from the KJB. As when a manuscript sermon on the KJB text of Hebrews 13:18, 'For we trust we have a good Conscience', dropping out of a book on military fortifications brought in by Corporal Trim, drops into *Tristram Shandy* (1759–67) and so into the reader's consciousness. Trim's reading of it is much mocked by his auditors, but he carries on through a large array of KJB quotations and examples, to the sermon's conclusions about scriptural regulations and divine law, especially for lawyers (Book II, ch. 17 (Book II published with Book I, 1759)). Assigned to 'Mr Yorick' in the novel, the sermon was one of Prebendary Sterne's own, preached to the judges and lawyers of Assize in York Minster in 1750 (published York, 1750). And what this arrival of a sermon in a novel of the 1750s confirms, like the Bible meditations of *Clarissa*, is not just that the English novel's morality was now firmly Bible-based, but that the only English Bible in play by this time was the KJB.[14]

That 'Bible' at the time meant the KJB was utterly clear when Alexander Cruden's astounding one-man *Concordance* to the Bible appeared in 1737 (it was revised in 1761, and again in 1769 – to take cognizance of the revised KJB of that year? See Cruden's characteristic explanatory entry on 'Scripture' in figure 57). Notably, Cruden (1699–1770) was not an Anglican, but a Scottish Calvinist, for many years an attender at the conservative Calvinist Dr John Guyse's Independent Meeting in London, and eventually buried in the Dissenters' burial ground in Deadman's Place, Southwark – thus a Dissenter for whom, along apparently with his co-religionists, the Bible had become axiomatically the KJB. Dr Guyse (a Bible parenthesiser himself) collaborated closely with the great Nonconformist hymn-writers Isaac Watts and the lesser but still important Philip Doddridge, whose canonical biblical hymns, as for instance Watts's 'Our God, Our Help in Ages Past', and Doddridge's 'Hark the Glad Sound! The Saviour Comes', were utterly KJB-driven. As Anglican Herbert's poems once announced their Scriptural origins in KJB texts, so now did these Nonconformist hymns. Characteristically, 'Hark the Glad Sound!' was in the Nonconformist hymn book as 'Christ's message, from Luke iv.18,19' – the KJB's St Luke, naturally. Ernest Rattenbury, Methodist expositor of the 'evangelical doctrines' of Charles Wesley's hymns, declared that 'if the Bible were lost', you could 'extract much of it' from Wesley's hymns. And it would be the KJB you extracted. The early 'Methodists' were in the main Anglicans like their leaders the Revds John and Charles Wesley, but the Methodist congregations they brought into being were soon mainly not. And nary a one was bothered by singing the Bible of the Anglican Church they'd abandoned and which abandoned them. By the time the Wesleys were flourishing evangelistically, the KJB had become the text of anglophone Christendom of every stripe.[15] Demonstrative of this tradition is Charles Wesley's *Short Hymns on Select Passages of the Holy Scriptures*, a volume whose verses are based on every book of the KJB: No. 931, for example, 'Thou Shepherd of Israel and Mine', is based on the KJB translation of Song of Solomon 1:7, 'Tell me, O thou whom my soul loveth, where thou makest *thy flock* to rest at noon.'

This literary omnipresence of the KJB can be observed dramatically emerging as the intertextual motor of the emerging mode of the English

Figure 57 Alexander Cruden, *A Complete Concordance to the Holy Scriptures of the Old and New Testament* (1738), entry for 'Scripture'. Oxford, Bodleian Library, Douce C subt.158.

John 8. 3. the *s.* brought a woman taken in adultery
Acts 4. 5. *s.* gathered against the apostles
6. 12. the *s.* brought Stephen to the council
23. 9. *s.* of the Pharisees part arose, and strove

SCRIP.

1 *Sam.* 17. 40. David put smooth stones in a *s.*
Mat. 10. 10. provide no *s.* for your journey,
              Mar. 6. 8. *Luk.* 9. 3. | 10. 4.
Luk. 22. 35. when I sent you without *s.* lacked ye
36. but now let him take his purse and *s.*

SCRIPTURE,

Or Writing. There is great dispute concerning the *first inventor of letters and writing. Some maintain that there was writing before the deluge, and that Adam was the inventor of letters. Others think, that Moses is the first author of whom we have any writings, and that before him there were no written monuments. Thro' the whole lives of the patriarchs, there are found no footsteps of any writing; neither does Moses quote any writing, that was extant before his own; for the book of the wars of the Lord mentioned Num. 21. 14. some think that it is a passage added to the text of Moses, or that it was a writing composed in his time. Others take it as a prophesy of what should afterwards be recorded in the books of Joshua and Judges; and instead of reading the text, It is said in the book of the wars of Lord, they say the Hebrew will bear to be read in the future tense, It shall be said in the book of the wars.*

All agree that it is an admirable invention: *To paint speech, and speak to the eyes, and by tracing out characters in different forms to give colour and body to thoughts. It is also agreed by all, that there is nothing extant this day in the world, either more ancient, or more authentick, than the books of Moses; but it does not follow from thence, that there was no writing before him. It appears, on the contrary, that writing was common enough at that time both among the Egyptians and Hebrews. This people seemed already prepared and accustomed to express their thoughts and sentiments after this manner. And it is to be supposed, that the chief of the nation read the tables of the law. Moses had been instructed in all the knowledge of the Egyptians, and, doubtless, had learned their manner of writing.*

The word Scripture generally stands for the *sacred books of the Old and New Testament, written by holy men, as they were inspired, instructed, and enabled by the Holy Ghost, 2 Tim. 3. 16. All Scripture is given by inspiration of God, and is profitable for doctrine, to declare and confirm the truth; for reproof, to convince of sin and confute errors; for correction, to reform the life; and for instruction in righteousness, i. e. to teach us to make a farther progress in the way to heaven; or, to instruct us in the true righteousness in which we may appear with comfort before God. Scripture is sometimes taken for some one sentence or passage of the sacred writings, Mar. 15. 28. The scripture was fulfilled, which saith, and he was numbred with the transgressors. The passage referred to is recorded in Isa. 53. 12. Scripture is also taken for the Holy Ghost, speaking in the scripture, and by whose inspiration the scripture was written, Gal. 3. 8. The scripture foreseeing that God would justify the heathen thro' faith, preached before the gospel unto Abraham, saying, In thee shall all nations be blessed. And in John 5. 39. Our Saviour says, Search the scriptures, for in them ye think ye have eternal life, and they are they which testify of me. q. d. Diligently examine the books of the Old Testament, which your selves acknowledge do set forth the true way to eternal life; and upon due trial you will find, that all those prophesies and types are fulfilled in me;*

me; *and that all the promises of life there made, have respect to me, and point me out as the true Messiah.*

The sacred writings of the Old and New Testament are called, *The Scriptures, The Bible, or The Book in the way of eminency and distinction; because they far excel all other books: For, (1) They contain the whole will of God necessary to be known for our Salvation. (2) They were inspired by the holy Ghost, 2 Tim. 3. 16. 2 Pet. 1. 21. (3.) They contain a wisdom far above all the wisdom of the world, 1 Cor. 2. 7. (4.) They were penned by the most excellent of men, for wisdom and holiness, as Moses, David, Solomon, the prophets, apostles, and evangelists. (5) They are most perfect, pure, deep, and immutable, and contain all things necessary for faith and manners, Psal. 19. 7. 2 Tim. 3. 16, 17. 1 Pet. 1. 23. (6) No scripture but this brings such glory to God, or hath such an efficacy in converting a soul, Psal. 19. 7, 8. Heb. 4. 12. (7) Tho' these books were written by divers men in divers ages, yet there is as great harmony in them, as if they had been written by one man.*

Dan. 10. 21. which is noted in the *s.* of truth
Mar. 12. 10. and have ye not read this *s.*
15. 28. the *s.* was fulfilled, which saith
Luk. 4. 21. he said, this day is this *s.* fulfilled
John 2. 22. they believed the *s.* and the word
7. 38. he that believeth on me, as *s.* saith
42. hath not the *s.* said, Christ cometh of David
10. 35. and the *s.* cannot be broken
19. 37. again another *s.* saith, they shall look
Acts 1. 16. this *s.* must needs have been fulfilled
8. 32. the place of the *s.* which he read, was this
35. Philip began at the same *s.* and preached
Rom. 4. 3. what saith the *s.* 11. 2. *Gal.* 4. 30.
9. 17. for the *s.* saith, 10. 11. 1 *Tim.* 5. 8.
Gal. 3. 8. the *s.* foreseeing that God would justify
22. the *s.* hath concluded all under sin
2 *Tim.* 3. 16. all *s.* is given by inspiration of God
Jam. 4. 5. do you think the *s.* saith in vain
1 *Pet.* 2. 6. also it is contained in the *s.*
2 *Pet.* 1. 20. no prophesy of *s.* is of private

SCRIPTURES

Mat. 21. 42. have ye never read in the *s.*
22. 29. ye do err, not knowing the *s. Mar.* 12. 24.
26. 54. but how then shall the *s.* be fulfilled
Mar. 14. 49. but the *s.* must be fulfilled.
Luk. 24. 27. he expounded to them in all the *s.*
32. heart burn, while he opened to us the *s.*
45. that they might understand the *s.*
John 5. 39. search the *s.* for in them ye think
Acts 17. 2. he reasoned with them out of the *s.*
11. were more noble, and searched the *s.* daily
18. 24. a Jew named Apollos, mighty in the *s.*
28. shewing by the *s.* that Jesus was Christ
Rom. 1. 2. promised by prophets in the holy *s.*
15. 4. thro' comfort of the *s.* might have hope
16. 26. and by the *s.* made known to all nations
1 *Cor.* 15. 3. died, || 4. rose according to the *s.*
2 *Tim.* 3. 15. from a child hast known the holy *s.*
2 *Pet.* 3. 16. wrest, as they do also other *s.*

SCROLL.

Isa. 34. 4. heavens be rolled together as a *s.*
Rev. 6. 14. and the heaven departed as a *s.*

SCUM.

Ezek. 24. 6. wo to the pot whose *s.* is therein
11. that the *s.* of it may be consumed
12. her great *s.* went not forth out of her, her
           s. shall be in the fire

SCURVY.

Lev. 21. 20. none shall approach that is *s.*
22. 22. the *s.* or scabbed not offer to the Lord.

SEA.

1 *Kin.* 7. 23. he made a molten *s.* 2 *Chron.* 4. 2.
24. knops compassing the *s.* round about
25. the *s.* was set above upon oxen, 2 *Chron.* 4. 4.
39. set the *s.* on the right side of the house
2 *Kin.* 16. 17. Ahaz took down the *s.* from the oxen
25. 13. the *s.* did Chaldees break in pieces, 16.
2 *Chron.* 4. 6. the *s.* was for the priests to wash in

Figure 58 Robinson Crusoe Reading the Bible to his Man Friday, engraving by Charles G. Lewis after Alexander Fraser, 1836. © The Trustees of the British Museum.

novel – that Protestant, Puritan, Nonconformist biblicist genre coming to birth in John Bunyan's ur-novel *The Pilgrim's Progress* (1678, 1684) and Daniel Defoe's first English novel proper *Robinson Crusoe* (1720). Both of them were Geneva Bible men, KJB hostiles by theological and ecclesiological disposition: Bunyan one of Cromwell's New Model soldiers, a self-taught Independent twice imprisoned (twelve years in the first instance) for preaching outside the licensed purlieus of the Church of England, hot against the Prayer Book ('I Will Pray With the Spirit' he declares at length in the teeth of the Restoration in 1662), so at home in the Genevan text that he imitates its marginal commentary practice in the extensive marginalia of *The Pilgrim's Progress*; and Defoe, that child of Dissent copying out the Geneva Pentateuch, received into membership of a Dissenting congregation, who fought on Monmouth's side against the Establishment forces of James II at the Battle of Sedgemoor, pilloried for his satirical pamphleteering against the foes of Nonconformity (as in, for instance, *The Shortest Way With The Dissenters* (1702)), his pioneer novel *Robinson Crusoe* (1719) constructed massively out of the puritanical habit of spiritual diary-keeping. To be sure, what the actual versions of the three 'very good' Bibles Crusoe happens to have brought with him to the island are is never specified, so we're left to guess which version he quotes from so frequently, which one he keeps modelling his behaviour and spirituality on, which one he reads savingly to his Man Friday (figure 58), and, most importantly, which one actually effects his conversion. Parataxis – narrative proceeding in a sequence of 'and … and … and' (Hebrew *waw* and Greek *kai*), the very great gift of Bunyan and Defoe to English narrative – could have been learned in any English Bible. But it is certainly affirmed by the KJB, which is the version becoming clearly audible in their writings.

Hybrid texts and alterations

One speculates that Nonconformists were helped in accepting the KJB by the hybrid editions, KJB text with the Geneva notes, which started to appear in England in 1642 (not insignificantly the year the Civil War broke out). Bunyan's mainly KJB quotations are frequently glossed by comments closely following Geneva notes. Hybrid sermonizing! As in *The Doctrine of the Law and Grace Unfolded* (1659). Was he using a Civil War hybrid? (figure 59).[16] It must, sooner or later, have dawned on the refuseniks that the KJB was itself a highly hybrid text, not least frequently following Geneva word for word. (Tyndale readers might well have recognised that many of the KJB's most memorable lines and phrases were purloined from Tyndale: the KJB translators weren't so cloth-eared as to miss out on 'Let there be light'; 'kill the fatted calf'; 'Ask and it shall be given you, seek and ye shall find'; 'a grain of mustard-seed'; 'one sinner that repenteth'; 'before the cock crow thou shalt deny me thrice', and so on, phrases poised for flight into the word-hoard of the English language).[17] And Crusoe's Bible is manifestly a hybrid.

The tipping point in Crusoe's conversion process is when he 'came to these Words, *He is exalted a Prince and a Saviour, to give Repentance, and to give Remission.*' – words from Acts 5:31 that are mainly the same in the KJB and Geneva; except that Defoe prefers the KJB's 'exalted' over Geneva's 'lift up'. So here, as elsewhere in the novel, the KJB is gaining the edge – just. But, even more characteristically, 'Remission' is Crusoe's own, substituted for 'forgiveness of sins' in both KJB and Geneva. 'Remission' has perhaps a stronger Calvinistic ring. It might be, of course, as is sometimes suggested, that as with so many of the textual variants *Crusoe* is rich in, Defoe is quoting the Bible from memory, and so misquoting a little. But whether conscious or not, this adaptive rewriting of his Bible texts – we can think of it as paraphrase, or even as *midrash* – is a personalizing of the Bible's English text, a making of the Bible Defoe/Crusoe's own that is indeed a kind of misreading. Here's an

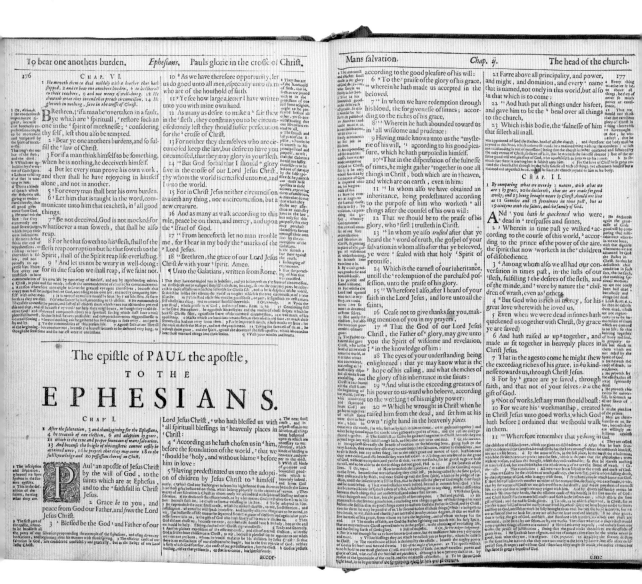

Figure 59 A hybrid 1642 King James Bible with Geneva Bible notes, showing the notes for Ephesians 1: 13, 4, the kind of annotating Bunyan replicated, and absorbed into his own Bible commentaries. Bib.Eng. 1642 C.1.

absolute respect for this life-changing book which is manifesting itself in this practical disrespect. This is the paradox that, of course, animates all translation, not least of the Bible – the radical alteration of originals in the name of aiding access to their reality: a disconcerting oxymoron doubled in the inevitably distortive business of poetic and fictional redoings of the English Bible's inevitable distortions. The poets' and hymn-writers' personalizings and paraphrasings, the novelists' expansions, Milton's filling in of narrative gaps in Genesis (and his Latin manipulations), Bunyan's strong allegorisings, Defoe's hybridisings, Clarissa's meditations, Yorick's sermonising, all the writerly chopping and changing of Bible texts, the repeated cuttings and expandings: they're all, ironically, the aweful textual violence of friends. All abuse.

Mr Shandy rebukes Corporal Trim for making his opening sentence from the sermon sound 'as if the Parson was going to abuse the Apostle'. Roman Catholic Dr Slop agrees, and thinks Trim is right to do so because abusing the text is what Protestant interpreters all do. And, of course, Sterne is merely pointing out plain truths. The sermonising is Protestant and it is textually abusive – like all Bible translating and above all like Sterne's biblicising fiction. The sermon proceeds by inventing 'characters' in little narratives, vignettes, short stories, to illustrate the ways of 'conscience'. Reading the Bible in Yorick's way is inventing, fictionalising, making things up. So this model sermon is also a model of the novel it's in (that's Sterne's usual metatextual way): a fiction of fine KJB using which is, per se, a devoted abusing.[18] And at one with all the aestheticisings of the English Bible which got such new life in the wake of the KJB. It's effectively homage by damage: tesselation, bricolage, cut up. Like Little Gidding's famous interpretative products, their Harmonies of the Gospels, used in the community's hourly Gospel readings, made by cutting up KJB copies and pasting the bits in new desired order on the sheets of new volumes. The scissored Gospels. Charles I got a copy for himself. George Herbert said of his that he was thankful he'd 'lived now to see women's scissors brought to so rare a use as to serve at God's altar.' (The British Library has four copies of these KJB Harmonies or Concordances.) Cutting and pasting: it is what, essentially, all the poets and novelists were doing, and went on doing. A devoted rereading process exemplified perhaps most vividly in Cruden's *Concordance*, that great textual machine for KJB access, constructed by cutting up the text into millions of little bits and reassembling them into their so useful new alphabetical order. A maintaining of the KJB's readerly life by textual surgery. Dissecting the text for textual resurrecting. Theology as, so to say, pathology. Which is wonderfully apt, you might think, for the Bible: a sort of model of the redemption by sacrifice, holocaust, crucifixion, that fills the pages of both Testaments (translated, of course).

Notes

1. Hugh Broughton, *A Censure of the Late Translation for our Churches* (Middleburg, 1611), n.pag.

2. Izaak Walton, *The Lives of John Donne, Sir Henry Wotton, Richard Hooker, George Herbert & Robert Sanderson*, ed. George Saintsbury (Oxford, 1927), p. 353.

3. Lancelot Andrewes, *XCVI Sermons*, ed. William Laud and John Buckeridge (London, 1629), pt 2, p. 143.

4. Ruth Smith, 'The Achievements of Charles Jennens (1700–1773)', *Music & Letters* 70 (1989), 161–90.

5. Wynne E. Baxter, 'Milton Bibles', *Notes & Queries*, 11th series, 3 (1911), 109–10; Michael Leib, 'John Milton', in Rebecca Lemon, Emma Mason, Jonathan Roberts and Christopher Rowland (eds), *The Blackwell Companion to the Bible in English Literature* (Malden, Mass. and Oxford, 2007), pp. 269–85.

6. Johnson owned a polygot Bible, several Greek New Testaments and Latin Bibles. His (Anglican) sermons, mostly delivered at St Margaret's, Westminster, are collected in Jean Hagstrum and James Gray (eds), *Sermons*, The Yale Edition of the Works of Samuel Johnson, Vol. XIV (New Haven and London, 1978). The Introduction tells much about Johnson's Anglican devotion and Bible reading. The Sermons include No. 23, "Where envying and strife is, there is confusion". James iii.16', to commemorate the martyrdom of Charles I – at one of the annual Prayer Book ordained services Johnson thought should never be abolished (it was, in 1859); see pp. 237–47.

7. See John Carey, Translator's Preface to *Christian Doctrine*, Complete Prose Works of John Milton, Vol. VI: *ca 1658–ca 1660*, ed. Maurice Kelley (New Haven and London, 1973), pp. xii–xvi.

8. David Norton, *A History of the Bible as Literature*, 2 vols (Cambridge, 1993), Vol. I: *From Antiquity to 1700*, p. 306.

9. Helen Wilcox (ed.), *The English Poems of George Herbert* (Cambridge, 2007).

10. *The Bodleian Manuscript of George Herbert's Poems: A Facsimile of Tanner 307*, intro. Amy M. Charles and Mario A. Di Cesare (Delmar, N.Y., 1984).

11. 'Religio Laici or a Laymans Faith. A Poem', in Paul Hammond (ed.), *The Poems of John Dryden*, 5 vols (London, 1995), Vol. II, Preface, pp. 86–7; poem, lines 145ff.

12. *A Proposal for Correcting, Improving and Ascertaining the English Tongue; in a Letter to the Most Honourable Robert Earl of Oxford and Mortimer, Lord High Treasurer of Great Britain* (London, 1712), pp. 32–4.

13. Richardson republished the novel's four Meditations, with many more claiming to come also from Clarissa and *Clarissa*, in *Meditations Collected from the Sacred Books; And Adapted to the Different Styles of a Deep Distress; Gloriously Surmounted by Patience, Piety, and Resignation. Being Those Mentioned in the History of Clarissa drawn up by her for her own use. To Each of which is prefixed A Short Historical Account, Connecting it with the Story* (1750).

14. The instant success of the first books of *Tristram Shandy* prompted Sterne to publish *The Sermons of Mr Yorick* (London, 1760) – though without the novel's Assize sermon. All of them are based on KJB texts.

15. J. Ernest Rattenbury, *The Evangelical Doctrines of Charles Wesley's Hymns* (London, 1941), p. 48. Cited by J.R. Watson, 'Eighteenth-Century Hymn-Writers' in Lemon et al. (eds), *The Blackwell Companion to the Bible in English*

*Literatur*e, pp. 329–44, here p. 335. Watson's article discusses the crowd of KJB-inspired Dissenting poets and hymnodists, Watts, Doddridge, William Cowper ('There is a fountain filled with blood / Drawn from EMMANUEL's veins'), John Newton ('O for a closer walk with God'; 'Amazing grace! (how sweet the sound)'), and the Baptist Benjamin Beddome, as well as Charles Wesley.

16. *The Doctrine of the Law and Grace Unfolded and I will pray with the Spirit*, ed. Richard L. Greaves (Oxford, 1976), p.131.

17. One of the many virtues of David Daniell, *The Bible in English: Its History and Influence* (New Haven and London, 2003) is its heroising of Tyndale and its demonstrations of Tyndale's vast donation to the Bible in English. David Crystal, *Begat: The King James Bible and the English Language* (Oxford, 2010), investigates the persistence of Bible phrases into the modern age.

18. Cf. Stephen Prickett, pointing out how Sterne's sermons (though not this one) novelise Biblical characters, inventing dialogue for them, and so forth: 'Introduction' to the Eighteenth Century and Romantics section of Lemon et al. (eds) *The Blackwell Companion to the Bible in English Literature*, pp. 313–28 (here pp. 321–2). It's what Defoe does widely with Bible stories, especially in his 'non-fictional' works: see Valentine Cunningham, 'Daniel Defoe' in ibid., pp. 345–58, and the discussion of the same interpretative process in Bunyan's fictions and Biblical polemics, in Valentine Cunningham, 'Glossing and Glozing: Bunyan and Allegory', in N.H. Keeble (ed.), *John Bunyan: Conventicle and Parnassus: Tercentenary Essays* (Oxford, 1988), pp. 217–40.

CHAP. XVI.

3 Paul willeth the brethren to greete many, 17 and aduiseth to them to take heede of those which cause dissension and offences, 21 and after sundry salutations endeth with praise and thankes to God.

I Commend vnto you Phebe our sister, which is a seruant of the Church which is at Cenchrea:

2 That yee receiue her in the Lord as becommeth Saints, and that yee assist her in whatsoeuer businesse she hath neede of you: for she hath beene a succourer of many, and of my selfe also.

3 Greete Priscilla and Aquila, my helpers in Christ Iesus:

4 (Who haue for my life layd downe their owne neckes: vnto whom not onely I giue thankes, but also all the Churches of the Gentiles.)

5 Likewise greet the Church that is in their house. Salute my welbeloued Epenetus, who is the first fruites of Achaia vnto Christ.

6 Greet Mary, who bestowed much labour on vs.

7 Salute Andronicus and Iunia my kinsmen, and my fellow prisoners, who are of note among the Apostles, who also were in Christ before me.

8 Greete Amplias my beloued in the Lord.

9 Salute Urbane our helper in Christ, and Stachys my beloued.

10 Salute Apelles approued in Christ. Salute them which are of ‖ Aristobulus ‖ houshold.

11 Salute Herodion my kinsman. Greete them that bee of the ‖ houshold of Narcissus, which are in the Lord.

12 Salute Tryphena and Tryphosa, who labour in the Lord. Salute the beloued Persis, which laboured much in the Lord.

13 Salute Rufus chosen in the Lord, and his mother and mine.

14 Salute Asyncritus, Phlegon, Hermas, Patrobas, Hermes, and the brethren which are with them.

15 Salute Philologus and Iulia, Nereus, and his sister, and Olympas, and al the Saints which are with them.

16 Salute one another with an holy kisse. The Churches of Christ salute you.

17 Now I beseech you, brethren, marke them which cause diuisions and offences, contrary to the doctrine which yee haue learned, and auoid them.

18 For they that are such, serue not our Lord Iesus Christ, but their owne belly, and by good wordes and faire speeches deceiue the hearts of the simple.

19 For your obedience is come abroad vnto all men. I am glad therefore on your behalfe: but yet I would haue you wise vnto that which is good, and ‖ simple concerning euill.

20 And the God of peace shall ‖ bruise Satan vnder your feet shortly. The grace of our Lord Iesus Christ be with you. Amen.

21 Timotheus my worke-fellow, and Lucius, and Iason, and Sosipater my kinsmen salute you.

22 I Tertius who wrote this Epistle, salute you in the Lord.

23 Gaius mine hoste, and of the whole Church saluteth you. Erastus the Chamberlaine of the city saluteth you, and Quartus a brother.

24 The grace of our Lord Iesus Christ bee with you all. Amen.

25 Now to him that is of power to stablish you according to my Gospel, and the preaching of Iesus Christ, according to the reuelation of the mystery, which was kept secret since the world began:

26 But now is made manifest, and by the Scriptures of the Prophets according to the commandement of the euerlasting God, made knowen to all nations for the obedience of faith,

27 To God, onely wise, bee glory through Iesus Christ, for euer. Amen.

¶ Written to the Romanes from Corinthus, and sent by Phebe seruant of the Church at Cenchrea.

❧The first Epistle of Paul the Apostle to the Corinthians.

CHAP. I.

After his salutation, and thankesgiuing, 10 he exhorteth them to vnity, and 12 reproueth their dissensions, 18 God destroyeth the wisedome of the wise, 21 by the foolishnes of preaching, and 26 calleth not the wise, mighty, and noble, but 27. 28 the foolish, weake, and men of no accompt.

PAul called to be an Apostle of Iesus Christ, through the will of God, and Sosthenes our brother,

2 Unto the Church of God which is at Corinth, to them that * are sanctified in Christ Iesus, called to be Saints, * with all that in euery place call vpon the Name of Iesus Christ our Lord, both theirs and ours.

3 Grace bee vnto you, and peace from God our Father, and from the Lord Iesus Christ.

4 I thanke my God alwayes on your behalfe, for the grace of God which is giuen you by Iesus Christ,

5 That in euery thing yee are enriched by him, in all vtterance, and in all knowledge:

6 Euen as the Testimony of Christ was confirmed in you.

7 So that yee come behind in no gift: waiting for the † comming of our Lord Iesus Christ,

8 Who shall also confirme you vnto the end, that ye may be blamelesse in the day of our Lord Iesus Christ.

9 * God is faithfull, by whom yee were called vnto the fellowship of his Sonne Iesus Christ our Lord.

10 Now I beseech you by the Name of our Lord Iesus Christ, that yee all speake the same thing, and that there be no diuisions among you: but that yee be perfectly ioyned together in the same minde, and in the same iudgement.

11 For it hath beene declared vnto me of you, my brethren, by them which are of the house of Chloe, that there are contentions among you.

12 Now this I say, that euery one of you saith, I am of Paul, and I of Apollo, and I of Cephas, and I of Christ.

13 Is Christ diuided? was Paul crucified for you? or were yee baptized in the name of Paul?

14 I thanke God that I baptized none of you, but * Crispus and Gaius,

15 Lest any should say, that I had baptized in mine owne name.

16 And I baptized also the houshold of Stephanas: besides, I know not whether I baptized any other.

17 For Christ sent me not to baptize, but to preach the Gospel: * not with wisedome of ‖ wordes, lest the crosse of Christ should be made of none effect.

18 For the preaching of the crosse is to them that perish, foolishnesse: but vnto vs which are saued, it is the * power of God.

19 For it is written, I will destroy the wisedome of the wise, and bring to nothing the * vnderstanding of the prudent.

20 * Where is the wise? where is the Scribe? where is the disputer of this world? hath not God made foolish the wisedome of this world?

21 * For after that, in the wisedome of God, the world by wisedome knew not God, it pleased God by the foolishnesse of preaching to saue them that beleeue.

22 For the * Iewes require a signe, and the Greekes seeke after wisedome.

23 But we preach Christ crucified, vnto the Iewes a stumbling blocke, and vnto the Greekes foolishnesse:

24 But vnto them which are called, both Iewes, and Greekes, Christ the power of God, and the wisedome of God.

25 Because the foolishnesse of God is wiser then men: and the weakenesse of God is stronger then men.

26 For yee see your calling, brethren, that not many wise men after the flesh, not many mighty, not many noble are called.

27 But God hath chosen the foolish things of the world, to confound the wise, and God hath chosen the weake things of the world, to confound the things which are mighty.

28 And base things of the world, and things which are despised, hath God chosen, yea and things which are not, to bring to nought things which are:

29 That no flesh should glory in his presence.

30 But of him are yee in Christ Iesus, who of God is made vnto vs wisedome, and righteousnesse, and sanctification:

Margin notes:

‖ Or, friends.

‖ Or, friends.

‖ Or, harmlesse, ‖ Or, treade.

* Acts 15.9.

* Rom. 1.7.

† Gr. Reuelation.

* 1.Thess. 5.24.

Gr. persons.

* Acts 18.24.

* Acts 18.8.

* 2.Pet. 1.16. Gr. speech.

Rom. 1.16.

* Esa. 29.14. Esa. 33.18.

* Rom. 1.20.

* Rom. 12.38.

31 That according as it is written, *Hee *Iere.9.23.
that glorieth, let him glorie in the Lord.

CHAP. II.

*He declareth that his preaching, & though it bring not ex-
cellencie of speech, or of 4 humane wisdome : yet con-
sisteth in the 4. 5 power of God : and so farre excelleth 6 the wisedome of this world, & 9 humane sence,
as that 14 the naturall man cannot understand it.*

AND I, brethren, when I came to you,
came not with excellencie of speech, or of   *Wisd.1.17.
wisedome, declaring vnto you the testimonie
of God.

2 For I determined not to know any thing
among you, saue Iesus Christ, & him crucified.

3 And I was with you in weakenesse, and in
feare, and in much trembling.

4 And my speech, and my preaching *was   *1.Pet.1.10.
not with enticing words of mans wisedome, but ||Or, perswa-
in demonstration of the Spirit, and of power :   sible.

5 That your faith should not stand in the
wisdome of men, but in the power of God.

6 Howbeit wee speake wisedome among
them that are perfect : yet not the wisedome of
this world, nor of the princes of this world, that
come to nought :

7 But wee speake the wisedome of God in a
mysterie, euen the hidden wisedome which God
ordained before the world vnto our glory.

8 Which none of the Princes of this world
knew : for had they knowen it, they would not
haue crucified the Lord of glory.

9 But as it is written, *Eye hath not seene,   *Esay 64.4.
nor eare heard, neither haue entred into the
heart of man, the things which God hath prepared for them that loue him.

10 But God hath reuealed them vnto vs by
his Sprit : for the Spirit searcheth all things,
yea, the deepe things of God.

11 For what man knoweth the things of a
man, saue the spirit of man which is in him?
Euen so the things of God knoweth no man,
but the Spirit of God.

12 Now wee haue receiued, not the spirit of
the world, but the Spirit which is of God, that
wee might know the things that are freely giuen to vs of God.

13 *Which things also we speake, not in the   *1.Pet.1.16.
wordes which mans wisedome teacheth, but
which the holy Ghost teacheth, comparing spirituall things with spirituall.

14 But the naturall man receiueth not the
things of the Spirit of God, for they are foolishnesse vnto him : neither can hee know them,
because they are spiritually discerned.

15 *But he that is spirituall, iudgeth all   *Prou.27.19.
things, yet he himselfe is iudged of no man. ||Or, discerneth.
                                                    ||Or, discerned.
16 * For who hath knowen the minde of the   *Rom.11.34.
Lord, that he may instruct him? But we haue   esay 40. 13.
the minde of Christ. ||Or, shall.

CHAP. III.

*1 Milke is fit for children. 3 Strife and diuision, argu-
ments of a fleshly minde. 7 He that planteth, and hee
that watereth, is nothing. 9 The Ministers are Gods
fellow-workemen. 11 Christ the onely foundation. 16
Men the Temples of God, which 17 must be kept holy,
19 The wisedome of this world is foolishnesse with God.*

AND I, brethren, could not speake vnto you,
as vnto spirituall, but as vnto carnall, euen
as vnto babes in Christ.

            Doo 4   2 I

7

The King James
Bible in America

Hannibal Hamlin

T HE FIRST COPY OF THE KING JAMES BIBLE on American soil is likely to have arrived on the *Mayflower*. Among those who landed on 11 November 1620 at Cape Cod, in what would become the State of Massachusets, was John Alden, a cooper from Southampton who had been hired as one of the *Mayflower* crew for the voyage. Alden elected to stay in the new colony. As Puritan separatists, the Pilgrims who settled what they named Plymouth naturally brought with them copies of the Geneva Bible. The Geneva was the most popular English translation between its first publication in 1560 and the mid-seventeenth century, but it was favoured especially by Puritans, the more evangelical among English Protestants. As an ordinary sea-farer, Alden may not have shared the religious beliefs of the *Mayflower* passengers, which would explain his choice of Bible. Whatever his beliefs, he brought from England a brand new 1620 edition of the KJB, printed in London by Robert Barker. It survives in the collection of the Pilgrim Hall Museum in Massachusetts (figure 60). (One can only speculate, but a 1599 Geneva Bible also owned by Alden may have been acquired after he joined the Plymouth community.) For the Pilgrims America was understood biblically as the promised land. A decade later, John Winthrop, the first governor of the Massachusetts Bay Colony, preached a sermon while he and the colonists were still on board their ship, *Arbella*, in which he compared the colony they longed to settle to the 'city on a hill' from Jesus' Sermon on the Mount (Matthew 5:14; implicitly likening the colonists to those Jesus named 'the light of the world'). That both John F. Kennedy and Ronald Reagan repeated Winthrop's phrase indicates the lasting sense many Americans still have of the United States as a privileged biblical nation.[1]

Of course, there were Bibles in America before the arrival of the *Mayflower*. The Spanish had been in Florida and Mexico, and the French in New France (what would become Canada) for decades, but their Bibles were almost certainly copies of the Latin Vulgate, and probably exclusively in the hands of priests and Jesuit missionaries. There were also Bibles at the Roanoke colony in Virginia, but since the tiny settlement had disappeared by 1590, long before 1611, these were likely also Geneva Bibles or possibly copies of the Bishops', which in the 1570s was published in several easily portable quarto editions as well as the more cumbersome folios. When the first permanent British colony was established in Jamestown in 1607, the completion of the KJB was still several years away. Copies of the KJB may have been imported shortly after 1611 – it would be interesting to think of a copy in the hands of the Powhatan princess Pocahontas, for instance, who received Christian instruction after she was taken captive in 1613 – but in the absence of documentation, John Alden's copy remains the first known on American soil.

The market for Bibles

Many King James Bibles arrived in America as the colonies grew during the seventeenth and eighteenth centuries, but the English royal monopoly on printing Bibles, only slightly disrupted during the Commonwealth, ensured that they remained an imported commodity. The first Bibles actually printed in America were not in English. In 1663, the Cambridge-educated missionary scholar and 'Apostle to the Indians' John Eliot published his translation of the Bible into the Algonquin dialect of Massachusetts, *Mamusse Wunneetupanatamwe Up-Biblum God* (the New Testament appeared first in 1661, see figure 61). Further editions were published in the following decades. The first Bible in a European language to be printed in America was Christopher Sauer's 1743 Luther Bible in German (Germantown, Pa.). A German immigrant himself, Sauer was an enterprising printer catering to the growing German community in Pennsylvania, at its eighteenth-century height fully one-third of the state's population. He deserves credit for a series of Bible printing firsts: the first American Bible on American-made paper (1763), and the first using American-made type (1776). Large numbers of German Bibles continued to be printed throughout the nineteenth century.

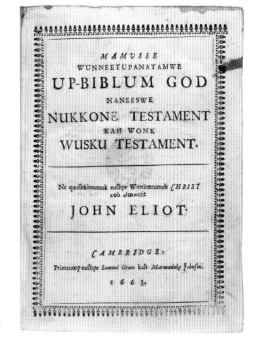

During the years of the American Revolution, imports of Bibles from Britain naturally dried up, due to the British naval blockade. Native demand was met by another intrepid hero of Bible printing, Robert Aitken. A Scots Quaker, Aitken established himself in Philadelphia in the 1770s, printing, among a miscellany of books sacred and secular, *The Pennsylvania Magazine*, edited by Tom Paine, radical revolutionary and author of the immensely popular *Common Sense*. In 1777 Aitken printed, at his own expense, a New Testament in the King James version. A metrical version of the Psalms, the 'Bay Psalm Book' (properly *The Whole Book of Psalms*), notorious for its singularly inept prosody, actually lays claim to being not only the first biblical publication in America but the first book printed in the colonies (Cambridge, Mass., 1640). But metrical psalters are not Bibles. Aitken's New Testament, however modest, in small duodecimo with the unadorned text taking up every inch of the paper, was a breakthrough, the first trickle of a rising flood that would become a tidal wave of American Bibles by the nineteenth century.

In 1782, Aitken printed the first complete American Bible, again at his own expense, despite an urgent petition for support to the Continental Congress. Congress did lend its support, but in spirit rather than cash. The 'Aitken' or 'Revolutionary' Bible (figure 62) was printed with an enthusiastic report on the edition from the Congressional Chaplains, William White and George Duffield (Episcopal and Presbyterian, respectively), as well as a congressional resolution signed by Charles Thomson, Secretary:

> *Resolved*. That the United States in Congress assembled highly approve the pious and laudable undertaking of Mr. Aitken, as subservient to the interest of religion, as well as an instance of the progress of arts in this country, and being satisfied from the above report of his care and accuracy in the execution of the work, they recommend this edition of the Bible to the inhabitants of the United States, and hereby authorize him to publish this Recommendation in the manner he shall think proper.[2]

It is ironic that the 'King James Bible' rather than the 'Authorized Version' is the nickname for this translation preferred in America, since it was only in America that this version was ever officially 'Authorized', though of course by Congress, not the Crown. Aitken tactfully removed any reference to King James and omitted both the dedication to James and the translators' preface. This was Congress's last involvement in Bible publishing, which may be just as well, since Aitken was rewarded for his efforts with bankruptcy. Lack of congressional money was not the sole cause, however, since Aitken's Bibles went on the market, in a remarkably optimistic print run of 10,000 copies, just as British imports recommenced. Better printed and for a cheaper price, British Bibles outsold Aitken's, despite the patriotic resolution of Philadelphia Presbyterians to purchase copies to distribute to the poor. Ever inventive, Aitken proposed to George Washington that Aitken's Bibles would make ideal parting gifts to the discharged soldiers of the Continental Army. General Washington liked the idea, but the suggestion had come too late. Aitken died in 1802 having lost, by his own account, over £3,000 on his Bible venture. It is a curious irony that the first printers of the KJB both in Britain (Robert Barker) and America were financially

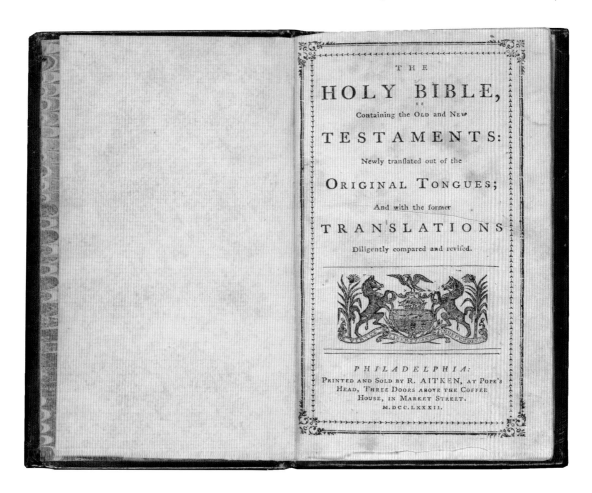

THE
HOLY BIBLE,
Containing the OLD and NEW

TESTAMENTS:
Newly translated out of the

ORIGINAL TONGUES;
And with the former

TRANSLATIONS
Diligently compared and revised.

PHILADELPHIA:
PRINTED AND SOLD BY R. AITKEN, AT POPE'S
HEAD, THREE DOORS ABOVE THE COFFEE
HOUSE, IN MARKET STREET.
M.DCC.LXXXII.

ruined as a result, especially since the Bible made the fortunes of most later publishers.

The many Bible publishers that quickly followed Aitken's lead did, in fact, get extremely rich. Not all American Bibles were King James Bibles; editions of the Catholic Douai–Rheims, for instance, as revised by Richard Challoner (1750) and others later, were printed in increasing numbers as waves of immigrants swelled the American Catholic population. But the KJB nonetheless dominated the market. King James Bibles were printed in the 1790s by Matthew Carey, Isaiah Thomas and Isaac Collins, among others, in Philadelphia, Worcester (Massachusetts) and Trenton (New Jersey). Further editions by other printers appeared in the next decade, produced in towns across the north-east. Carey alone was responsible for over sixty editions between 1801 and 1824, hawked across the country by his indefatigable travelling salesman – another innovation – Mason 'Parson' Weems. Weems is famous for his biography of Washington, which included the legend of honest George owning up to chopping down the cherry tree, but

Figure 62 The 'Aitken' or 'Revolutionary' Bible (1782), the first complete Bible to be printed in America. Library of Congress, Bible Collection, Rare Books and Manuscripts Division.

his business correspondence with Carey establishes him as a homespun humorist on a par (perhaps unintentionally) with Mark Twain and Will Rogers. He helped earn Carey a fortune by selling his Bibles from town to town. He cursed bookbinders (apparently always a headache), saying, 'Never did a Wild Asse's Colt so tremble at thought of a Lion as I do at thought of the Binders'. Yet he wrote to Carey from New York that their plan to publish a new Bible had 'knock'd up just such a dust here among the Printers as would a stone if thrown smack into the center of a Hornet's nest.' Later he compared Bible sales to the marriage market, complaining that some would have 'but one *bible*, as one *Wife*, in their life time … and to have *that* one of the best sort'. Apparently also a skilled fiddle player, he is said to have escaped a beating from highway robbers by charming them with a quick tune.[3]

Weems also recognised that as the number of Bibles on the market grew, it was essential to make sure that Carey's Bibles contained 'more Curious things than were ever seen in any other bible'.[4] Carey thus included engraved illustrations, maps, and other extras like tables of measures and names, chronologies, interpretive notes and essays, as did his competitors. Many quarto-sized Bibles were targeted at families. Genealogical information, including births, marriages and deaths, had been written onto the blank leaves of printed Bibles since the sixteenth century; recognising this practice, nineteenth-century publishers began to include preprinted Family Record pages. Some Bibles later in the century even included pages into which family photographs could be inserted. Annotation and illustration increased to the point where they threatened to overwhelm the biblical text. 'Scott's Bible' (published originally in England by Revd Thomas Scott) was printed in as many as five volumes with more commentary on the page than text. Desperate to make their Bibles stand out from the crowd, publishers constantly sought out new gimmicks. Bibles promised to be 'Self-Interpreting' (New York: Hodge & Campbell, 1792) and self-pronouncing (*The Phonotypic Bible* [Bath: I. Pitman; Boston: Andrews & Boyle, 1845] and *The Holman New Self-pronouncing Sunday-school Teacher's Bible* [Philadelphia: A.J. Holman & Co., *c.* 1898]), and one *Collateral Bible* advertised that 'all the corresponding texts are brought together into one view, and arranged in a familiar and easy manner' (Philadelphia, S.F. Bradford; New York, E. Bliss & E. White, 1826–28). The comfortingly named *Village Testament* (New York: Conner & Cooke, 1833) was 'adapted to Bible classes and Sunday schools' by Revd William Patton. *The Comprehensive Bible* (Hartford, Conn.: Andrus & Judd, 1836), naturally, had it all: 'the Old and New Testaments according to the authorized version, with the various readings and marginal notes usually printed therewith, a general introduction … parallel passages … philological and explanatory

Figure 63 The story of Jonah, as depicted in the lavishly illustrated Harper's *Illuminated Bible*, published in the 1840s. Library of Congress, Bible Collection, Rare Books and Manuscripts Division.

JONAH CAST FORTH FROM THE WHALE.

9 And he said unto them, I *am* a Hebrew;
and I fear ‖the LORD, the God of heaven,
[o]which hath made the sea and the dry *land*.
10 Then were the men †exceedingly afraid,
and said unto him, Why hast thou done this?
For the men knew that he fled from the
presence of the LORD, because he had told
them.
11 ¶ Then said they unto him, What shall
we do unto thee, that the sea †may be calm
unto us? for the sea ‖†wrought, and was
tempestuous.
12 And he said unto them, [p]Take me up,
and cast me forth into the sea; so shall the
sea be calm unto you: for I know that for
my sake this great tempest *is* upon you.
13 Nevertheless the men †rowed hard to
bring *it* to the land; [q]but they could not: for
the sea wrought, and was tempestuous against
them.
14 Wherefore they cried unto the LORD,
and said, We beseech thee, O LORD, we beseech thee, let us not perish for this man's
life, and [r]lay not upon us innocent blood:
for thou, O LORD, [s]hast done as it pleased
thee.
15 So they took up Jonah, and cast him
forth into the sea: [t]and the sea †ceased from
her raging.
16 Then the men [u]feared the LORD exceedingly, and †offered a sacrifice unto the LORD,
and made vows.

B.C. cir. 862.

‖ Or, *JEHOVAH*.
o Ps. 146, 6. Acts 17, 24.
† Heb. *with great fear.*
† Heb. *may be silent from us.*
‖ Or, *grew more and more tempestuous.*
† Heb. *went.*
p John 11, 50.
† Heb. *digged.*
q Prov. 21, 30.
r Deut. 21, 8.
s Ps. 115, 3.
t Ps. 89, 9. Luke 8, 24.
† Heb. *stood.*
u Mark 4, 41. Acts 5, 11.
† Heb. *sacrificed a sacrifice unto the* LORD, *and vowed vows.*

x Matt. 12, 40, & 16, 4. Luke 11, 30.
† Heb. *bowels.*
a Ps. 120, 1, & 130, 1, & 142, 1. Lam. 3, 55, 56.
‖ Or, *out of mine affliction.*
b Ps. 65, 2.
‖ Or, *the grave*, Isai. 14, 9.
c Ps. 88, 6.
† Heb. *heart.*
d Ps. 42, 7.
e Ps. 31, 22.
f 1 Kings 8, 38.
g Ps. 69, 1. Lam. 3, 54.
† Heb. *cuttings off.*
h Ps. 16, 10.
‖ Or, *the pit.*

17 ¶ Now the LORD had prepared a great
fish to swallow up Jonah. And [x]Jonah was
in the †belly of the fish three days and three
nights.

CHAPTER II.

1 The prayer of Jonah. 10 He is delivered from the fish.

THEN Jonah prayed unto the
LORD his God out of the fish's
belly,
2 And said, I [a]cried ‖by reason
of mine affliction unto the LORD,
[b]and he heard me; out of the
belly of ‖hell cried I, *and* thou heardest my
voice.

3 [c]For thou hadst
cast me into the deep,
in the †midst of the
seas; and the floods
compassed me about:
[d]all thy billows and
thy waves passed over
me.
4 [e]Then I said, I am
cast out of thy sight;
yet I will look again [f]toward thy holy temple.
5 The [g]waters compassed me about, *even* to
the soul: the depth closed me round about,
the weeds were wrapped about my head.
6 I went down to the †bottoms of the
mountains; the earth with her bars *was* about
me for ever: yet hast thou brought up my
life [h]from ‖corruption, O LORD my God.

notes.' *The Illustrated Polyglot Bible* (Philadelphia, 1869) seems at first to have been targeted indecisively at families that were both illiterate and learned, but its title is misleading: the many American 'polyglots' were usually entirely in English. Even new printing techniques like stereotyping and phonotype were advertised on title pages, though how this might have benefited the reader was anybody's guess.

American illustrated Bibles culminated in *The Illuminated Bible*, published by Harper & Brothers in New York in the 1840s (figure 63). The history of the Bible in America cannot be wholly detached from its history in Britain, and the Harpers may have been influenced by publications like the lavish four-volume *Holy Bible, embellished by the most eminent British artists* (London: T. Cadell, 1816–24). Harpers' *Illuminated Bible* featured not just a wealth of illustration, however (1,600 in all, with some copies including colour); these were printed with the new technology of electrotyping, allowing large print runs without sacrificing high-quality images, and making it possible for the first time to intersperse text and images on the page. Harper & Brothers also printed the Bible in fifty-four instalments at a time when serial publication was all the rage: Dickens's *Pickwick Papers*, *Nicholas Nickleby* and *The Old Curiosity Shop*, for instance, had appeared in instalments between 1836 and 1841, and readers on both sides of the Atlantic had waited desperately for news of the fate of *The Old Curiosity Shop*'s Little Nell. Harpers' *Illuminated Bible* shared the sentimental sensibility of Dickens's and other popular novels. The illustrations featured women more than men, captured at moments of great emotional distress. Even the dramatic image of Jonah being gobbled up by a curiously toothy whale is framed, gratuitously, by two robed female figures. The title page of the New Testament features a puzzling image that looks at first like a Madonna and child, surrounded by perhaps Elizabeth and John the Baptist. This would be a logical image for the opening of the New Testament, but what puzzles is that the infant Jesus seems dead. On closer inspection, the subject turns out to be 'Rachel weeping for her children', the lines from Jeremiah quoted in the account of the Slaughter of the Innocents, an emotion-packed event that naturally involved many weeping mothers and terrified children. For whichever of its many features, *The Illuminated Bible* was a great success, selling out quickly and justifying additional printings.

The KJB in American literature

By the mid-nineteenth century, King James Bibles (principally, but among others) were being printed in America in astonishing numbers. 3,415 different editions of Bibles and New Testaments were printed in America between 1777 and 1850, three times as many as in Britain over the same period. And print runs were colossal. The American Bible Society, founded in 1816, alone accounted for a million Bibles a year by the 1860s, all KJB.[5] One result of the biblical saturation of the country – though one might also argue it was the demand that called for the supply – was that American culture was a biblical culture. American literature, for example, was steeped in the Bible. This was true even in earlier (British) America, as evidenced by the wealth of biblical allusion and meditation in the poems of Edward Taylor, Anne Bradstreet and Phillis Wheatley (the first two British-born, the latter African), as well as biblical adaptations like Michael Wigglesworth's popular *Day of Doom* (1662), a verse recounting of Revelation. Two of America's major poets, Walt Whitman and Emily Dickinson, though as different as can be imagined in most ways, both wrote under the influence of the KJB. Whitman's vast *Leaves of Grass* (1855), which he himself described as a 'New American Bible', took its prose-poetic line, as Blake had before him, from the rhythmic prose of Isaiah and other Old Testament prophets:

> Solitary at midnight in my back yard, my thoughts gone from me a long
>   while,
> Walking the old hills of Judaea with the beautiful gentle God by my side,
> Speeding through space, speeding through heaven and the stars,
> Speeding amid the seven satellites and the broad ring, and the diameter
>   of eighty thousand miles,
> Speeding with tail'd meteors, throwing fire-balls like the rest,
> Carrying the crescent child that carries its own full mother in its belly,
> Storming, enjoying, planning, loving, cautioning,
> Backing and filling, appearing and disappearing,
> I tread day and night such roads.[6]

Emily Dickinson's contrastingly tiny lyrics took their verse forms from Protestant hymnody, but their content (often) from her reading of the Bible, though her reading tended to be independent and boldly revisionary:

> Abraham to kill him
> Was distinctly told –
> Isaac was an Urchin –
> Abraham was old –
>
> Not a hesitation –
> Abraham complied –
> Flattered by Obeisance
> Tyranny demurred –

> Isaac – to his children
> Lived to tell the tale –
> Moral – with a Mastiff
> Manners may prevail.[7]

Many of Whitman's and Dickinson's contemporaries – Ralph
Waldo Emerson, Nathaniel Hawthorne, Henry David Thoreau, Henry
Wadsworth Longfellow – also responded to or wrestled with the Bible
in their writing.

Perhaps the greatest American novel of the nineteenth century,
Herman Melville's *Moby-Dick*, is a thoroughly, if often heretically, biblical
work. Melville's protagonist famously introduces himself in the novel's
first line – 'Call me Ishmael' – with a name that instantly recalls the
Bible. Never a popular American biblical name, 'Ishmael' refers to just
one person: Abraham's first son, born of Hagar, the servant of his infertile
wife, Sarah. After Sarah herself bears a son, Isaac, Hagar and Ishmael
are, at Sarah's insistence, driven out into the desert. Surprisingly, however,
an angel arrives to save them, announcing that, although it is Isaac whose
line will become Israel, Ishmael too will found a great nation, traditionally
understood to be the Arabs, and by Muslims the nation of Islam. Like
the biblical Ishmael, Melville's is a wanderer and an outcast, though the
desert he travels on is the sea rather than sand. An even stranger biblical
name in *Moby-Dick* is Captain Ahab's, since Ahab is the King of Israel
who 'did evil in the sight of the Lord above all that were before him' (1
Kings 16:30). Melville's naming is appropriate – the Old Testament Ahab
built himself a house made of ivory, while the novel's Ahab has an ivory
leg, ivory being produced by sperm whales as well as elephants (1 Kings
22:39). *Moby-Dick* is rich in biblical allusions, but the most pervasive
ones are to the book of Jonah. An early chapter features the sermon of
Father Mapple, delivered from a shiplike pulpit (strikingly illustrated by
Rockwell Kent in a 1930 edition), instructing the Nantucket whaling
community on the lessons of Jonah. A later chapter, 'Jonah Historically
Regarded', parodies the popular contemporary historical interpretation
of the Bible. The obvious candidate for the 'Jonah' of the *Pequod* is its
mad captain, Ahab. As a result of Ahab's obsession with hunting the
white whale, the *Pequod* and its crew are wrecked, all perishing except
one, whose survival is described in words taken from Job: 'And I alone
am escaped to tell thee' (1:15–19). It is no coincidence that, like Jonah,
the book of Job refers to the whale, Leviathan, whom God in his power
can draw up 'with a hook' (41:1).

The biblical strain in American literature can be heard from its
earliest days to modern times. The prophetic lines of Whitman were
adapted to the Beat Generation by Allen Ginsberg in his hip jer-

emiad *Howl*. Emily Dickinson's metaphysical lyrics influenced the biblically allusive poems of Elizabeth Bishop. The Bible (always the KJB) shaped both the style and the plots of novels, including William Faulkner's *Absalom, Absalom*, John Steinbeck's *The Grapes of Wrath*, Cormac McCarthy's *Blood Meridian* and Marilynne Robinson's *Gilead*. The biblical influence on the African-American literary tradition is especially strong, as evidenced by the novels of Toni Morrison and Edward P. Jones. Introduced to African slaves partly as a means of maintaining discipline (emphasising Paul's injunctions in Colossians, Ephesians and Timothy on obeying earthly masters), the Bible was quickly appropriated by the slaves and read as a consolation for the oppressed and as a promise of emancipation and redemption. African-American 'spirituals' (from Colossians 3:16, 'Let the word of Christ dwell in you richly in all wisdom; teaching and admonishing one another in psalms and hymns and spiritual songs, singing with grace in your hearts to the Lord') were rooted in the language and imagery of the KJB: 'Go down, Moses', 'There is a balm in Gilead', 'Deep River', 'Wrestle on, Jacob'.

During the American Civil War, both Southern slaveholders and Northern abolitionists found the justification for their beliefs in the Bible. Abraham Lincoln's Gettysburg Address is biblically allusive in its language and style, as in the antiquated 'four score and seven years' or the phrase 'shall not perish' (taken from John 3:16).[8] On the opposite side were works like Josiah Priest's *Bible Defence of Slavery* (Glasgow, Ky., 1853), which argued that Africans, as the descendants of Noah's cursed son Ham, were slaves by divine decree. Legend has it that Lincoln attributed the cause of the Civil War to a biblically saturated novel, Harriet Beecher Stowe's *Uncle Tom's Cabin*. The novel was an astonishing bestseller, and not only in America. In Britain it sold well over a million copies in its first five years, and it was translated into French, German, Spanish, Italian, Swedish, Russian, and even Finnish, Armenian, Hindi and Chinese.[9] The eponymous Uncle Tom is devoted to his Bible, as is the saintly child Little Eva, and Stowe's chapter titles are often drawn from biblical verses: 'The grass withereth – the flower fadeth' (ch. 22, from Isaiah 40:8), or 'The dark places of the earth are full of the habitations of cruelty' (ch. 32, from Psalm 74).[10] The novel galvanised anti-slavery feeling; a popular story has it that Lincoln, on meeting Stowe, said 'So this is the little lady who made this big war'. The story may not be true, but the statement might be accurate. It is true, on the other hand, that at the end of the Civil War, African Americans in Baltimore presented Lincoln with a pulpit edition of the KJB, bound in purple velvet, gold-detailed, with an embossed cover design representing the Emancipation. The cost was $580.75, equivalent to almost $8,000 today.[11]

Rhetorical traditions

In addition to influencing African-American literature, the KJB also shaped the language of African-American preaching and public oratory (though, as Lincoln's speeches show, it influenced non-African-American rhetorical traditions as well).[12] In his speech 'What to the Slave is the Fourth of July' (1852), Frederick Douglass quoted Isaiah ('"The arm of the Lord is not shortened", and the doom of slavery is certain'), as well as Psalm 137 ('By the rivers of Babylon, there we sat down'), likening the African-American slaves to the Israelites in exile.[13] In his most famous speech, 'I Have a Dream', delivered on the steps of the Lincoln Memorial in 1963, Martin Luther King (figure 64) used to powerful effect the Old Testament rhetorical figure of anaphora, and began by alluding to Lincoln's Gettysburg Address with the same biblical language of time: 'five score years ago'. A particular powerful biblical borrowing was King's statement that 'we will not be satisfied until "justice rolls down like waters, and righteousness like a mighty stream".'[14] The phrase is from Amos 5:24. (The translation is the American Standard Version [ASV, 1901]; the only difference from the KJB in this passage is the word 'justice', as opposed to 'judgment').

In 2009, from the steps of the Capitol at the opposite end of the Washington Mall from the Lincoln Memorial, the Revd Joseph Lowery in turn echoed Martin Luther King's famous speech. Lowery's benediction at the inauguration of President Barack Obama, the first African-American president and thus in part the realisation of King's dream, wove King's lines from Amos together with adaptations of Isaiah (2:4, swords into ploughshares) and Jonah (4:6, sitting under the gourd):

> With your hands of power and your heart of love, help us then, now, Lord, to work for that day when nations shall not lift up sword against nation, when tanks will be beaten into tractors, when every man and every woman shall sit under his or her own vine and fig tree and none shall be afraid, when justice will roll down like waters and righteousness as a mighty stream.[15]

Minutes earlier, Barack Obama had himself quoted the King James version of 1 Corinthians 13, saying that though it was a young nation, it was time for America to 'set aside childish things'.[16] Whatever the achievements and failings of the King James translators, as churchmen they clearly had a keen sense of the high style of spoken English, which is one reason politicians still turn to its elevated diction and poetic cadences when they want to speak with authority.

In the twentieth and twenty-first centuries, the position of the King James Bible in America has been changing. Many churches still use it, and it is the basis for some of the most important modern translations.

Figure 64 Revd Martin Luther King delivers his address at the Lincoln Memorial in Washington DC, during the civil rights March on Washington, 28 August 1963. Reproduction Number: LC-DIG-ppmsca-19406. Courtesy Library of Congress.

Just as the King James translators incorporated without change much of the language of Tyndale and Coverdale (the Great Bible is the source of 'righteousness as a mighty stream'), so the American Standard translators left unchanged much of the King James, as indeed did its subsequent revision, the Revised Standard Version (RSV) of 1952. Luther Weigle, the RSV committee chair, wrote that the translation was a 'revision which seeks to preserve all that is best in the English Bible as it has been known and used throughout the years', and that the translators had striven to maintain 'those qualities which have given the King James Version a supreme place in English literature'.[17] The history of the influence of the English Bible is thus a continuous tradition from Tyndale and Coverdale, through the KJB, to the modern revisions of the ASV and RSV.

Despite the long American preference for the British KJB, however, the history of Bible translation in America is distinctly different from that of Britain. The Revised Standard Version is a notable case in point. American Bible scholars were largely excluded from involvement in the English Revised Version (1885), though they had initially been invited to participate. Dissatisfied with the results of the British translators, American scholars produced in the ASV and RSV their own major revisions of the KJB. Ironically, the American RSV became the longest-respected twentieth-century Bible translation in Britain.[18] One concern of American translators was rendering the Bible in a distinctively American English. They were anticipated in this by the lexicographer Noah Webster, who produced his own revision of the KJB in 1833. As in his more successful dictionary, the goal of Webster's Bible was to update the archaic language of the 1611 translation and to convert English into American idioms. Webster's revision proved timid and inconsistent, however, and had little impact. More radical in its attempt to Americanise was the 1848 New Testament of Andrew Comstock, in 'Komstok's Purfekt Alfabet', but Comstock's translation broke from the KJB entirely.[19] A number of other American Bible translations have been produced by individual scholars, including the first complete Bible translated anywhere by a woman, Julia Evelina Smith (later Parker, after she married), in 1876, as well as more recent translations by Richmond Lattimore, Robert Alter, Everett Fox and Willis Barnstone.

The KJB in popular culture

The readers still holding on firmly to the KJB are of several sorts. There are those who love the long cultural traditions associated with the Bible that dominated English-speaking Christianity for centuries. There are also those who argue that, despite the advances in linguistic and textual scholarship and the discovery of ancient manuscripts at Qumran and Nag Hammadi, the KJB, for all its infelicities, is still the best English Bible available.[20] A peculiarly American backlash against new translations has spawned a 'King James Only' movement with some peculiar consequences. This is perhaps just the latest development of the fundamentalist longing to preserve the textual and theological integrity of the Bible against all threats, dating back to resistance against the German Higher Criticism of the nineteenth century. The anti-intellectualism of the King James Onlyists is particularly fierce, however: a bumper sticker available online reads, 'If it ain't King James, it ain't the Bible', and one North Carolina church hosts an annual Halloween book burning, casting into the flames all Bibles other than the King James.[21] The history of the Bible in English has taken some odd turns since Wyclif and Tyndale.

Yet the contemporary Bible reader does face a vast number of alternative translations, in a bewildering array of formats. Between 1945 and 1990, David Daniell notes, 'over twelve hundred new translations into English of the Bible, or parts of it, were made from the original Hebrew and Greek'.[22] The large majority of these are American, including the ASV quoted by King and Lowery, the RSV (1952), the *New World Translation of the Holy Scriptures* (1961), the *New American Bible* (1970), the *Good News Bible* (1976), the New International Version (1978), the *Jewish Publication Society Tanakh* (1985), the New Revised Standard Version (1989), the Contemporary English Version (1995), *The Message* (2002), the *Holman Christian Standard Bible* (2004), the New English Translation (2005), and the *Orthodox Study Bible* (2008), among others. Even the King James version has spawned a New King James Version (1982) and a 21st Century King James Version (1994), as well as revisions under other titles like the American and Revised Standard Versions. As Bible historian Paul Gutjahr puts it, the KJB has, after several centuries, been dethroned, but no other has been able to take the crown; the KJB is now one translation among a democracy of English Bibles.[23]

Despite the loss of its predominant position in the American Bible market, the KJB seems to retain the cultural authority it gained through publication in staggering numbers of copies, recitation in church and home, and in its presence in American literary and political culture. The KJB's influence also extends to American popular culture. In *A Charlie Brown Christmas*, seen by millions of Americans every year since its first broadcast in 1965, Linus (read by child-actor Chris Shea, aged seven) explains the meaning of Christmas by reciting Luke's Nativity account in the KJB. The Jamaican Rastafarian and Reggae star Bob Marley read the KJB regularly, sang its language in songs like 'Exodus' and 'Wings of a Dove', and was buried with one in his hand. 'Exodus' transposes the story of Moses, Israel and Egypt to the Rastafarian Jamaica, calling for God to send them another Moses. 'Wings of a Dove' takes its title and lyrics from Psalm 55.

Marley also owned a copy of the Gideon Bible, a form of the KJB that has a significant place in American and international culture. Formed in 1899 in Wisconsin, the Gideons took on the mission of providing King James Bibles to travellers. They have since distributed over 1.5 billion copies, and the Gideon Bible has become a familiar feature of hotel rooms across America and the world. Gideon Bibles are mentioned in songs by the Beatles ('Rocky Racoon'), Frank Zappa ('Room Service'), Jimmy Buffett ('This Hotel Room'), and Loudon Wainright III ('Motel Blues'). Gideon Bibles also appear in the films *Mission Impossible* (1996) and *Memento* (2000). In the 2010 film *The Book of Eli*, starring Denzel Washington and Gary Oldman, survivors of a nuclear apocalypse battle over the single surviving copy of the KJB (in this case, not a Gideon), which is seen as the key to restoring civilisation. Perhaps the most sublime use of the KJB in modern times was the recitation of the opening of Genesis by astronauts Frank Borman, James Lovell and William Andres aboard Apollo 8 as they watched the Earthrise while orbiting the Moon in 1968 (figure 65). According to *TVGuide* (10–16 May 1969), the live television broadcast on Christmas Eve was watched by a quarter of the people on the Earth, one billion people in sixty-four countries. One story tells of a Japanese reporter covering the Apollo 8 flight in Houston who called NASA Public Affairs to request a copy of the speech the astronauts were reading. The NASA official told the reporter to get the book out of his hotel room drawer and turn to page one. The reporter found the Gideon Bible with the text of Genesis and commented, 'NASA Public Affairs is very efficient – they had a mission transcript waiting in my hotel room.'[24] The US Postal Service issued a stamp commemorating the event, featuring the astronauts' photograph with the words 'In the beginning, God...' To date, no other English Bible translation has been read from outer space.

Figure 65 'Earthrise': in a live television broadcast on Christmas Eve 1968, astronauts on board Apollo 8 read from the opening of the book of Genesis in the King James translation. © NASA.

Notes

1. Kennedy repeated the phrase in a speech to the General Court of Massachusetts on 9 January 1961, arguing that the metaphor still applied, and that the eyes of the world were upon Massachusetts and America. Reagan used the same biblical figure in his speech accepting the Republican nomination for president in 1984.

2. *The Holy Bible* (Philadelphia, 1782). Interestingly, Charles Thomson himself was later responsible for an important translation of the Bible, the first anywhere in English from the Greek Septuagint. It was printed in Philadelphia in 1808 by Jane Aitken, the daughter of Robert.

3. Paul C. Gutjahr, *An American Bible: A History of the Good Book in the United States, 1777–1880* (Stanford, Calif., 1999), pp. 24–7.

4. Ibid., p. 27.

5. David Daniell, *The Bible in English: Its History and Influence* (New Haven and London, 2003), p. 635.

6. Walt Whitman, 'Song of Myself', *Leaves of Grass* (1891), *Complete Poetry and Collected Prose* (New York, 1982), p. 223.

7. Emily Dickinson, 'Abraham to kill him' (1317), *The Complete Poems of Emily Dickinson*, ed. Thomas H. Johnson (Boston and Toronto, 1951, repr. 1960), pp. 571–2.

8. www.ourdocuments.gov/doc.php?flash=old&doc=36 (accessed 6 August 2010). The Gettysburg Address is an unusually short speech. Lincoln's longer speeches, at his Inaugurations for instance, incorporate many more biblical allusions and influences.

9. Daniell, *The Bible in English*, p. 714; Gutjahr, *An American Bible*, p. 159; Tao Jie, '*Uncle Tom's Cabin*: The First American Novel Translated into Chinese', *Prospects* 18 (1993), 517–34.

10. Daniell, *The Bible in English*, pp. 715–16.

11. Nathan O. Hatch and Mark Noll (eds), *The Bible in America: Essays in Cultural History* (Oxford and New York, 1982), Introduction, p. 5. According to the online calculator at www.westegg.com/inflation (accessed 6 August 2010), the cost would have been equivalent to $7,865.99 in 2009.

12. Further examples of biblical political language include Franklin Delano Roosevelt, who said in his first Inauguration speech that America was 'stricken by no plague of locusts' (i.e. the Great Depression wasn't a divine punishment), and John F. Kennedy, who quoted Isaiah 58:6 and Romans 12:12 (both KJB) in his Inauguration speech. Both speeches are accessible at *The American Presidency Project*, www.presidency.ucsb.edu/inaugurals.php (accessed 6 August 2010).

13. *TeachingAmericanHistory.org*, http://teachingamericanhistory.org/library/index.asp?document=162 (accessed 6 August 2010).

14. *TeachingAmericanHistory.org*, http://teachingamericanhistory.org/library/index.asp?document=40 (accessed 6 August 2010).

15. *The Washington Post*, http://voices.washingtonpost.com/inauguration-watch/2009/01/transcript_of_rev_lowerys_inau.html (accessed 6 August 2010).

16. *The White House Blog*, www.whitehouse.gov/blog/inaugural-address/ (accessed 6 August 2010).

17. Daniell, *The Bible in English*, pp. 738–9.

18. Ibid., p. 741.

19. Harold P. Scanlin, 'Bible Translation by American Individuals', in Ernest S. Frerichs (ed.), *The Bible and Bibles in America* (Atlanta, Ga., 1988), pp. 43–82, here p. 50.

20. The best arguments for the merits of the KJB as a translation are by Gerald Hammond, *The Making of the English Bible* (Manchester, 1982), and Robert Alter, 'The Glories and Glitches of the King James Bible: Ecclesiastes as Test Case', in Hannibal Hamlin and Norman W. Jones (eds), *The King James Bible after Four Hundred Years: Literary, Linguistic, and Cultural Influences* (Cambridge, 2010), pp. 45–58.

21. See the website for Amazing Grace Baptist Church (Canton, N.C.) (accessed 6 August 2010), www.amazinggracebaptistchurchkjv.com/index.html.

22. Daniell, *The Bible in English*, p. 764.

23. Gutjahr, 'From Monarchy to Democracy: The Dethroning of the King James Bible in the United States', in Hamlin and Jones (eds), *The King James Bible after Four Hundred Years*, pp. 164–78.

24. The story of the Japanese reporter may be apocryphal (it appears online at www.astronautix.com/flights/apollo8.htm; accessed 6 August 2010), but a Gideon Bible does have a documented place in the story, since the idea to read from Genesis apparently came from Simon Bourgin, who consulted a Gideon Bible he stole from a hotel room. See Robert Zimmerman, *Genesis: The Story of Apollo 8* (New York, 1998), pp. 197–202.

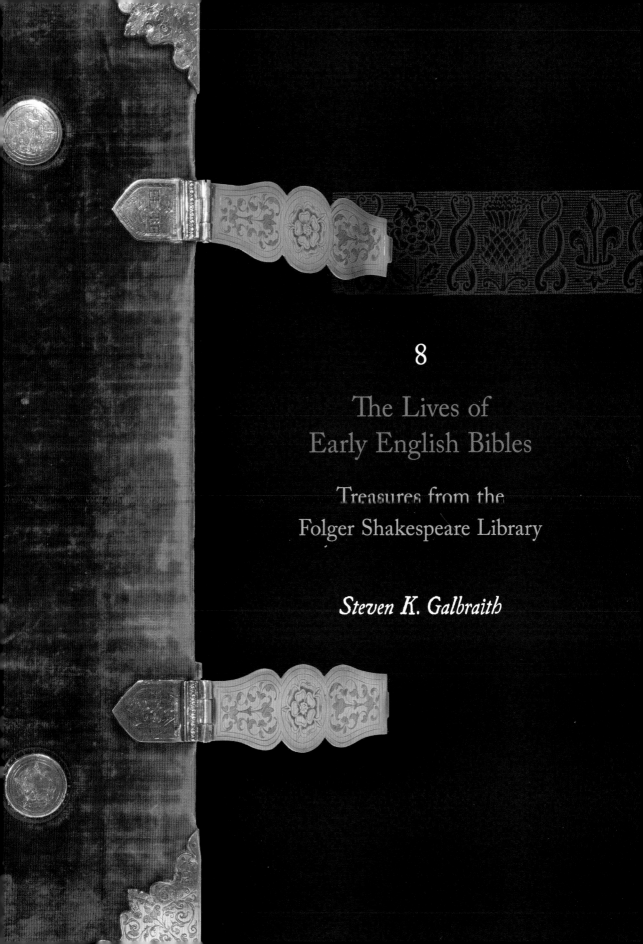

8

The Lives of
Early English Bibles

Treasures from the
Folger Shakespeare Library

Steven K. Galbraith

THE FOLGER SHAKESPEARE LIBRARY in Washington DC opened its doors on 23 April 1932, a gift from Henry and Emily Jordan Folger to the American nation and, in turn, to the world. Although Shakespeare was originally central to the Folgers' collecting, over the decades the scope of the library expanded to printed books, art, manuscripts, and other artefacts that document more completely the early modern era in Britain and Continental Europe. At the heart of the Folger Library is the third largest collection of books printed in England or in the English language from 1475 to 1640, behind only the British Library and the Bodleian Library in Oxford.

The 400th anniversary of the publication of the King James Bible provides the opportunity for the Folger Shakespeare Library to highlight some of its treasures related to the evolution of the English Bible and to the creation and afterlife of the KJB. These treasures not only hold great value as historic artefacts, but also tell compelling stories about the men and women who interacted with them. Like many of the Bibles that preceded it, the KJB first appeared in the form of a large folio book and thereafter was produced in a variety of forms for a variety of readers. Through an examination of the physical properties of these books, we may begin to reconstruct their lives and those of their owners. Often we can document how the books were used, and trace how they travelled from generation to generation. Ultimately we begin to understand that, in addition to being holy books, Bibles were works of art, sites for recording family histories, and gifts both familial and royal. From a trio of elegant royal Bibles, to a travel-sized book of Psalms, to a gift of affection from a father to his daughter, these treasures survive as historical artefacts that shed light on the various lives of English Bibles during the early modern period and beyond.

Elizabeth I's Bishops' Bible

Many of the Folger's most prized artefacts are related to Elizabeth, including a copy of the first edition of the Bishops' Bible (1568) that was probably the very copy presented to Queen Elizabeth I by Matthew Parker, Archbishop of Canterbury.[1] Parker, who initiated and organised

Figure 66 *pp. 182–183* The binding of Queen Elizabeth I's copy of the Bishops' Bible (1568). Folger Shakespeare Library.

Figure 67 *right* A coloured engraved portrait of William Cecil from Queen Elizabeth I's copy of the Bishops' Bible. Cecil delivered the gift bible on behalf of Archbishop Matthew Parker, who was too unhealthy to travel. Folger Shakespeare Library.

¶ The argument of the firſt pſalme.

¶ The firſt pſalme ſeemeth to be a preface vnto the reſidue. It declareth that the iuſt man only hath the true felicitie in this woꝛlde, whoſe delight is wholly in practiſing the lawe of God. As foꝛ the vngodly man, although he ſeeme foꝛ a tyme to pꝛoſper and to floꝛiſhe, yet his ende is very miſerable and wꝛetched.

1 Leſſed is the man that walketh not in the counſell of the vngodly : noꝛ ſtandeth in the way of ſinners, noꝛ ſitteth in the ſeate of the ſcoꝛnefull.

2 But his delight [is] in the lawe of God : and in [God] his lawe exerciſeth him ſelfe day and night.

3 And he ſhalbe lyke a tree planted " by the waters ſyde, that bꝛyngeth fooꝛth her fruite in due ſeaſon : and whoſe leafe wy= thereth not, foꝛ whatſoeuer he doth (a) it ſhall pꝛoſper.

4 [As foꝛ] the vngodly [it is] not ſo [with them :] but they [are] like the chaffe which the winde ſcattereth abꝛode.

5 Therefoꝛe the vngodly ſhall not [be able to] " ſtande in the iudgement : neither the ſinners in the congregation of the righteous.

6 Foꝛ God (b) knoweth the way of the righteous : and the way of the vngodly ſhall periſhe.

¶ The argument of the. ij. pſalme.

¶ All conſpiracies of the Gentiles, Iewes, Pꝛinces, Magiſtrates, and Kinges, againſt Chꝛiſte, be but altogether vayne, foꝛ God hath marueylouſly appointed hym Loꝛde and king ouer al people, to the vtter confuſion of his aduerſaries. In exhortation to kinges and Iudges foꝛ to be learned, foꝛ to ſerue God, and foꝛ to receaue his ſonne Chꝛiſte : foꝛ happy are they that truſt in hym.

1 Why do the Heathen ſo furiouſly rage together: and why do the people imagine a vayne thing?

2 The kynges of the earth ſtande vp : and the rulers take counſell together againſt god, and againſt his annointed.

3 (a) Let vs bꝛeake [ſay they] their bondes a ſunder : and caſt away their coꝛdes from vs.

4 He that dwelleth in heauen wyll laugh them to ſcoꝛne : the Loꝛde wyll haue them in deriſion.

5 Then wyll he ſpeake vnto them in his wꝛath : and he wyll aſtonie them with feare in his ſoꝛe diſpleaſure.

6 [Saying] (b) euen I haue annointed [him] my kyng : vpon my holy hyll of Sion.

7 I wyll declare the decree, God ſayde

vnto me : thou art my ſonne, this day I haue begotten thee.

8 Deſire of me, and I wyll geue thee the heathen foꝛ thyne inheritaunce : and the vttermoſt partes of the earth foꝛ thy poſſeſſion.

9 Thou ſhalt bꝛuiſe them with a rod of iron : and bꝛeake them in peeces like a potters veſſell.

10 Wherfoꝛe be you nowe wel aduiſed O ye kinges : be you learned ye [that are] iudges of the earth.

11 Serue ye God in feare : and reioyce ye with a trembling.

12 Kiſſe ye the ſonne leſt that he be an= grye, and [ſo] ye periſhe [from] the (c) way, if his wꝛath be neuer ſo litle kind= led : bleſſed are all they that put their truſt in hym.

A (ij)   The

the translation now known as the Bishops' Bible (as used by the KJB translators), wrote a letter dated 5 October 1568 to William Cecil, Lord Burghley, Elizabeth's chief adviser. It reads:

> Sir after my right hartie Comendacions, I was in purpose to have offred to the Quenes highnes the first fruites of our Labors in the recognising the Bible, But I feale my health to be such, that as yet I dare not adventure. Whervppon for that I wold not have the Queens highnes and your honor to be long delayed, nor the poore printer after his great charges to be longer deferred, I have caused one booke to be bound as you see which I hartelye pray yow to present favorablie to the Queens Maiestie, with your frendlie excuse of my disabylitie, in not coming my self.[2]

Being too unhealthy to deliver a presentation copy of the newly printed Bible to the Queen, Parker asks Cecil to present the specially bound copy for him. Parker also prepared a letter to Elizabeth that Cecil delivered along with the book. It begins:

> After my most Lowlie submission to your Maiestie, with my hartie reioyce of your prosperous progresse and retorne, pleaseth yt your highnes to accept in good parte, the endevor and diligence, of sum of vs your chapleins, my brethren the Bisshoppes, with other certaine Learned men, in this newe edicion of the bible, I trust by comparisone of divers translacions put forth in your realme will apeare as well the workemanshippe of the printer, as the Circumspeccion of all such as have traveiled in the recognicion.[3]

The presentation copy that Parker caused 'to be bound' is probably the copy that survives at the Folger Shakespeare Library. The evidence for drawing such a conclusion is based on the physical evidence present in the book itself, in particular the book's binding. The Folger Bishops' Bible is bound in crimson red velvet (figure 66). Velvet bindings were a particular favourite of the Queen, who appears to have preferred them to leather.[4] Other decorative touches appear to personalize the book for its royal recipient. Four round raised silver bosses found on both sides of the book are engraved with the Tudor rose. The silver centre plates are engraved with Queen Elizabeth's royal arms flanked by 'EL' and 'RE', standing for 'Elizabetha Regina' or 'Queen Elizabeth'. The same initials are engraved on the silver clasps. The book's gilt edges have been gauffered or decorated with heated tools, creating floral and guilloche patterns.[5] Decorative touches continue inside the book. The portraits of Robert Dudley, Earl of Leicester and Elizabeth's favourite, and William Cecil, who delivered the book to Elizabeth, are hand-coloured (figure 67). All told, these fine embellishments suggest a very impressive presentation copy from Parker and his bishops to the Queen as evidence of the 'first fruites' of their labours.

Measuring 430 × 290 × 120 mm, this weighty book was probably used as a lectern copy in one of Elizabeth's private chapels. How a Bishops' Bible travelled the great historical distance from Elizabeth's lectern to Washington DC is not entirely clear, but its last two centuries of ownership are well-documented. Three bookplates on the book's inside front cover identify two owners. Two bookplates show the Honywood family arms with a cheveron between three hawk heads. One reads 'Markshall' and 'Ph. Honywood'. The other simply has 'Ph. Honywood', but has been dated 'Feb. 1776' in manuscript. This is surely General Philip Honywood of Marks Hall in Essex. When he died in 1788, he bequeathed his estate to a relative named Filmer Honywood, who eventually bequeathed his estate to his nephew William Honywood. The book passed through two more generations, ending up with William Philip Honywood (1823–1859). In 1895, his widow Frances Emma died and his library eventually went up for sale at Sotheby, Wilkinson & Hodge in 1898.[6]

The book's next owner was a carpet manufacturer and book collector named Michael Tomkinson (1841–1921).[7] His bookplate can be found on the front board between the Honywood arms. After Tomkinson's death in 1921, his library went on sale at Sotheby, Wilkinson & Hodge, who found themselves once again auctioning Elizabeth's Bishops' Bible. For a description of the book, they returned to their catalogue entry of 1898, which claimed the following provenance: 'The tradition attached to this volume is that it was presented by Queen Elizabeth to a member of the Honywood Family.'[8] The bookseller Maggs Brothers purchased the book at auction and sold it the following year to Henry Folger in 1923. In describing the book, Maggs clearly labelled it 'The Royal Copy, originally Belonging to Queen Elizabeth' and offered an alternative version of its history, writing:

> At the time of the Commonwealth, and when the Royal Library was dispersed by the Parliament, this Bible fell into the hands of Sir Thomas Honywood, one of the most powerful of Cromwell's supporters, and it was sold in 1898 or thereabouts by Sir John William Honywood, the last of the family, and came into the Collection of Michael Tompkinson [sic].[9]

Maggs's narrative is plausible, but not likely. General Philip Honywood and Sir Thomas Honywood were both descendants of Robert Honywood (1525–1576), but there is no direct line between them. Also, the book cannot be traced to the dispersal of the Royal Library or directly to Sir Thomas Honywood. What about the tradition of the book being a gift from Queen Elizabeth to a member of the Honywood Family? There could be some truth in this claim. The Honywoods were a prominent family during Elizabeth's reign. Robert Honywood's wife

Mary (1527–1620), for example, was a well-known Protestant supporter who received mention in Thomas Fuller's *Worthies of England* (1662), where her devotion to Protestant martyrs is recorded: 'In the days of Queen *Mary* she used to visit the Prisons, and to comfort and relieve the Confessors therein.'[10] Nevertheless there is no evidence to say confidently that the book was a gift from Elizabeth. Thus, the book's life during the period between Elizabeth I and General Philip Honywood remains unknown.

Prince Henry's King James Bible

Although not a part of the Folger collection, just a few miles away in Washington DC in the library of the Washington National Cathedral resides another important royal Bible. The Cathedral has had a library since 1927, but the Rare Books Library (which opened in 1965) is relatively new: its creation was inspired, in fact, by a service held in 1961 to commemorate the 350th anniversary of the KJB.

One of the highlights of the library's opening exhibition, entitled 'In the Beginning was the Word', was a remarkable book on loan from the great book collector H.H. Houghton: a first edition of the 1611 KJB that once belonged to James I's son, Henry Frederick, Prince of Wales. This copy is what is referred to as a 'He Bible', for the first issue of the first edition has the line in Ruth 3:15 reading 'He went to the city' rather than 'She went to the city'. Prince Henry's Bible was one of two 1611 King James Bibles in Houghton's collection. In a 1957 article for *Book Collector*, William H. Bond visited Houghton's Wye Plantation home on the Eastern Shore of Maryland and took a tour of his collection. He

reports, 'Two magnificent copies in contemporary red morocco of the 'He' Bible. One of these, with Prince Henry's arms on the cover, has the engraved title in its earliest state; the other, with the arms of St George's Chapel, Windsor, has the letterpress title.'[12] It is not surprising that Houghton would collect two copies with extraordinary provenance. 'Two governing principles' of Houghton's collecting, notes Bond, were association and provenance.[13] The St George's Chapel copy, known as the 'Garter copy', was sold in Houghton's estate sale in 1979, while Prince Henry's copy found a home in the Washington National Cathedral.

Figure 68 The copy of the 1611 King James Bible bound for Prince Henry features his royal arms on the front and back covers. Courtesy of the Washington National Cathedral.

Henry's arms stamped onto the front and back red morocco binding supply evidence that the book was bound for the prince (figure 68). The binder surrounds the arms with intricate ornamental gilt tooling. Royal symbols such as the crowned thistles on the corners of the

binding and Tudor roses sprinkled around the border are joined by fleurs-de-lys and intricate floral patterns. Flanking the crown atop Henry's arms are two squirrels. The appearance of squirrels is actually an important clue to determining the history of the Bible, for binders can be identified by the tools they used. The presence of small squirrels confirms that the binding was prepared by a binder who has come to be known by scholars as the 'Squirrel Binder'. The identification of the 'Squirrel Binder' also helps to confirm the book's royal provenance. Active from approximately 1610 to 1635, the 'Squirrel Binder' appears to have worked as the binder for Edward Herbert, first Baron Herbert of Cherbury and also to have bound books for several members of the royal court, including James I, Charles I and Prince Henry. The design of the binding is consistent with other bindings found on books from Prince Henry's collection. Before his death in 1612, Henry built on his acquisition of Lord Lumley's famous library in 1609 to have one of the largest private libraries in England. He typically rebound the books he acquired: surviving books from his library indicate that he favoured bindings with his royal arms stamped onto the front and back boards.

How the book went from the royal court to Harmsworth is as yet unknown. Houghton's book label is affixed to the upper left of the inside front paste-down leaf. Along the bottom of the same page someone has written in pencil: 'Henry Prince of Wales's Copy (1594–1612) with his arms'. Other than that, no further evidence of provenance can be found in the book. A little research reveals that the copy was in the collection of Robert Leicester Harmsworth, before being purchased by Houghton, but for now the trail ends there.

A King James Bible bound for Queen Anne

Binders have an afterlife of sorts, as the equipment they used passes on to subsequent generations of their trade. The 'Squirrel Binder' continued to work until around 1640, but the tools he used for his ornate designs appear on book bindings well into the eighteenth century. One well-known bookbinder who came to own some of the 'Squirrel Binder's' stock (though perhaps not the squirrels) was Robert Steel.[14] Active in the later part of the seventeenth century through to the early eighteenth century, Steel was one of England's finest binders from that period. He learned the trade from Samuel Mearne, bookbinder to Charles II. In 1705 a London bookseller named John Dunton (1659–1733) described Steel and his work:

I may call him my occasional Binder; for, when I met with a nice Customer, no binding would serve him but Mr. Steel's; which, for the fineness and

Figure 69 A 1701 King James Bible bound for Queen Anne by Robert Steel. Folger Shakespeare Library.

goodness of it, might vie with the Cambridge Binding; but, as celebrated a Binder as Steel is, he is a man very humble and lowly in his own eyes, far from insinuating his own praise, and very rarely speaks of himself or his own actions, but never of other Binders with contempt or disrespect.[15]

Steel's skills are in full display in an elegantly bound 1701 KJB that survives at the Folger Shakespeare Library.[16] Judging from the details on its binding, the book appears to have been presented to Queen Anne in around 1705 (figure 69). As with Prince Henry's Bible, Queen Anne's ownership is suggested by her coat of arms tooled into the centre of the front and back dark blue goatskin binding. Moreover, Queen Anne's cipher is tooled on each corner of the binding's second panel and on each of the seven panels on the spine. Perhaps the book's most striking feature is the large silk ties with gold tassels. A Book of Common Prayer from the same year bound by Steel in a similarly decorated dark olive goatskin survives, indicating that the two books may have been given together as a presentation copy to Queen Anne.[17]

A Bible taken 'beyond the seas'

Association copies connected to royals and other famous figures are historical treasures, but copies associated with lesser-known or unknown owners often teach us the most about how books were used. For example, surviving in the Folger collection is a remarkable copy of *The third part of the Bible*, containing Job, the Psalms, Proverbs, Ecclesiastes and the Song of Solomon.[18] On the verso of a vellum leaf used as an endpaper is the following inscription: 'This was ye only booke I carried in my pockett when I travelld beyond ye seas ye 22^d year of my Age; & many years after Just. Isha[m]' (figure 70). The 'Just. Isham' who inscribed this note is Sir Justinian Isham (1611–1675), second baronet of Lamport Hall, Northamptonshire. Supporting this identification is an armorial bookplate of the Isham family on the inside front cover and a manuscript IOU contract between sisters Susan and Elizabeth Stuteville written on the back paste-down leaf. The Stuteville family was closely associated with the Ishams.

As Isham's inscription suggests, at the age of twenty-two he did indeed travel 'beyond ye seas', journeying to the Netherlands in 1633.[19] Justinian's older sister Elizabeth kept a diary in her youth and recorded her brother's departure and return in language similar to that used in Justinian's inscription. She writes, 'my B[rother] went beyond sea' and later 'my B[rother] came from beioynd sea [*sic*]'.[20]

Many book owners from the early modern period inscribed their names into their books and perhaps even supplied a date. But few

Figure 70 An inscription from a copy of *The third part of the Bible* (1626) reading 'This was ye only booke I carried in my pockett when I travelld beyond ye seas ye 22^d year of my Age; & many years after Just. Isha[m]'. Folger Shakespeare Library.

provide details about how they used the book or where they kept it. While it is taken for granted that books in smaller formats often travelled in the pockets of their owners, it is helpful to have direct confirmation from a contemporary owner. Isham's KJB is a small book measuring 110 x 55 mm, just the right size for travelling in one's pocket. It seems practical, too, that he chose only to travel with one volume. He appears to have chosen the third volume because it contains the Psalms. A manuscript index in the book's back endpapers suggests that Isham was especially engaged with the Psalms. Here he records the numbers of particular Psalms appropriate for particular occasions: morning, evening, mercy, sickness, joy, communion and comforts. The psalms section of the book is also where he wrote the most manuscript notes.

Justinian Isham's Bible was printed in 1626, so it may have been in his possession from the time he was sixteen years old or older, until he left for the Netherlands when he was twenty-two. It may have been given to him by his father, for we know that his sister Elizabeth received such a gift. In a diary entry from 1634, when Elizabeth Isham was twenty-five years old, she writes 'my father gave me an imbroidered Bible'. In the early part of the seventeenth century, it would not have been unusual to receive an embroidered Bible as a gift.

Figure 71 Four embroidered copies of the King James Bible or parts thereof printed between 1633 and 1640. The book *below right* contains the New Testament and Psalms bound in a *dos-à-dos* or 'back to back' fashion. Folger Shakespeare Library.

Embroidered King James Bibles

The King James Bible was first printed during a period in which 'there was a considerable vogue for small-format devotional books with embroidered covers, often depicting religious imagery but not uncommonly plants, landscapes and a variety of other possibilities.'[21] Small-format versions of the KJB were perfect candidates for a decorative embroidered binding. Several examples survive at the Folger Shakespeare Library, illustrating a variety of bindings. The four shown in figure 71 are editions of the KJB or parts thereof printed between 1633 and 1640. Elizabeth Isham's gift Bible may have looked like any of the four. The largest is an edition of the Bible bound with the Psalms. On its cover is a pelican, a medieval symbol for Christ. It was once believed that mother pelicans would feed their young with their own blood in the absence of other nourishment and this self-sacrifice found an association with Christ's passion. The other three books show a variety of flowers, usually composed of silk and silver threads on white satin. One of the three contains the New Testament and Psalms bound in a dos-à-dos or 'back to back' fashion, meaning the two books share the same back board and open from opposite sides.

Like Isham's Bible, these embroidered Bibles were small enough to fit into one's pocket and probably often travelled in that manner. Book owners such as Elizabeth Isham might have embroidered bindings for their books, but typically embroidered bindings were the work of professionals. The language of Elizabeth Isham's entry is telling: she did not embroider the binding herself, but rather was given a Bible that was already embroidered.

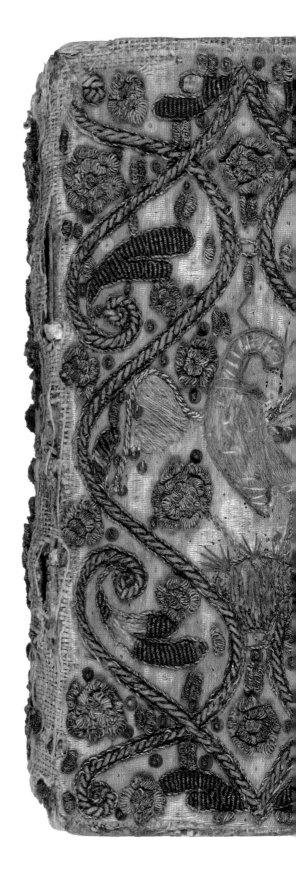

'The Gift of Her Father'

Bibles given as gifts between friends or family members are reminders of the personal relationships that so many have had with Bibles. We see a similar relationship when families use their Bible's blank leaves to record significant events such as births, christenings, weddings and deaths: it is a way of connecting family to the Bible or connecting family and friends through the Bible. With this in mind, this chapter concludes with a 1676 KJB bound with the Psalms that was a gift for a young woman named Rebekah Fisher from her father William Fisher in 1678.[22]

What makes this particular Bible so remarkable are the ways in which the book has been personalised as a gift. Facing each other in the book's front endpapers are two additions to the book that record the book's provenance (figure 72). Before the book was bound, Fisher's father commissioned a printed book label that recorded Rebekah's birth and baptism. It reads: 'Rebekah Fisher, Daughter of William and Mary Fisher, Was born the 7th of January, 1660. And Baptixed [*sic*] the 17th of the same.' This label is bound into the book facing an endpaper with a manuscript inscription recording the gift: 'Rebekah: Fisher: Her: Booke: The Gift of: Her Father in the Year: :1678:.' Rebekah would have been eighteen when she received the Bible; considering the mention of her birth date on the book label, it may have been a gift for her birthday. The personalisation of the book extends to the binding, where Fisher's initials, 'R.F.', are gilt-stamped on the front cover. Stamping the owner's initials onto the book's binding is a fairly common practice, but an added embellishment found on the remaining lower clasp is quite unusual. On its back is engraved 'Fisher 78'. Perhaps the now-missing upper clasp was once engraved, too.

Like many Bibles, Fisher's was passed along to her descendants for at least another century. An inscription in one of the front endpapers reads, 'William Fisher Dimond the gift of his grandmother Sarah Lucas and delivered to him on her death 29 January 1787': it seems this special Bible was gifted many times in its life.

Figure 72 A King James Bible (1676) with a book label and inscription from 1678 recording that the Bible was a gift from William Fisher to his daughter Rebekah. Her last name and the date are engraved on the surviving lower clasp *shown on p.198*. The Folger Shakespeare Library.

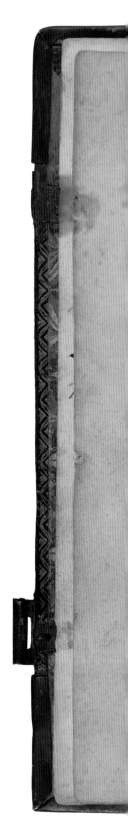

Rebekah Fisher, Daughter of *William* and *Mary Fisher*,

Was born the 7th of *January*, 1660.

And Baptized the 17th of the same.

Rebekah: Fisher: Her: Booke: The Gift of, Her Father in the Year: 1678:

The lives of early English Bibles

From the court of Queen Elizabeth to the pocket of a seafaring young man, the lives of early English Bibles are as diverse as the surviving Bibles themselves. Their lives intersect with a great many people, from the men and women who translated, printed and bound the books, to the generations of book owners who held them in their hands. A century of English Bible translations in print led to the landmark publication of the King James Bible, which after its first printing in 1611 appears in a variety of forms for a variety of readers. A young man carries a pocket-sized edition of the Psalms with him while travelling from England to the Netherlands. A large folio Bible is bound in an ornate style for the Queen. A young woman receives a personalised Bible from her father in her eighteenth year. Evidence of these events survives because the books survive. More than just conveyers of text, these books endure as historical artefacts documenting religious, political and social history. They present only a few of the many stories that early English Bibles have to tell and they are a part of a narrative that travels alongside the story of the English Bible and the creation and afterlife of the KJB.

Notes

1. *The. holie. Bible.* (London, [1568]). Folger STC 2099 Copy 3.

2. Alfred W. Pollard, *Records of the English Bible: The Documents Relating to the Translation and Publication of the Bible in English, 1525–1611* (London, 1911), pp. 292–3.

3. Ibid., p. 294.

4. David Pearson, *English Bookbinding Styles, 1450–1800: A Handbook* (London and New Castle, Del., 2005), p. 21. For a description of bindings on Queen Elizabeth's books, including many velvet bindings, see Cyril Davenport, *Royal English Book Bindings* (London and New York, 1896), pp. 35–52.

5. For a detailed binding description, see Frederick A. Bearman, Nati H. Krivatsy and J. Franklin Mowery, *Fine and Historic Bookbindings from the Folger Shakespeare Library* (Washington D.C., 1992), pp. 130–31.

6. Sotheby, Wilkinson & Hodge, *Catalogue of Valuable Books and Manuscripts, including the Library of the late William Philip Honywood, Esq., of Marks Hall, Essex …* ([London], 1898).

7. Sotheby's sold the book to the bookseller Tregaskis, who appears to have sold it to Tomkinson.

8. Sotheby, Wilkinson & Hodge. *Catalogue of the Extensive and Valuable Library the Property of the late Michael Tomkinson, Esq., of Franche Hall …* (London, 1922), p. 101.

9. Maggs Bros., *Shakespeare and Shakespeareana: A Catalog issued in Commemoration of the Tercentenary of the First Folio Shakespeare A.D. 1623–1923* (London, 1923), p. 136.

10. Thomas Fuller, *The History of the Worthies of England* (London, 1662), Vol. II, p. 86.

11. *The Holy Bible* (London, 1611).

12. William H. Bond, 'Contemporary Collectors XII: Arthur Amory Houghton Jr.', *The Book Collector* 6.1 (1957), 28–40, here p. 29.

13. Ibid., p. 28.

14. Maggs Bros., *Bookbinding in the British Isles: Sixteenth to the Twentieth Century*, 2 vols (London, 1996), Vol. I, p. 132.

15. John Dunton, *The life and errors of John Dunton, citizen of London …* (London, 1818), p. 262.

16. *The Holie Bible* (London, 1701). Folger 207–237b.

17. Maggs Bros., *Bookbinding*, Vol. I, p. 180.

18. *The third part of the Bible* (London, 1626). Folger STC 2278, copy 1.

19. R. Priestley, 'Isham, Sir Justinian, second baronet (1611–1675)', *ODNB*, accessed 13 April 2010.

20. Elizabeth Isham's diaries have been transcribed and published online. See Elizabeth Clarke and Erica Longfellow, 'Constructing Elizabeth Isham', Centre for the Study of the Renaissance, University of Warwick, 28 January 2009; www2.warwick.ac.uk/fac/arts/ren/projects/isham/, accessed 5 May 2010.

21. Pearson, *English Bookbinding Styles*, p. 21.

22. *The Holy Bible* (London, 1676). Folger 265–076.

Figure 73 The monument
to Henry Savile at Merton
College, Oxford. Photograph ©
Tim Rawle.

The Translators of the King James Bible

FIRST
WESTMINSTER COMPANY

Genesis to Second
Book of Kings

Lancelot Andrewes (Head): Dean of Westminster
John Overall: Dean of St. Paul's
Hadrian à Saravia: Prebendary of Westminster, Canterbury and
    Worcester
John Layfield (Leifield): Rector of St Clement Danes, London
William Bedwell (Beadwell): Rector of St Ethelburga, London
Richard Thomson (Tomson): Fellow of Clare Hall, Cambridge
Robert Tighe (Teigh): Archdeacon of Middlesex and Vicar of All
    Hallows-by-the-Tower, London
Francis Burleigh: Fellow of Chelsea College, London
Geoffrey King: Fellow of King's College, Cambridge
Richard Clarke (Clark): Vicar of Minster on the Isle of Thanet,
    Kent

SECOND
WESTMINSTER COMPANY

Romans to Jude

William Barlow (Head): Dean of Chester
John Spenser (Spencer): Fellow, and afterwards President, of
    Corpus Christi College, Oxford
Roger Fenton: Fellow of Pembroke Hall, Cambridge
Michael Rabbett: Vicar of St Vedast-alias-Foster, London
Thomas Sanderson: Rector of All Hallows-the-Great, London
Ralph Hutchinson: President of St John's College, Oxford
William Dakins: Professor of Divinity, Gresham College, London

FIRST
CAMBRIDGE COMPANY

First Book of Chronicles to the
Song of Solomon

Edward Lively (Head): Regius Professor of Hebrew, Cambridge
John Richardson: Rector of Upwell, Norfolk
Laurence Chaderton (Chatterton): Master of Emmanuel College,
    Cambridge
Francis Dillingham: Vicar of Wilden, Bedfordshire
Thomas Harrison: Fellow of Trinity College, Cambridge
Roger Andrewes: Rector of Ongar, Essex
Andrew Bing (Byng): Fellow of St John's College, Cambridge

**SECOND
CAMBRIDGE COMPANY**

The Apocrypha

John Duport (Head): Master of Jesus College, Cambridge
William Branthwaite (Branthwait): Fellow of Emmanuel College,
  Cambridge
Samuel Ward (Warde): Fellow of Sidney Sussex College, Cambridge
Andrew Downes (Downs): Regius Professor of Greek, Cambridge
John Bois (Boys): Rector of Boxworth, Cambridgeshire
Jeremiah Radcliffe: Vicar of Orwell, Cambridgeshire
Robert Ward: Prebendary of Chichester

**FIRST
OXFORD COMPANY**

Isaiah to Malachi

John Harding (Head): Regius Professor of Hebrew, Oxford
John Rainolds (Reynolds): President of Corpus Christi College,
  Oxford
Thomas Holland: Rector of Exeter College, Oxford
Richard Kilby (Kilbye): Rector of Lincoln College, Oxford
Miles Smith: Prebendary of Hereford and Exeter
Richard Brett: Rector of Quainton, Buckinghamshire
Possible: William Thorne, Dean of Chichester. John Harding's
  predecessor as Professor of Hebrew at Oxford

SECOND OXFORD COMPANY

*Gospels, Acts of the Apostles,
and Revelation*

Thomas Ravis (Head): Dean of Christ Church, Oxford
Sir Henry Savile: Warden of Merton College, Oxford; Provost of
  Eton College, Berkshire
George Abbot: Dean of Winchester
John Harmar (Harmer): Regius Professor of Greek, Oxford; Warden
  of St Mary's College, Winchester
John Perne (Perin): formerly Regius Professor of Greek, Oxford
Giles Thomson (Thompson): Fellow of All Souls College, Oxford;
  Dean of Windsor
Richard Edes: Dean of Worcester
John Aglionby: Principal of St Edmund Hall, Oxford
James Montague: Dean of Worcester
Ralph Ravens: Rector of Great Easton, Essex
Leonard Hutten: Canon of Christ Church, Oxford

Further Reading

CHAPTER 1   Rebecca Barnhouse and Benjamin C. Withers (eds), *The Old English Hexateuch: Aspects and Approaches* (Kalamazoo, Mich., 2000).

David Daniell, *The Bible in English: Its History and Influence* (New Haven and London, 2003).

Mary Dove, *The First English Bible* (Cambridge, 2007).

Kantik Ghosh, *The Wycliffite Heresy: Authority and the Interpretation of Texts* (Cambridge, 2002).

S.L. Greenslade (ed.), *The Cambridge History of the Bible*, Vol. III (Cambridge, 1963).

Anne Hudson, *The Premature Reformation: Wycliffite Texts and Lollard History* (Oxford, 1988).

Richard Marsden, *The Text of the Old Testament in Anglo-Saxon England* (Cambridge, 1995).

J.F. Mozley, *Coverdale and His Bibles* (London, 1953).

Orlaith O'Sullivan (ed.), *The Bible as Book: The Reformation* (London, 2000).

Jaroslav Pelikan, *The Reformation of the Bible: The Bible of the Reformation* (New Haven and London, 1996).

Paul G. Remley, *Old English Biblical Verse: Studies in Genesis, Exodus and Daniel* (Cambridge, 1996).

Michael G. Sargent (ed.), *The Mirror of the Blessed Life of Jesus Christ* (Exeter, 2005).

CHAPTER 2   Patrick Collinson, 'The Jacobean Religious Settlement: The Hampton Court Conference', in Howard Tomlinson (ed.), *Before the Civil War* (London, 1983).

Alan Cromartie, 'King James and the Hampton Court Conference', in Ralph Houlbrooke (ed.), *James VI and I: Ideas, Authority and Government* (Aldershot, 2006).

Peter Lake, *Anglicans and Puritans? Presbyterian and English Conformist Thought from Whitgift to Hooker* (London, 1988).

Diarmaid MacCulloch, *The Later Reformation in England 1547–1603* (London, 1990).

James McConica (ed.), *The History of the University of Oxford*, Vol. III: *The Collegiate University* (Oxford, 1986).

Victor Morgan, *A History of the University of Cambridge*, Vol. II: *1546–1750* (Cambridge, 2004).

Adam Nicolson, *Power and Glory: Jacobean England and the Making of the King James Bible* (London, 2003); published in the USA as *God's Secretaries: The Making of the King James Bible* (New York, 2003).

CHAPTER 3   Adam Nicolson, *Power and Glory: Jacobean England and the Making of the King James Bible* (London, 2003).

Olga S. Opfell, *The King James Bible Translators* (Jefferson, N.C., 1982).

Vivienne Westbrook, 'Translators of the Authorized Version of the Bible', *Oxford Dictionary of National Biography*, online (Oxford, 2004–).

CHAPTER 4   Stephen G. Burnett, *From Christian Hebraism to Jewish Studies* (Leiden, 1996).

Allison P. Coudert and Jeffrey S. Shoulson, *Hebraica Veritas? Christian Hebraists and the Study of Judaism in Early Modern Europe* (Philadelphia, 2004).

Basil Hall, 'Biblical Scholarship: Editions and Commentaries', in S.L. Greenslade (ed.), *The Cambridge History of the Bible*, 3 vols (Cambridge, 1963), Vol. III, pp. 38–93.

Gerald Hammond, *The Making of the English Bible* (Manchester, 1982).

Gareth Lloyd Jones, *The Discovery of Hebrew in Tudor England: A Third Language* (Manchester, 1983).

David Norton, *A Textual History of the King James Bible* (Cambridge, 2005).

CHAPTER 5   F.E. Brightman, *The English Rite*, 2 vols (London, 1915).

Ian Green, *Print and Protestantism in Early Modern England* (Oxford, 2000).

Gerald Hammond, *The Making of the English Bible* (Manchester, 1982).

Judith Maltby, 'The Prayer Book and the Parish Church: From the Elizabethan Settlement to the Restoration', in *The Oxford Guide to the Book of Common Prayer: A Worldwide Survey*, ed. Charles Hefling and Cynthia Shattuck (Oxford, 2006).

David Norton, *A Textual History of the King James Bible* (Cambridge, 2005).

CHAPTER 6   Gordon Campbell, *Bible: The Story of the King James Version* (Oxford, 2010).

David Daniell, *The Bible in English* (New Haven and London, 2003).

David Norton, *A History of the Bible as Literature*, 2 vols (Cambridge, 1993).

Rebecca Lemon, Emma Mason, Jonathan Roberts and Christopher Rowland (eds), *The Blackwell Companion to the Bible in English Literature* (Malden, Mass. and Oxford, 2007).

CHAPTER 7   Robert Alter, *Pen of Iron: American Prose and the King James Bible* (Princeton, N.J., 2010).

Ernest S. Frerichs (ed.), *The Bible and Bibles in America* (Atlanta, Ga., 1988).

Paul C. Gutjahr, *An American Bible: A History of the Good Book in the United States, 1777–1880* (Stanford, Calif., 1999).

Nathan O. Hatch and Mark Noll (eds), *The Bible in America: Essays in Cultural History* (Oxford and New York, 1982).

Vincent L. Wimbush (ed.), assisted by Rosamond C. Rodman, *African Americans and the Bible: Sacred Texts and Social Textures* (New York, 2000).

CHAPTER 8   Frederick A. Bearman, Nati H. Krivatsy and J. Franklin Mowery, *Fine and Historic Bookbindings from the Folger Shakespeare Library* (Washington D.C., 1992).

Elizabeth Clarke and Erica Longfellow, 'Constructing Elizabeth Isham', Centre for the Study of the Renaissance, University of Warwick, 28 January 2009; www2.warwick.ac.uk/fac/arts/ren/projects/isham/.

David Pearson, *English Bookbinding Styles, 1450–1800: A Handbook* (London and New Castle, Del., 2005)

Alfred W. Pollard, *Records of the English Bible: The Documents Relating to the Translation and Publication of the Bible in English, 1525–1611* (London, 1911).

Contributors

Valentine Cunningham is Fellow and Tutor in English at Corpus Christi College, Oxford and Professor of English Literature in the Faculty of English, University of Oxford.

Steven K. Galbraith is Andrew W. Mellon Curator of Books in the Folger Shakespeare Library, Washington DC.

Hannibal Hamlin is Associate Professor in the Department of English at Ohio State University.

Gareth Lloyd Jones is Emeritus Professor in the School of Theology and Religious Studies, Bangor University.

Diarmaid MacCulloch is Fellow of St Cross College, Oxford and Professor of the History of the Church in the University of Oxford.

Judith Maltby is Fellow and Chaplain of Corpus Christi College, Oxford and Reader in Church History in the University of Oxford.

Peter McCullough is Sohmer Fellow and Tutor in English at Lincoln College, Oxford, CUF lecturer in the Faculty of English, University of Oxford, and Lay Canon (History) of St Paul's Cathedral.

Helen Moore is Fellow and Tutor in English at Corpus Christi College, Oxford, and CUF lecturer in the Faculty of English, University of Oxford.

Julian Reid is Archivist at Merton and Corpus Christi Colleges, Oxford.

Elizabeth Solopova is a research fellow in the Faculty of English, University of Oxford.

Index